IMAGES
of America

MOUNT DORA

IMAGES
of America

MOUNT DORA

Lynn M. Homan and Thomas Reilly

ARCADIA
PUBLISHING

ISBN 978-0-7385-0568-8

Published by Arcadia Publishing
Charleston, South Carolina

Printed in the United States of America

Library of Congress Catalog Card Number: 00-102250

For all general information contact Arcadia Publishing at:
Telephone 843-853-2070
Fax 843-853-0044
E-Mail sales@arcadiapublishing.com
For customer service and orders:
Toll-Free 1-888-313-2665

Visit us on the Internet at www.arcadiapublishing.com

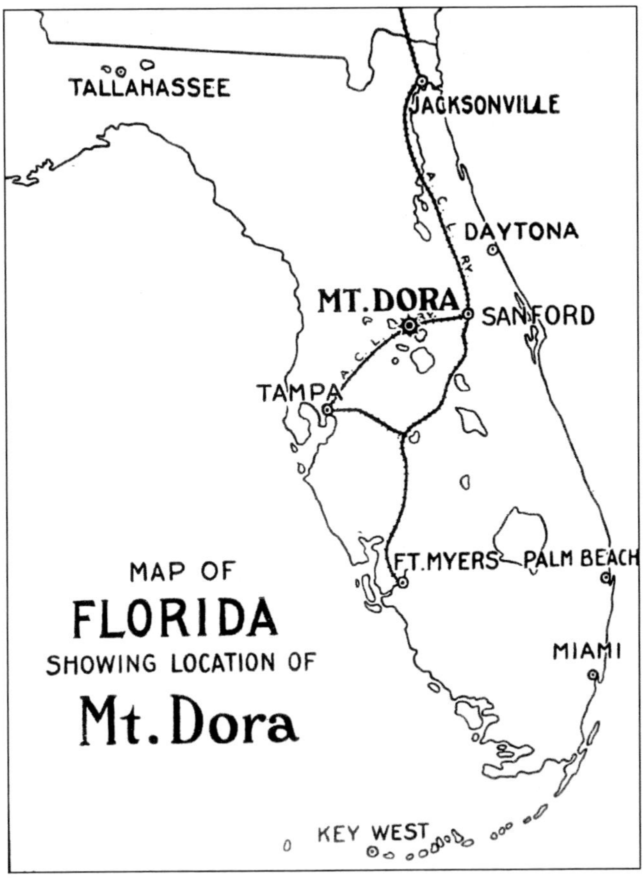

Contents

ACKNOWLEDGMENTS

In compiling a book on a particular community, the images collected by and the reminiscences of the residents are most valuable. Readers interested in detailed family information on some of the early citizens of Mount Dora may wish to consult *The Story of Mount Dora, Florida*, by R.J. Longstreet, and *Memories of Mount Dora and Lake County*, by David Edgerton. The *Mount Dora Topic* also has a complete set of newspapers dating from 1926. Available to researchers, these provide an informative look at local events. We especially appreciate the opportunity to utilize the archival collections of Historic Mount Dora, Inc. We are also most grateful for the help given us by Lucretia Freed-West, the very enthusiastic and knowledgeable president of that group. She not only provided access to the photographic collections of Historic Mount Dora, Inc., but also rendered considerable assistance with the identification of specific images. Unless otherwise stated, all photographs contained in *Mount Dora* belong to Historic Mount Dora, Inc.

INTRODUCTION

Located approximately 50 miles north of Disney World, the modern-day linchpin of Florida tourism, is the small community of Mount Dora. Epitomizing the development of the Sunshine State by men and women from the Midwest and the Northeast, the story of Mount Dora is the story of much of Florida.

In the history of any area, facts are frequently lost over the years. Legend is sometimes more exciting and romantic than reality. Much of the story is left to individual recollection and interpretation, which often vary substantially depending upon who tells the story. Such is the case with accounts of Mount Dora. Much of the town's history is frequently related in terms of different points of view.

What is indisputable is that there is a city named Mount Dora and a lake named Lake Dora. The derivation of the names of both the lake and the city are probably a combination of truth and folklore. It seems to be a certainty that in the 1840s, government surveyors were sent to Florida to undertake the mapping of the largely uninhabited land in the central portion of the state. Much to their surprise and certainly relief, they wandered upon a cabin that had been constructed by early settlers Jim and Dora Ann Drawdy. The Drawdys shared their hospitality and supplies with the surveyors. According to a remembrance by early Mount Dora resident John P. Donnelly, "...out of consideration for her gentle courtesy and kindness the lake was named 'Dora' " by the surveyors. The exact date of the survey cannot be fixed with certainty nor can the exact date of the naming of the lake.

Just as much uncertainty exists regarding the first name of the town that grew up along the banks of Lake Dora. In 1880, the fledgling settlement bore the name Royellou. This particular appellation was a combination of the names of the children of the town's postmaster—Roy, Ellen, and Louis Tremain. Other versions of the designation include Royallen, Royallien, Royallieu, Royaliew, Royalliew, Royallow, Royalune, and Royalview. Whatever it was dubbed, this name lasted only from 1880 to 1883.

Today, traveling to Mount Dora is easy. Florida's network of superhighways will deposit the visitor not far from this throwback to the turn of the 20th century. Not always such an easy trip, it once was a long and hard journey by foot, wagon, or steamship. Without any doubt, one of the seminal events in the history of Mount Dora was the long-awaited arrival of railroad service to the town. Although journeys were still long and tiring, the timing of a trip to Mount Dora from the Midwest or Northeast could now be measured in a matter of days or hours instead of weeks. The occasion of the first railroad service into town deserved a major celebration;

townsfolk celebrated with brass bands and speeches. Long tables were set with food, and a free dinner was offered for all that arrived by train.

Certainly not as important but just as interesting in the history of Mount Dora is the 1930 visit of former President Calvin Coolidge and his wife, Grace. The town fathers of Mount Dora, without a doubt, intended to mine Coolidge's visit for all it was worth. True to form, the laconic Coolidge generally chose not to cooperate, spending little time with the locals other than to take part in the dedication of a new addition to the Lakeside Inn. Fishing trips and long nights discussing politics with the President never came to fruition. Silent Cal lived up to his reputation, kept largely to himself, and had little to say.

Life in rural Mount Dora in the years just before and after the turn of the 20th century must certainly have been kinder and gentler than in the big cities of the industrialized Midwest and Northeast. At the same time, life in Mount Dora must have been quite similar to circumstances in small towns throughout America. There was good and bad to be found, just as in every other American community, large or small.

Looking at the city streets, beautiful lake, and turn-of-the-20th-century homes, it is easy to imagine life long ago in Mount Dora as an inordinately idyllic lifestyle. It was not always that way, however. Mount Dora also experienced its share of problems. In the late 1800s and early 1900s, several major freezes struck hard and ruined lives and fortunes. Like almost every other Florida community, Mount Dora pushed itself into major real estate and land development during the 1920s. Many of the promoters lost everything in the collapse of the real estate boom that preceded the stock market crash and Great Depression.

The city was not free from crime and contentious race relations. As early as 1926, one of the major news stories dealt with an armed robbery of one of the downtown businesses. There were muggings and even murders; much of the crime was unfairly blamed on the town's African-American population. Restricted to a separate but not equal life in what was described as "East Town," African Americans were treated in a manner that, at best, could be termed paternalistic.

From the beginning, one of Mount Dora's strongest assets was its beautiful Lake Dora. For many years, barely a week went by without the newspaper printing a story about a visiting fisherman and his conquest of the bass and catfish found in Lake Dora. Eventually, agricultural pollution threatened the life of the lake, however, and with this pollution came the demise of the tourist industry. Mount Dora's citizens rallied to the cause, as they set about to reverse the damage and return the lake to the pristine condition of earlier times. Likewise, when the rerouting of a major thoroughfare threatened to cut right through the city and destroy its very nature, residents were divided on the issue of development versus preservation. Led by Richard Edgerton, owner of the Lakeside Inn, the group favoring rerouting of the highway triumphed. The new road bypassed the downtown, creating a certain amount of economic hardship, but eventually, it proved to be the correct decision for the community.

Today, Mount Dora seems to be recreating a viable identity for itself. Citizens are working together, redevelopment efforts are thriving, and property values are increasing. The town's resident population is growing, as more and more people find Mount Dora a desirable place in which to live. At the same time, the economic benefits of historic preservation are becoming apparent, as tourists flock to Mount Dora in search of the community's old-fashioned charm and architectural distinctiveness.

One

Then and Now

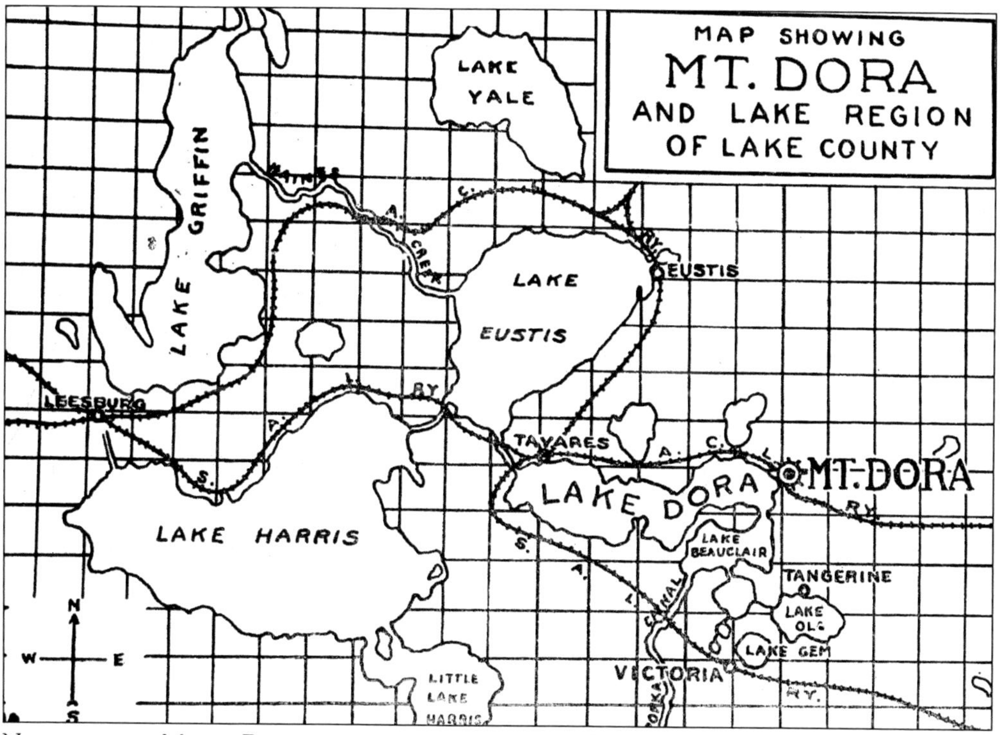

Newcomers to Mount Dora encounter unique topographical features. Whether today or more than 100 years ago, traveling on foot, by horseback, train, or automobile, they find something relatively uncommon in Florida—hills. Roads meandering through gently rolling countryside with small hills and valleys quickly dispel the myth that all of Florida is flat. Visitors are also struck by the presence of water everywhere. In almost any direction there are rivers, canals, and lakes—by some accounts, nearly 1,400 lakes! The 1925 *Florida Gazetteer* referred to Lake Dora, on the shores of which Mount Dora is located, as "the queen of the 1,400 perennially fed lakes of Lake County." Some things have changed since the first visitors arrived; others have not. Travel along on a short journey between the past and present, then and now.

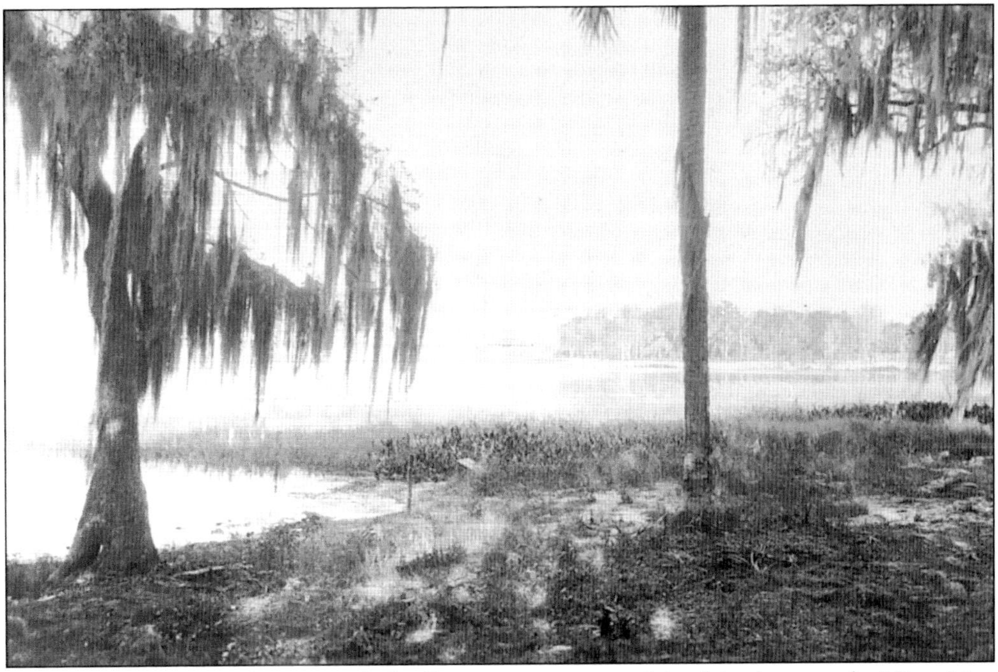

The first visitors must have seen Lake Dora as it is pictured in this photograph. Mist rising from the water, trees draped in Spanish moss, marshy grasses, and sandy shores would have been common sights in the mid-1800s. While today there are perhaps more people and fewer animals, much of the scenery and plant life remains the same.

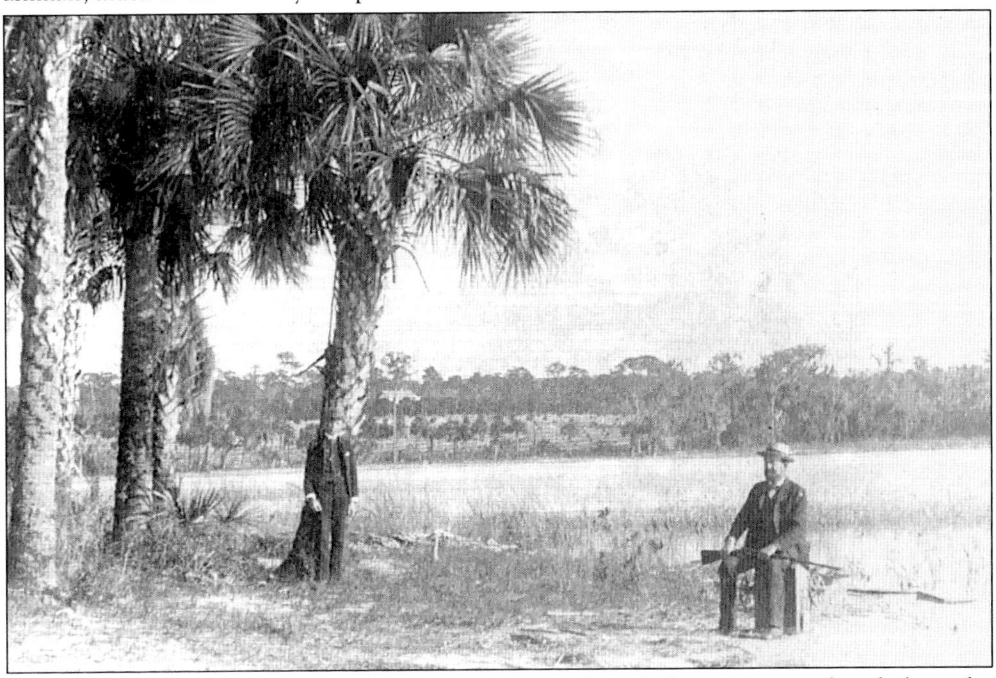

During the winter of 1888, William Hicks and an unidentified companion relaxed along the shore of Lake Dora. Despite the presence of the rifle, the men appear rather elegantly attired for a hunting expedition.

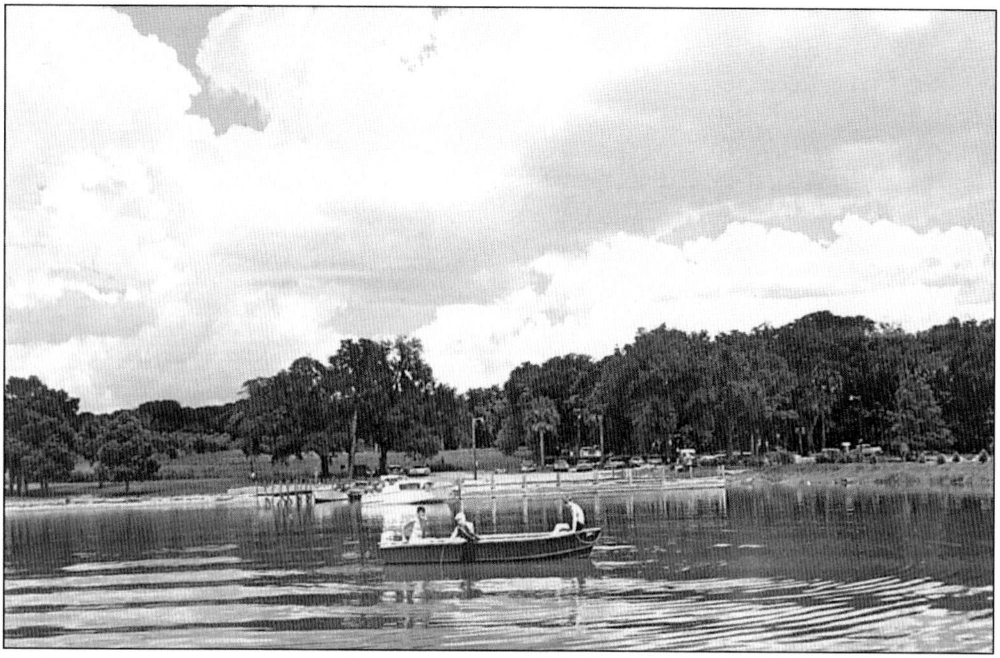

In this more contemporary view, boaters enjoy an afternoon on Lake Dora. In the background, the boat ramps and picnic facilities of Gilbert Park, located at Tremain Street and Liberty Avenue, are visible.

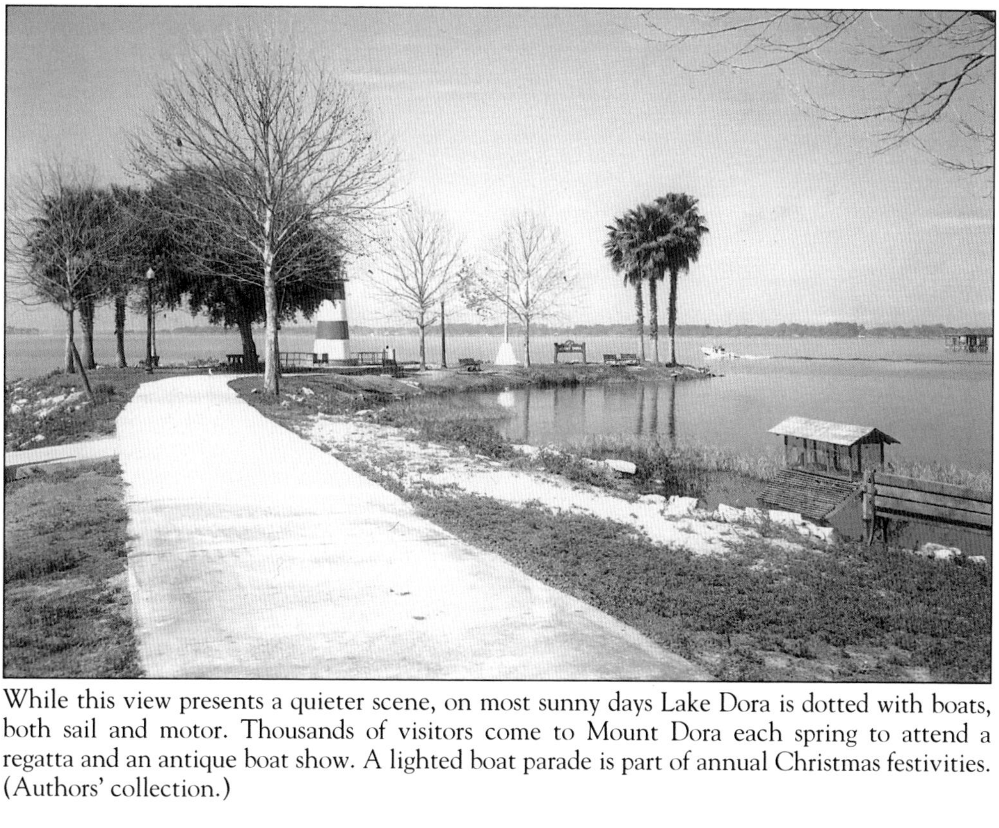

While this view presents a quieter scene, on most sunny days Lake Dora is dotted with boats, both sail and motor. Thousands of visitors come to Mount Dora each spring to attend a regatta and an antique boat show. A lighted boat parade is part of annual Christmas festivities. (Authors' collection.)

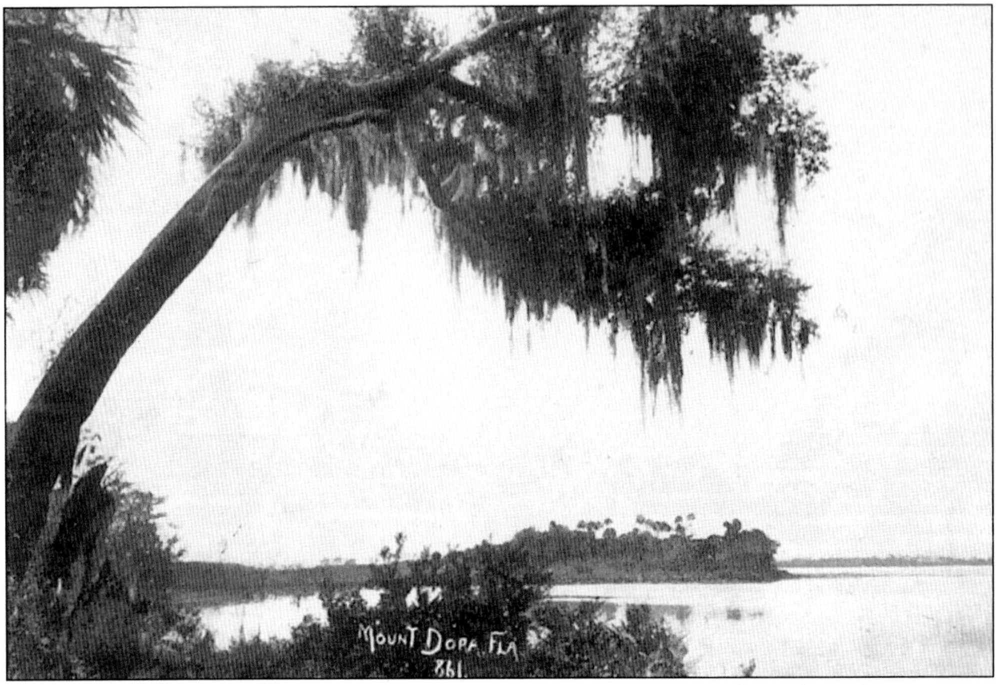

Lake Dora's Palm Island presented a pristine appearance in 1906, when the only occupants were visitors who came by boat. This postcard view of the island shows the area prior to the addition of any modern recreational amenities.

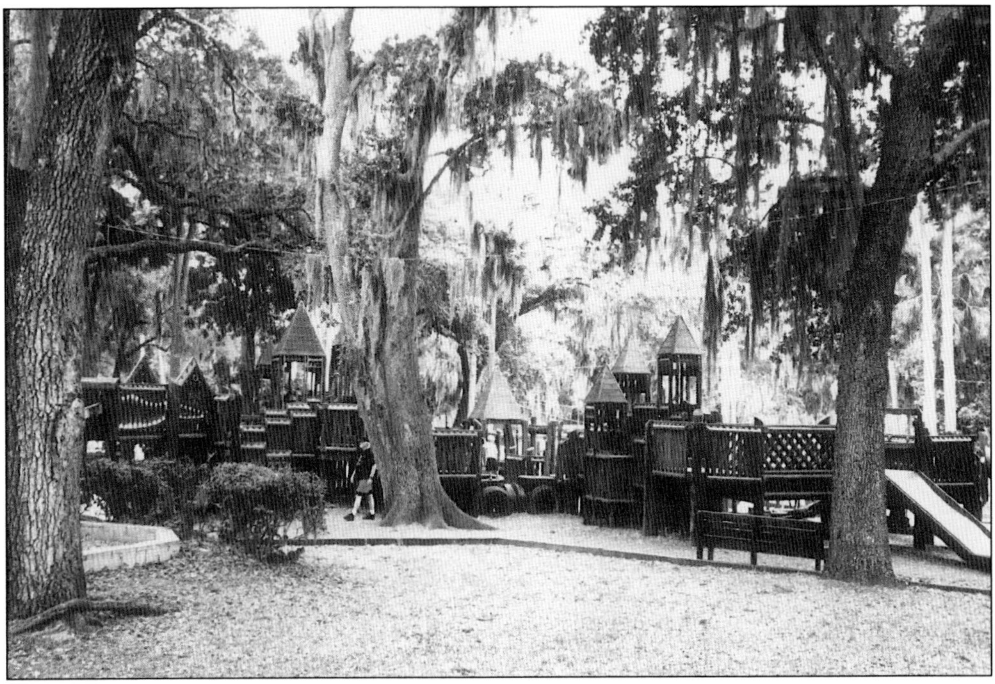

Today Gilbert Park features an intricate playground that must be a fun experience for children of all ages. In the 1980s, construction of a boardwalk in the adjacent Palm Island Park allowed nature lovers and birdwatchers to explore the park's wetlands.

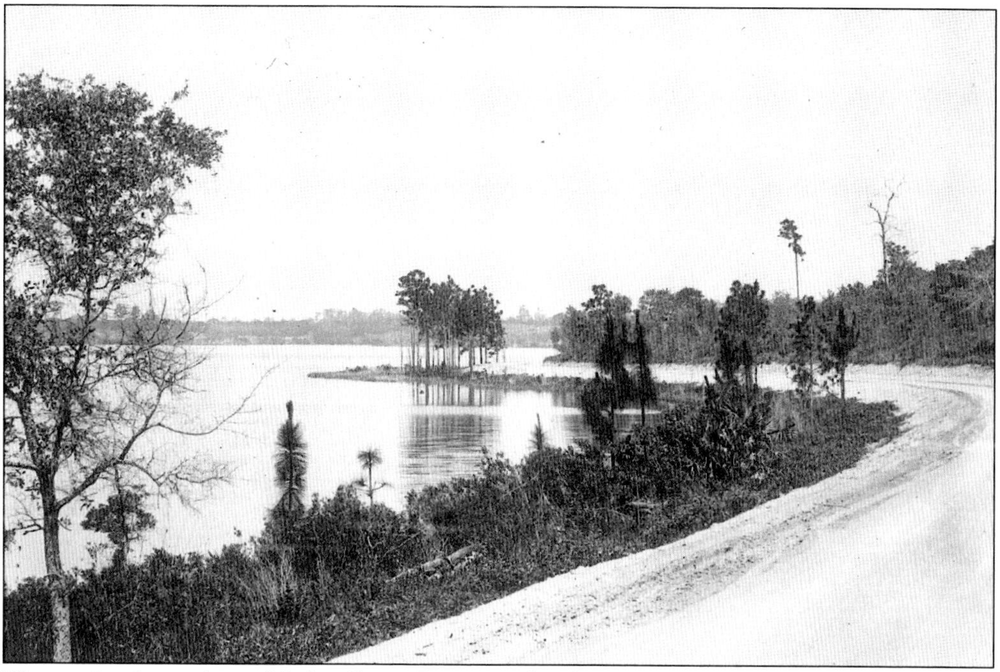

This early photo showed Lake Shore Drive in the days when it was just an unpaved road encircling Lake Dora. Although the first settlers, fearing maladies accompanying "damp air," preferred to build their homes further from the lake, subsequent residents opted for the waterfront views available along the shoreline.

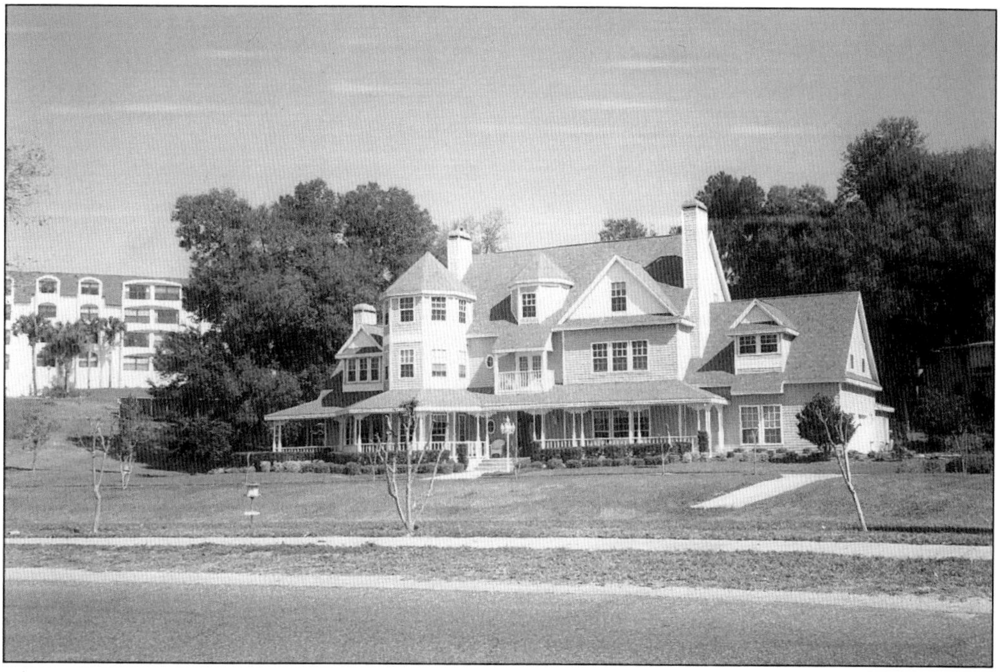

The same area of Lake Shore Drive today is much more heavily traveled. Railroad tracks curve between the lake and the old highway leading to neighboring Tavares. A number of large homes and several bed-and-breakfast inns overlook the lake. (Authors' collection.)

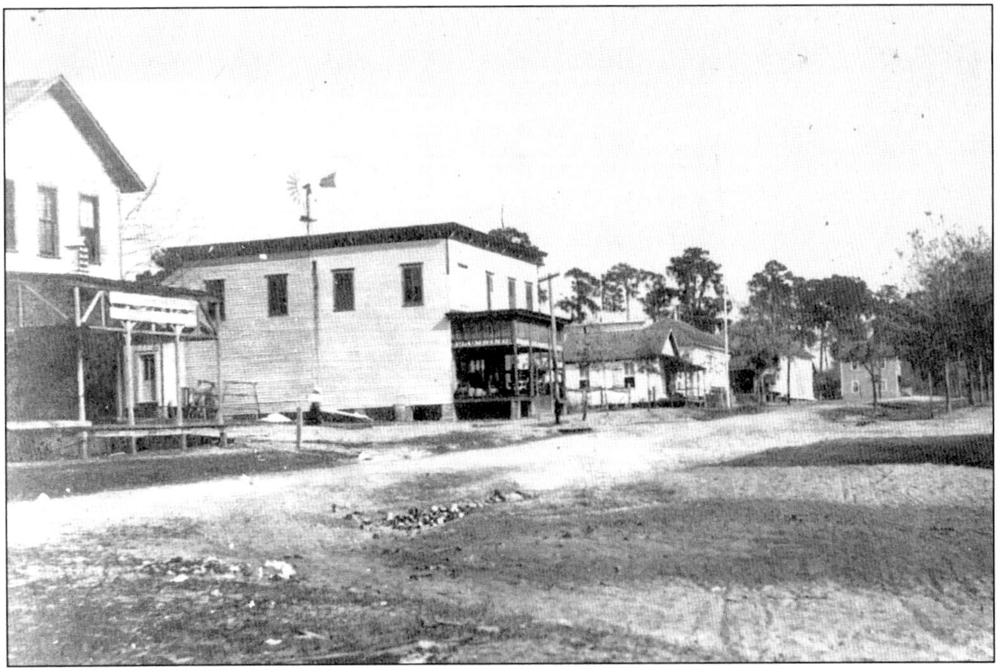

Mount Dora's business district has changed considerably over the years. In 1900, Fourth Avenue presented a drastically different appearance than it does today. The buildings lining the street were wooden, the paving dirt.

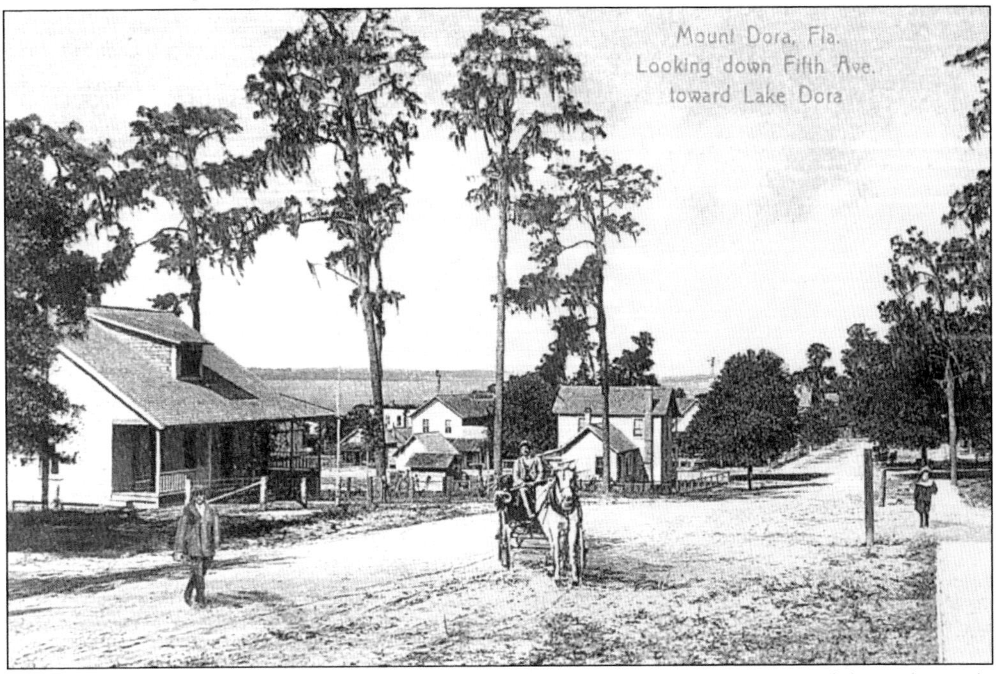

The gentle incline of Mount Dora's Fifth Avenue can be seen in this postcard from the early 1900s. A horse and buggy travels up the dirt street, while Lake Dora is visible in the background. Perhaps early visitors chose to make their homes in the area because the rolling countryside was reminiscent of their former homes in the North.

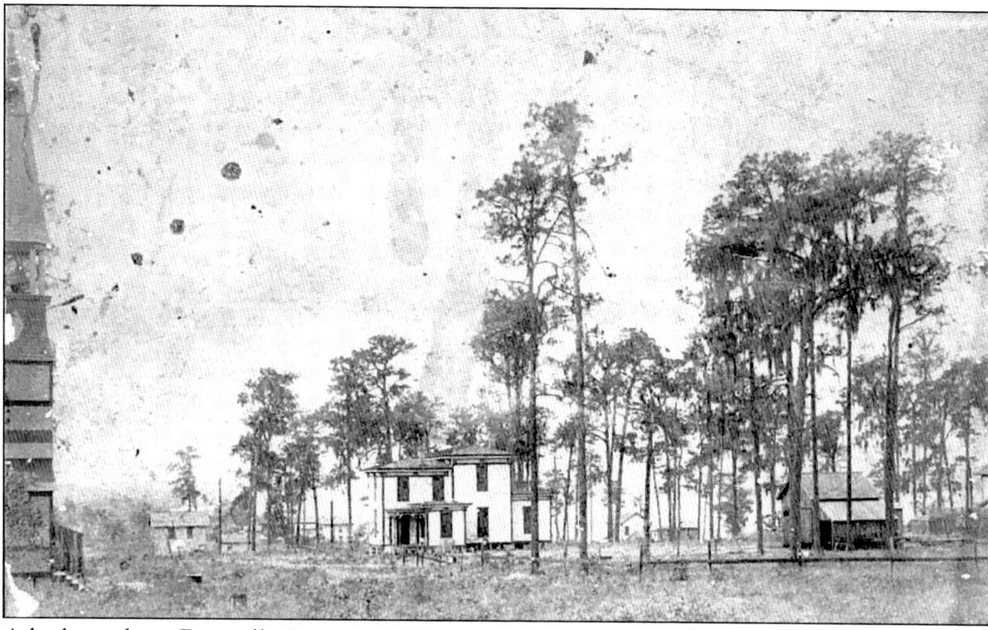

A look south on Donnelly Street in 1888 provided the viewer with little idea of the changes to come. The Congregational Church on the left was just two years old. By the time the Donnelly House, one of Mount Dora's most famous landmarks today, was built just a few short years later, the houses visible in this photograph would have been demolished.

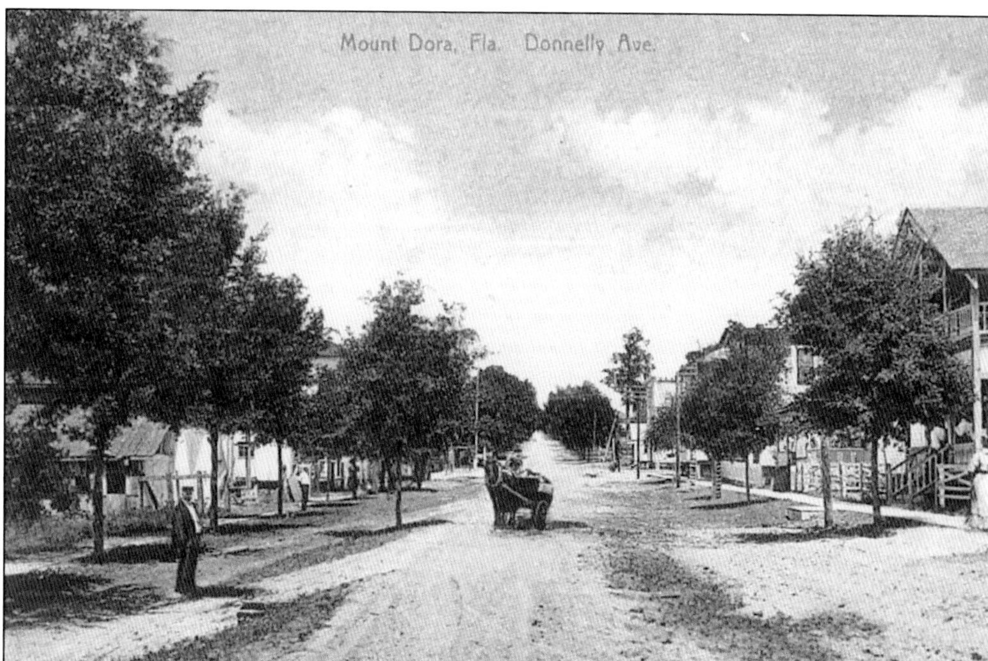

More residents meant more houses and wider streets. Although it was still unpaved when this 1890s image was taken, Donnelly Street was no longer just a dirt path, and it shows the possibility of becoming a major artery in the growing community.

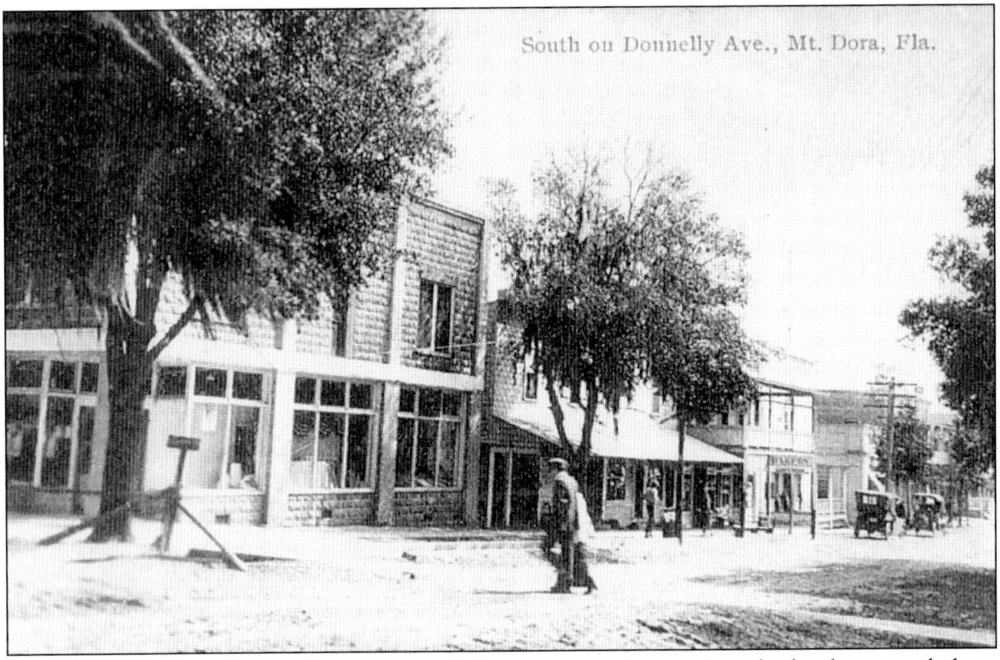

This postcard view of Donnelly Street, *c.* 1910, shows that Mount Dora had at least one bakery at the time. While many of the buildings are frame construction, the one on the corner features a rusticated block exterior. Progress has arrived in the form of the automobile.

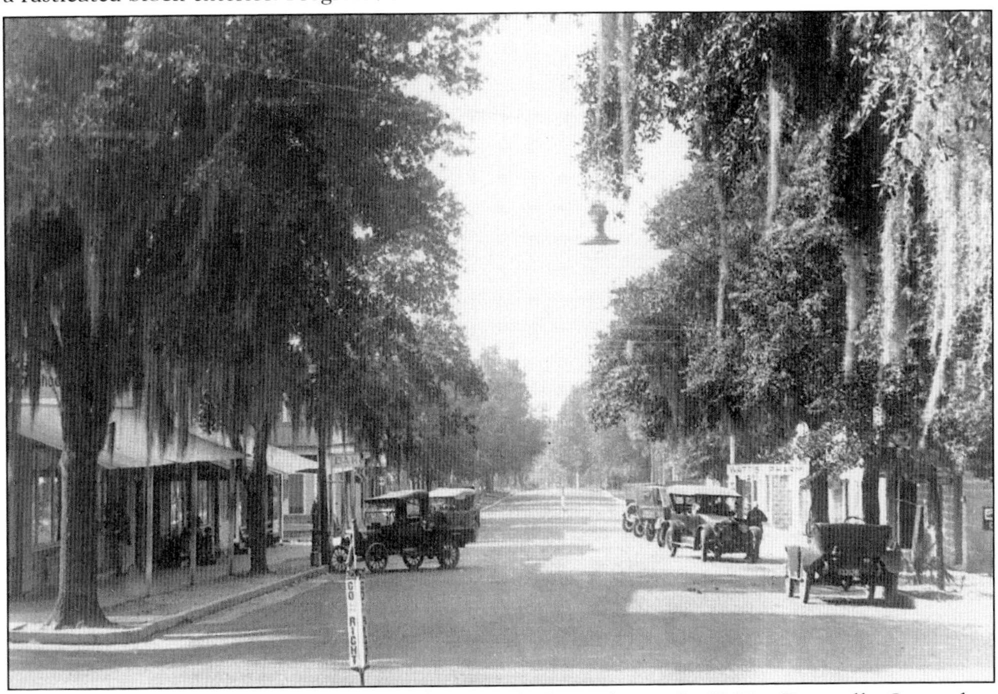

Traffic congestion is apparent in this photograph from the early 1920s. Donnelly Street has not only been paved, but a traffic sign ordering drivers to "go right" has been added. With one exception, angled parking seems to be the norm. Police Chief George Dahlin patrolled Mount Dora on motorcycle, enforcing the rules.

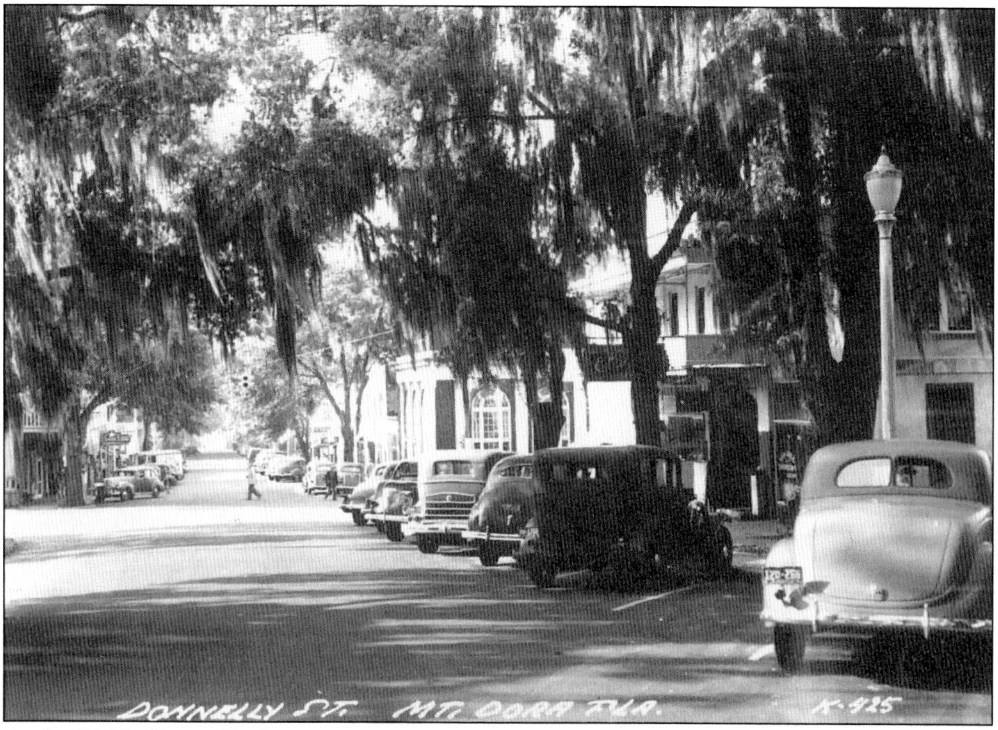

By the 1940s, Donnelly Street has taken on the look of a modern downtown business district. Planted by early resident J.P. Donnelly, the trees, which appeared as small saplings three photographs earlier, are now draped in Spanish moss and majestically shade the street.

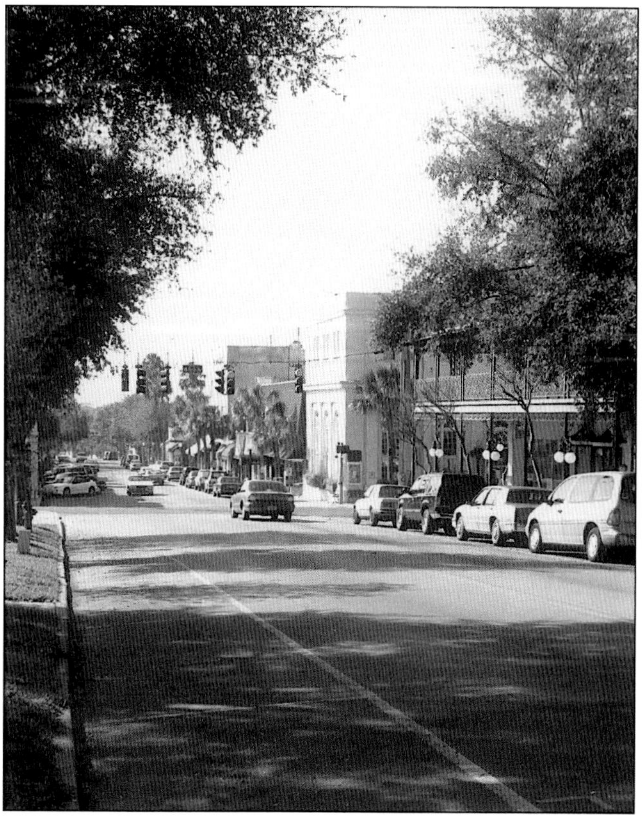

Some of the trees still remain on Donnelly Street today, but the traffic has increased substantially. Crowded with both residents doing their routine shopping and tourists eager to experience the lure of the galleries and antique shops, the area bustles with activity. (Authors' collection.)

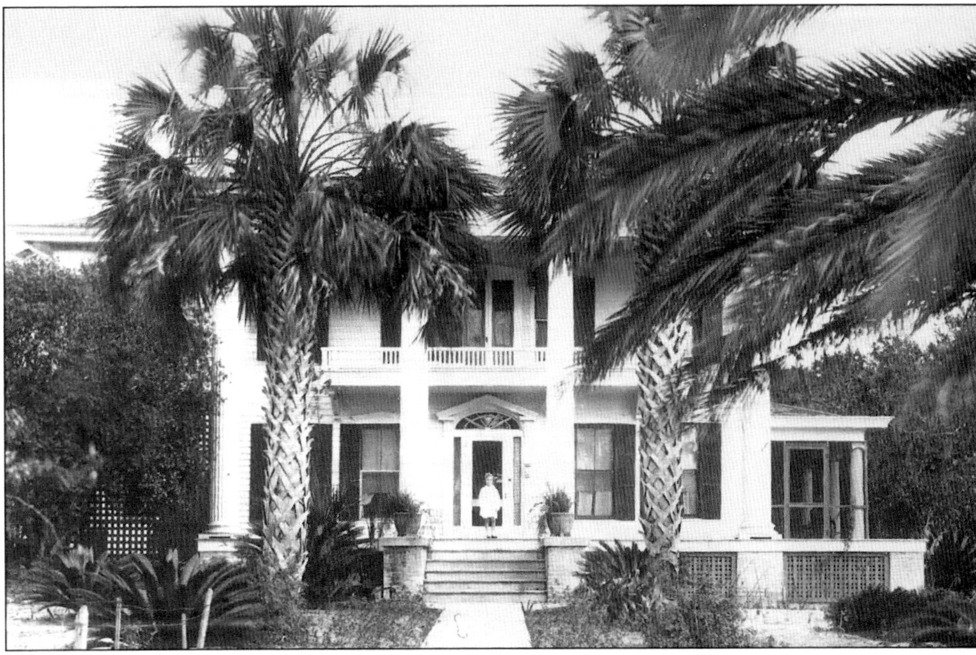

Built by the Reverend Henry Guller in the early 1880s, Guller House went through several changes in ownership before being sold to the city of Mount Dora during the Great Depression for $15,000. Used as city hall until 1963, Guller House was dismantled and reassembled in the nearby community of Astatula.

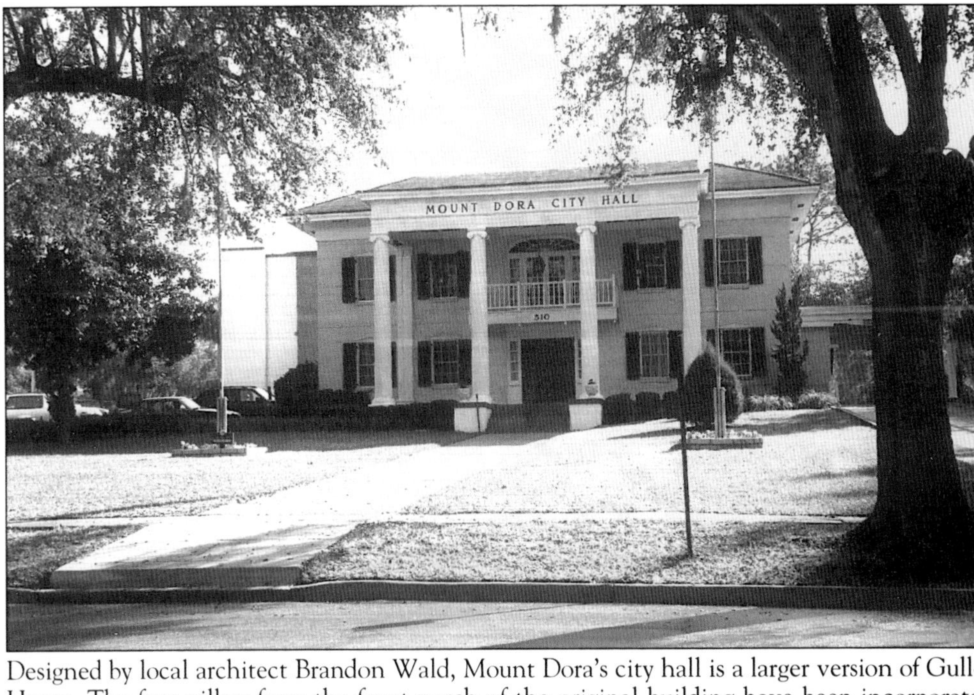

Designed by local architect Brandon Wald, Mount Dora's city hall is a larger version of Guller House. The four pillars from the front porch of the original building have been incorporated into the more efficiently designed contemporary version. Located next to Community Hall on Baker Street, city hall overlooks Donnelly Park. (Authors' collection.)

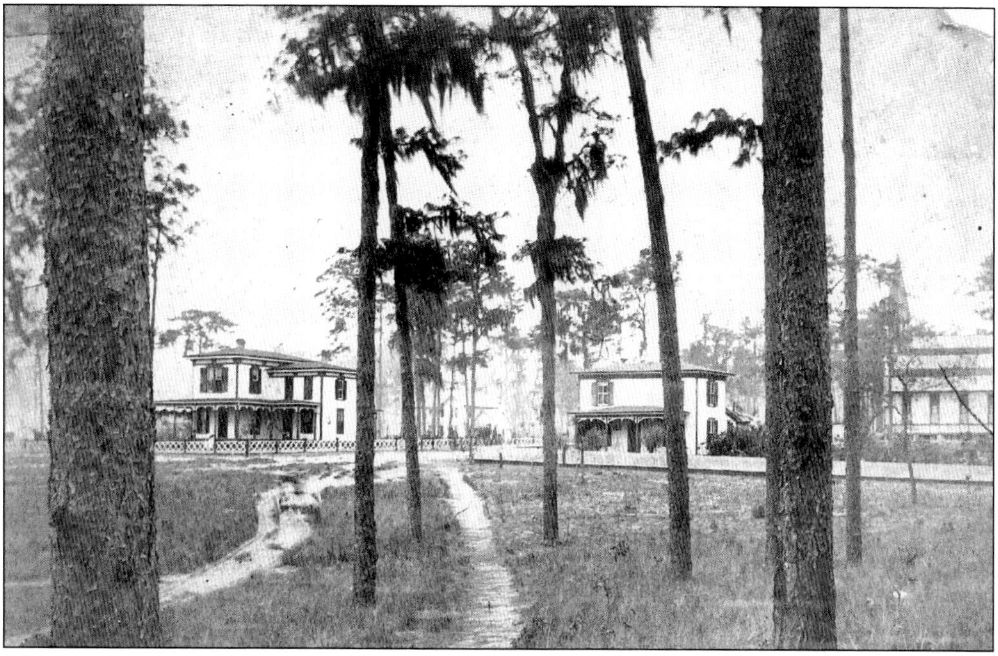

This 1888 view of a grassy lot with a few scattered trees shows the area that would eventually become Donnelly Park. In the background on the far right is the Congregational Church. The Else residence is shown on the left; Dr. Lewis's house is in the center.

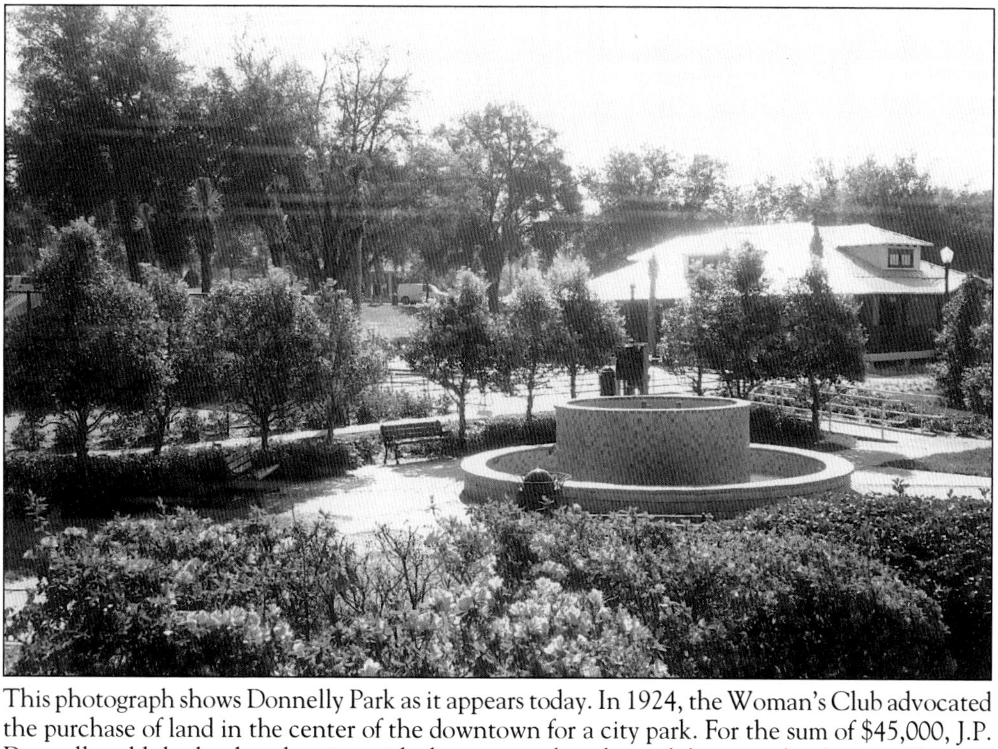

This photograph shows Donnelly Park as it appears today. In 1924, the Woman's Club advocated the purchase of land in the center of the downtown for a city park. For the sum of $45,000, J.P. Donnelly sold the land to the city, with the proviso that the park be named in honor of his late wife, Annie McDonald Stone Donnelly. (Authors' collection.)

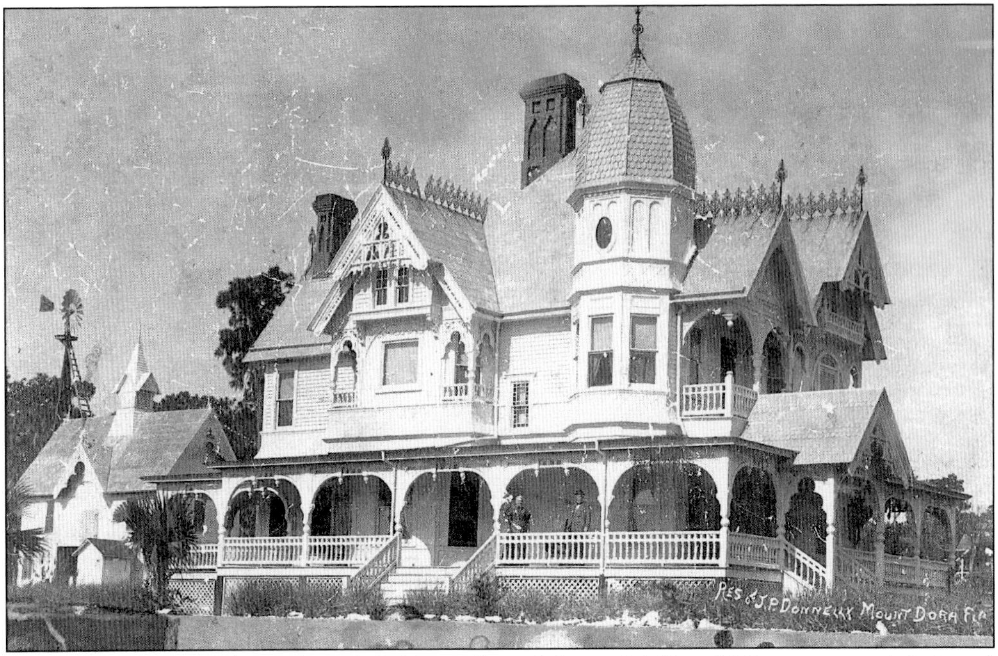

Two of the town's early residents, J.P. Donnelly and Annie McDonald Stone, merged their real estate holdings when they married in 1881. A portion of their combined properties included what today is downtown Mount Dora. Donnelly built this house as a gift for his wife in 1893.

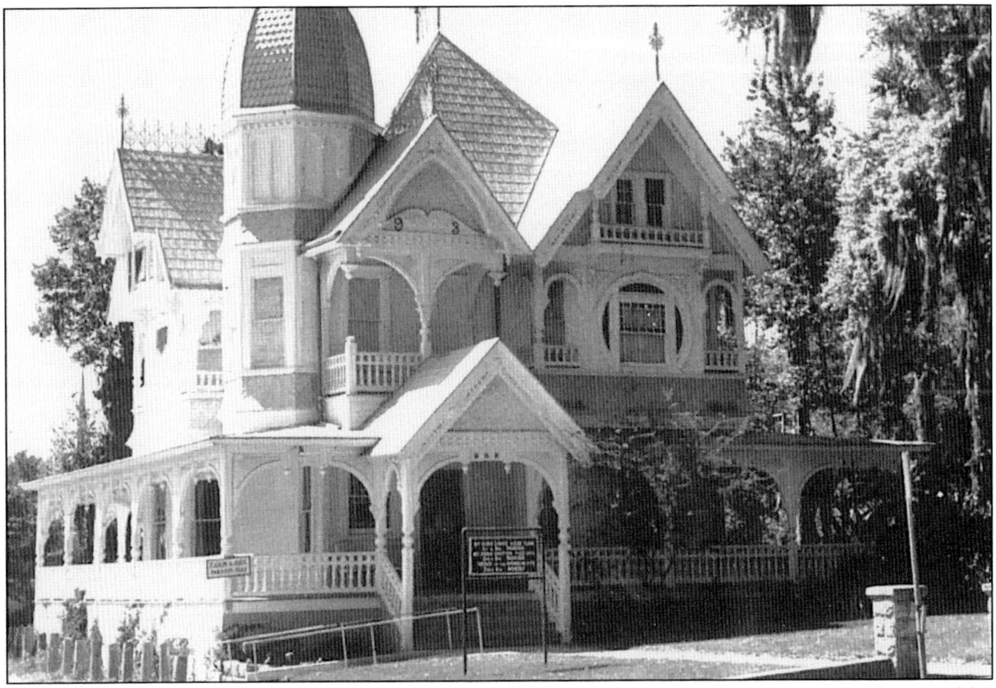

Visitors to Mount Dora who gush about the "wonderful Victorian homes" and "just like New England" are referring to Donnelly House. An eye-catching example of Queen Anne architecture, the house is listed on the National Register of Historic Places and is currently home to Masonic Lodge #238.

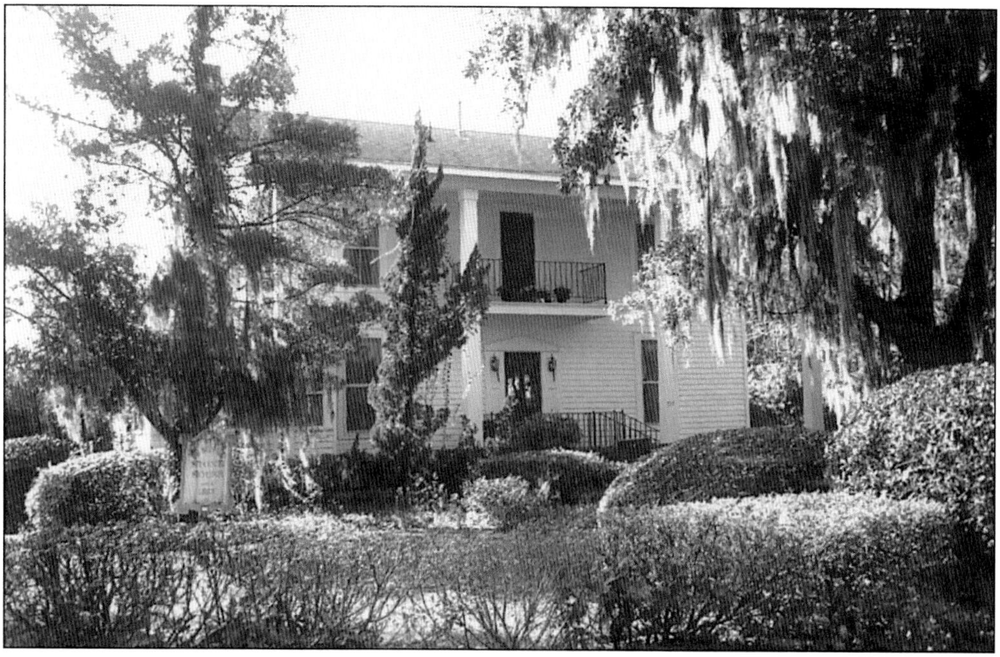

Annie McDonald Stone built this stately residence prior to her marriage to J.P. Donnelly. Set amidst tall moss-draped trees at 717 McDonald Street, the house is one of the most elegant in Mount Dora. A sign in the front yard denotes the significance of the house to local history. (Authors' collection.)

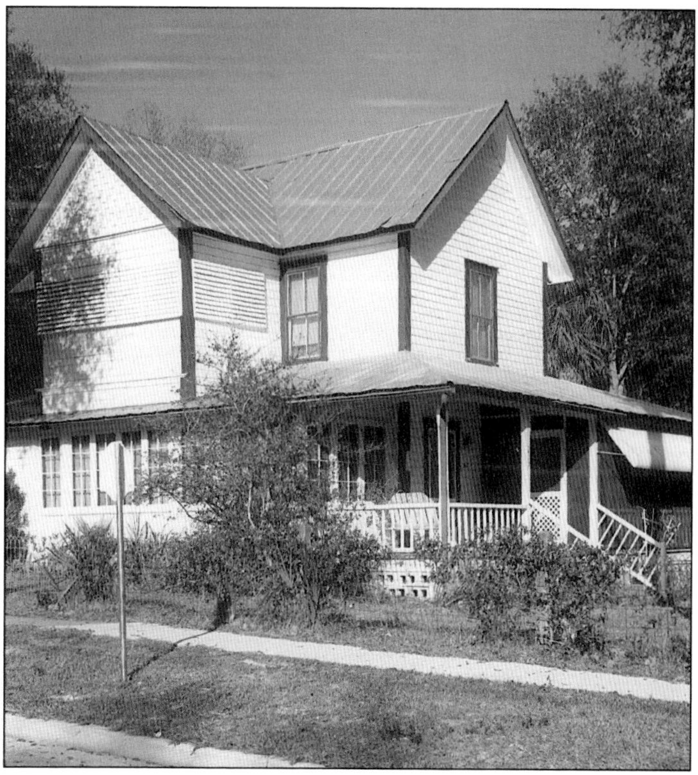

Home of another one of the city's early residents, this frame vernacular house was built by Col. John Alexander in the late 1880s. A founder of Mount Dora's Methodist Church, Alexander was also one of the partners, along with Annie McDonald Stone and John McDonald, who built the hotel that became the Lakeside Inn. (Authors' collection.)

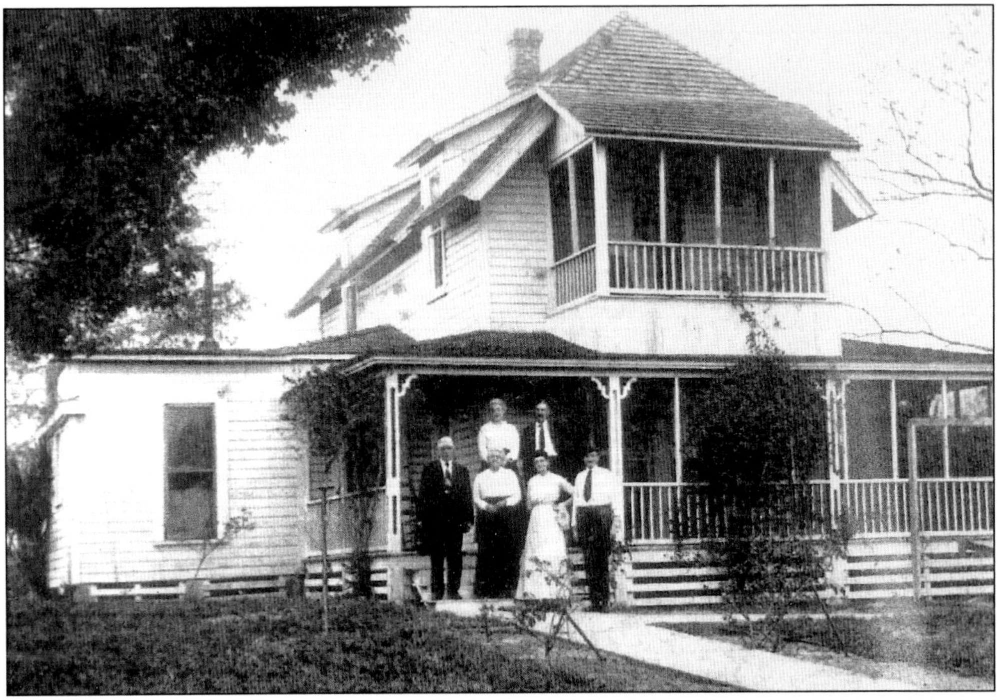

In 1883, Horatio Gates and his family, originally from Elyria, OH, built this house. At the age of 15, daughter Edith Gates became the first teacher of the public school in what was to become Mount Dora. Her sister, Gertrude, taught there during the 1893–94 school year.

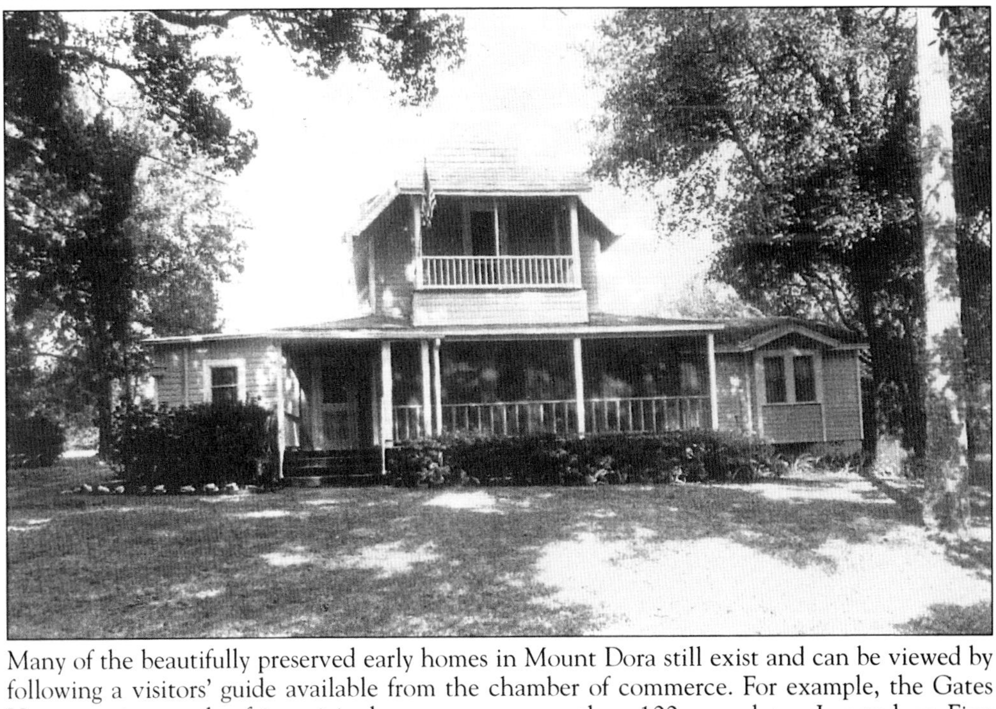

Many of the beautifully preserved early homes in Mount Dora still exist and can be viewed by following a visitors' guide available from the chamber of commerce. For example, the Gates House retains much of its original appearance more than 100 years later. Located on First Avenue, the residence was also home to one of Mount Dora's mayors.

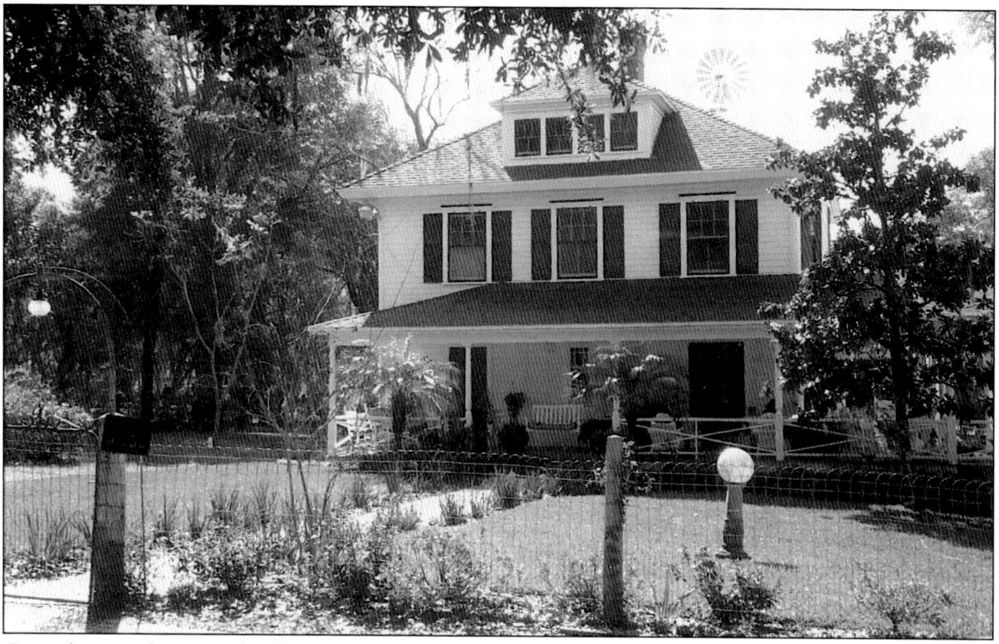

Complete with a windmill attached to the roof of an outbuilding, the William Watt House is still visible at the corner of Third and Grandview. The owner of many acres of citrus, Watt invented corrugated cardboard as a packing medium for his oranges. Although only a few trees remain in the yard today, it is easy to envision Watt's residence surrounded by groves. (Authors' collection.)

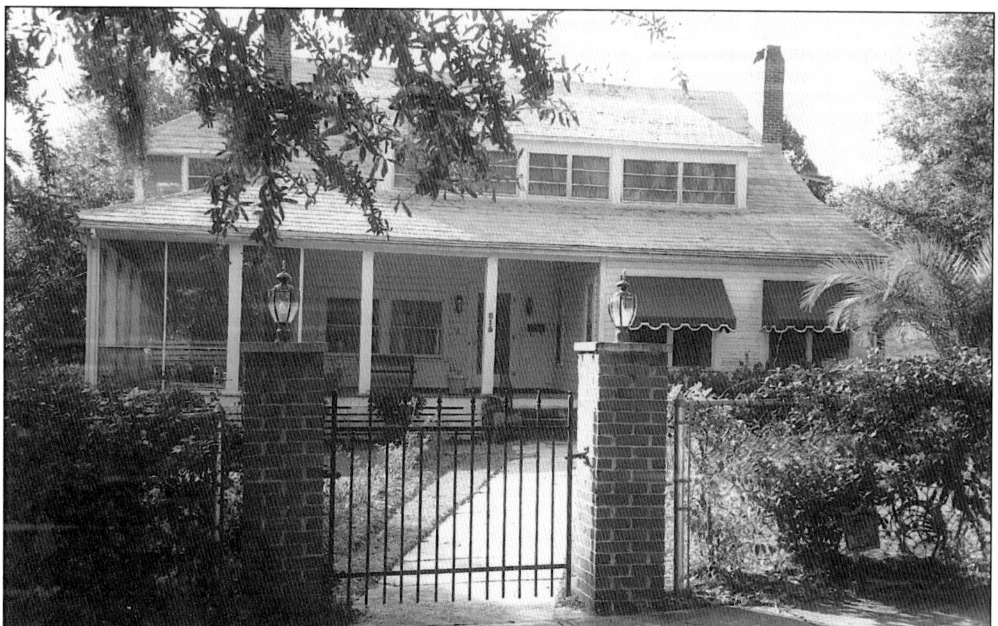

With a wide porch that wraps around three sides of the house, the J.H. Crane House at 815 McDonald Street was built by Gertrude Thorne in 1906 as a sanitarium. Several years later, she sold the home to Crane, the teacher at the Mount Dora public school and subsequent principal of Educational Hall. (Authors' collection.)

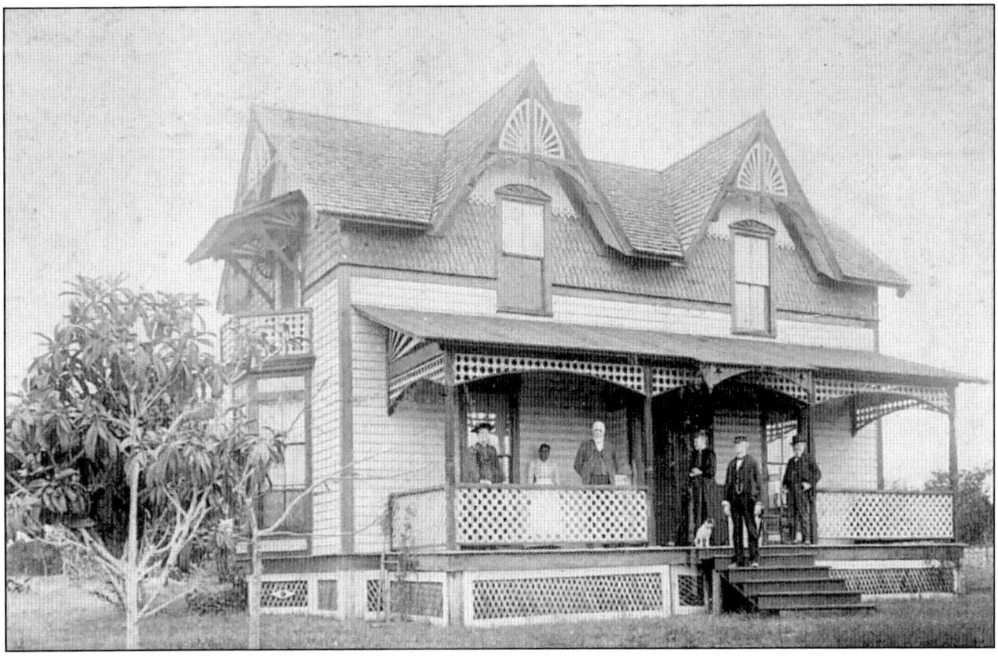

Fred and Nellie Risley came to Mount Dora in 1882. A builder and contractor by profession, Risley built several notable hotels in Florida including the Longwood Hotel, Sanford House, and Enterprise Hotel. The house was destroyed by fire in 1925.

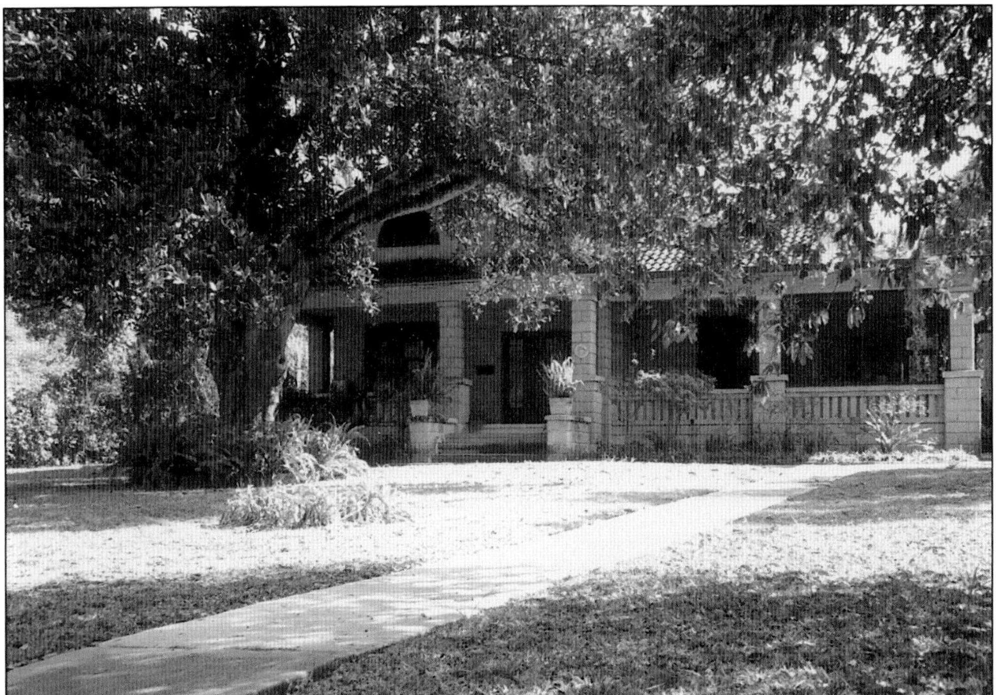

Located on North Tremain Street, this house was built by the Risley's son Carl after the destruction of the family home in 1925. Situated behind the original house was Carl Risley's cement business, the source of most of Mount Dora's original sidewalks. (Authors' collection.)

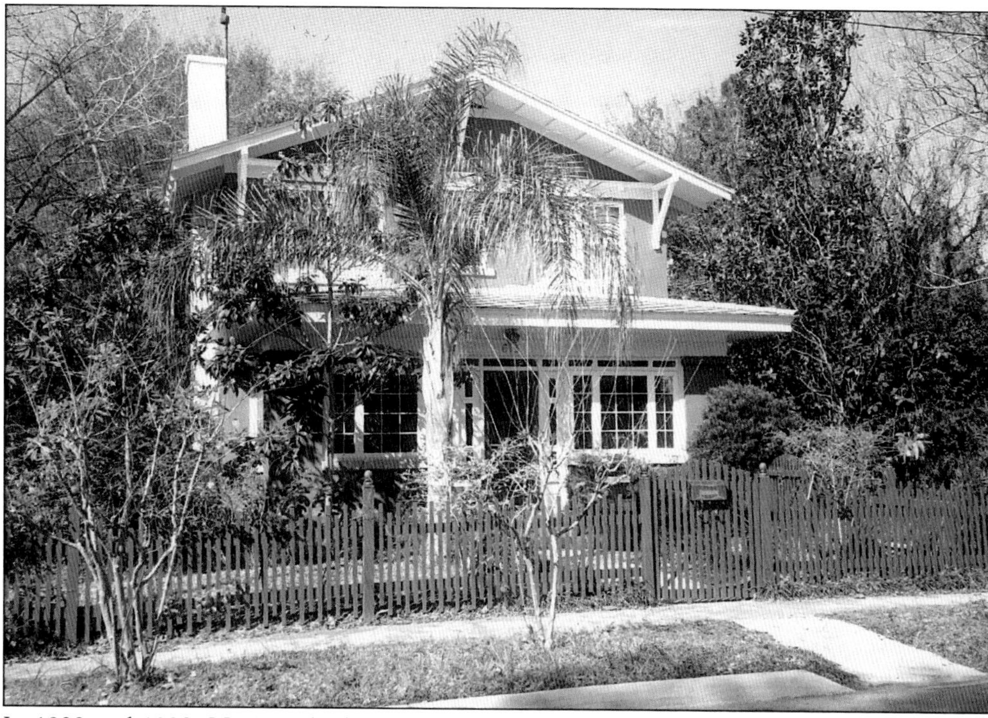

In 1922 and 1923, J.J. West built two nearly identical houses on Grandview Street as homes for his sister and himself. A fervent believer in Florida's growth, West played a leading role in Mount Dora's real estate boom. (Authors' collection.)

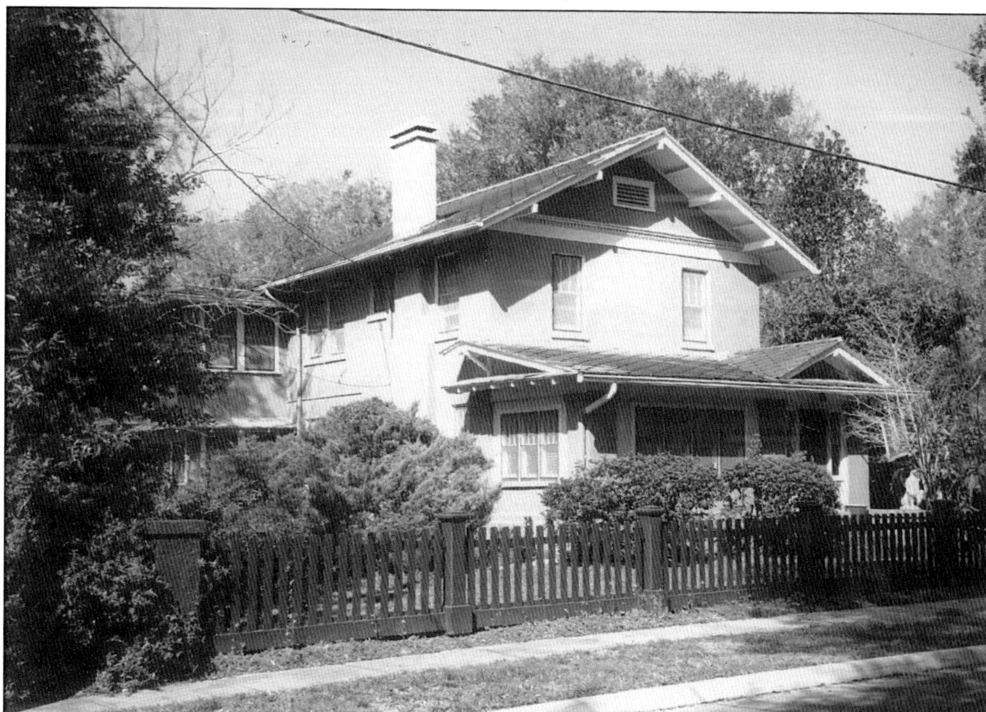

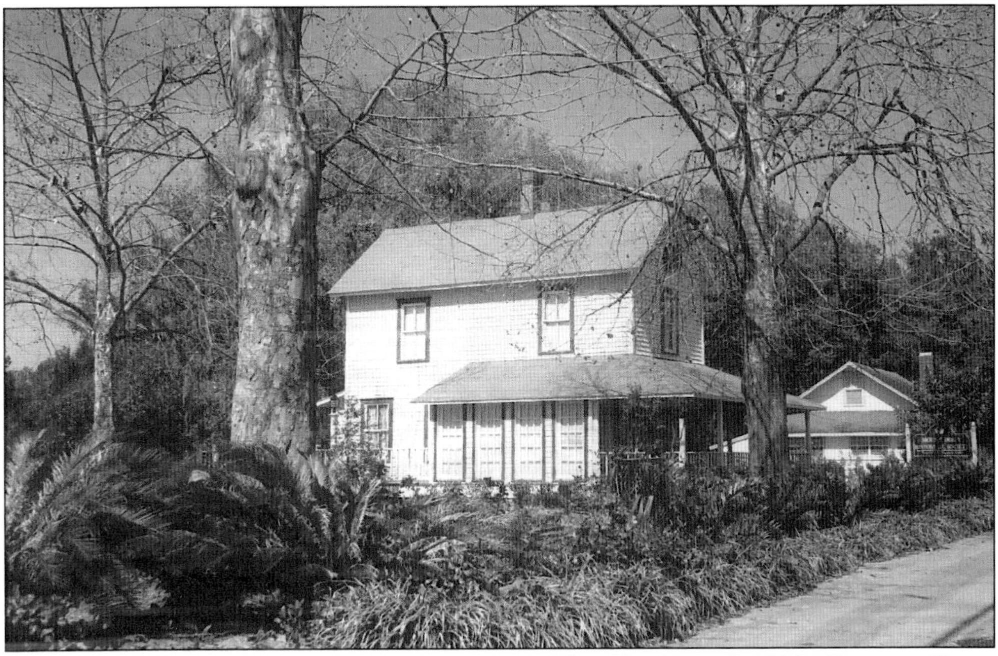

Now headquarters for Historic Mount Dora, Inc., the Charles and Alfida Simpson House was moved to 2015 North Donnelly Street in 1993. Built around 1900, the house was facing destruction until it was saved by local preservationists. (Authors' collection.)

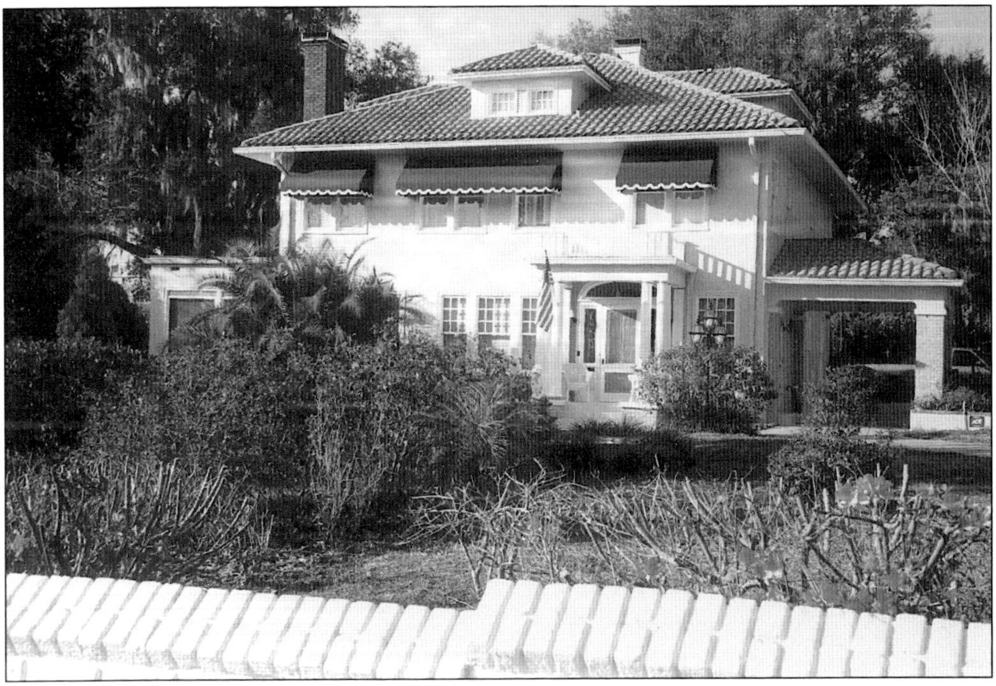

The residence of another one of Mount Dora's developers, L.R. Heim, is typical of the Spanish or Mediterranean Revival style of architecture so popular in Florida during the 1920s. Painted a soft pink color and sporting a red clay tile roof, the house survives today as one of Mount Dora's bed-and-breakfast inns. (Authors' collection.)

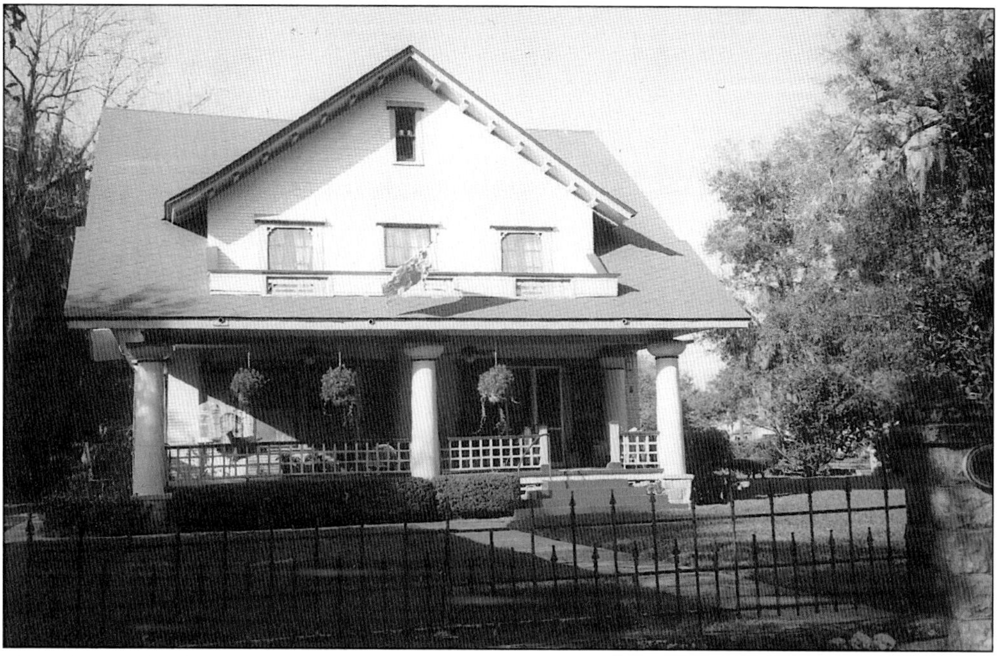

The Wardell-Wilmot House is a perfect example of a Craftsman bungalow. Built in 1917, the residence occupies one-half of the 300 block of West Ninth Avenue. Constructed from blueprints available from *The Craftsman* magazine, Sears Roebuck, Montgomery Ward, and other companies, the houses could also be purchased as kits. Bungalows came in a variety of designs and were extremely popular in the years prior to World War II. (Authors' collection.)

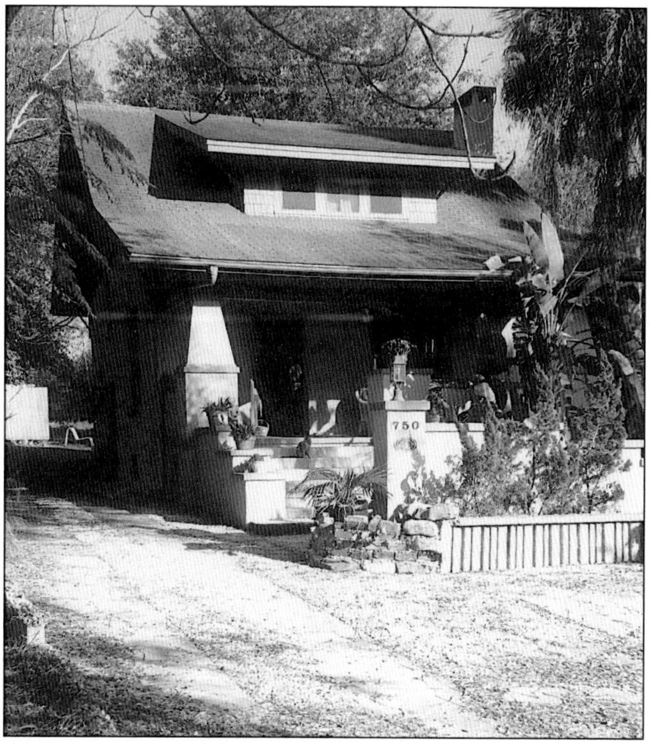

Built in 1923, the residence located at 750 North Grandview Street is another example of the bungalow type of architecture. Its low, sweeping roofline with parallel gable angles and the masonry porch piers with elephantine columns are characteristic of this style, a design that began in California and rapidly spread across America.

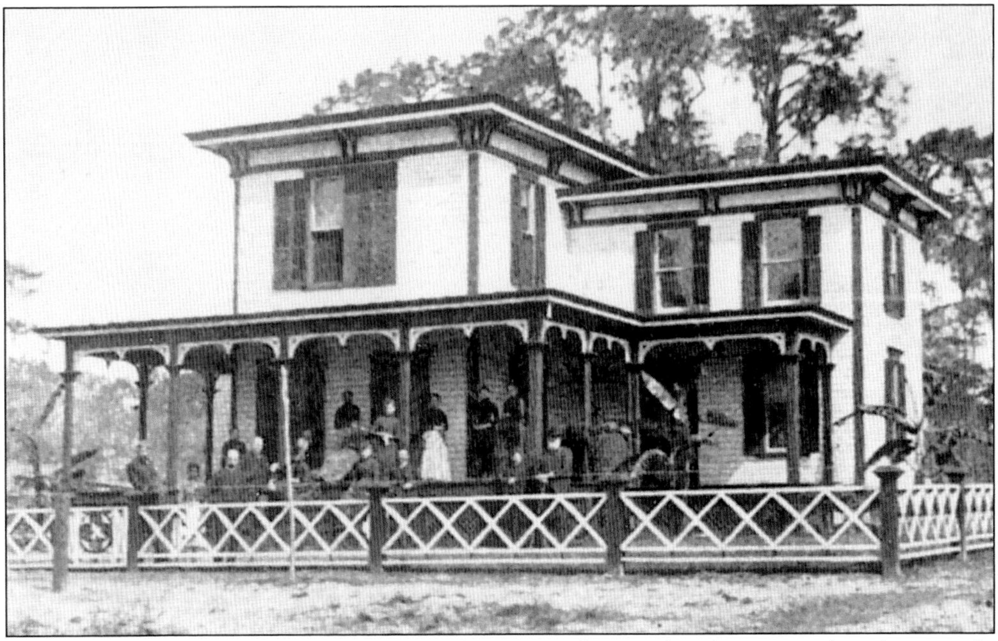

The porch of the Else-Backus House was the scene of a social gathering in this photograph. Mr. and Mrs. Thomas Else of Philadelphia bought the house from J.P. Donnelly as a winter residence. Later, their nephew, George Backus, and his family also became seasonal residents of Mount Dora. When purchased in 1890 for a selling price of $1,950, the property was said to include one-half block of land, the 11-room house, a barn, and some 40 orange trees.

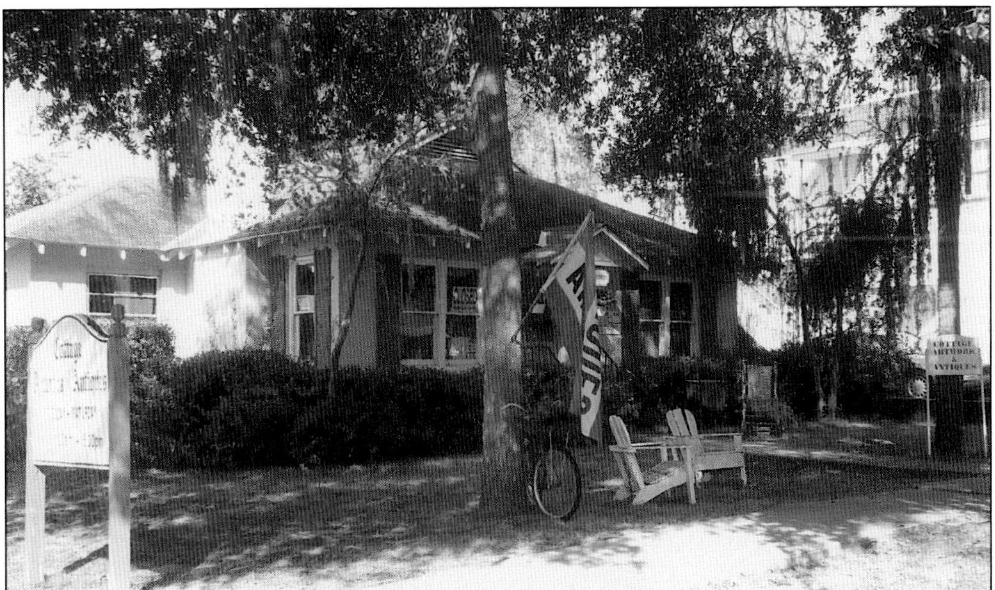

Despite the best efforts of preservationists, over the years many historic structures have disappeared. Demolished in July 1932, the Else-Backus House no longer exists; the barn and orange groves have also disappeared. All four corners of the intersection of Sixth and Donnelly Street are instead occupied by commercial entities, such as this rather quaint antique shop. (Authors' collection.)

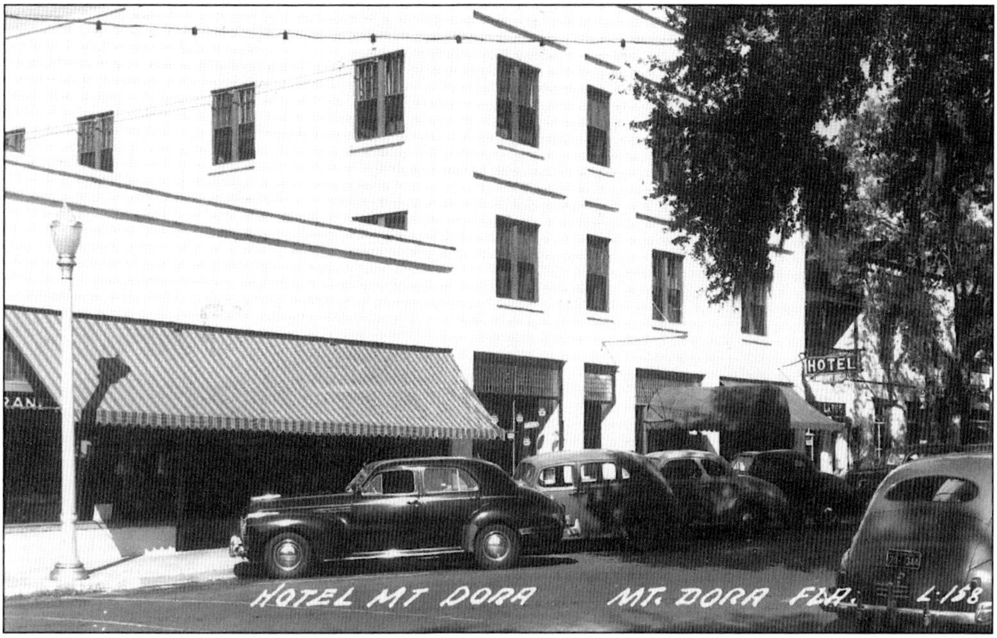

Visitors to Mount Dora have always needed a place to stay. In 1922, the Florida land boom created an influx of visitors, inspiring construction of the Mount Dora Hotel. In the late 1940s, when this photograph was taken, hotel guests may have been former servicemen who first visited Florida for military training during World War II.

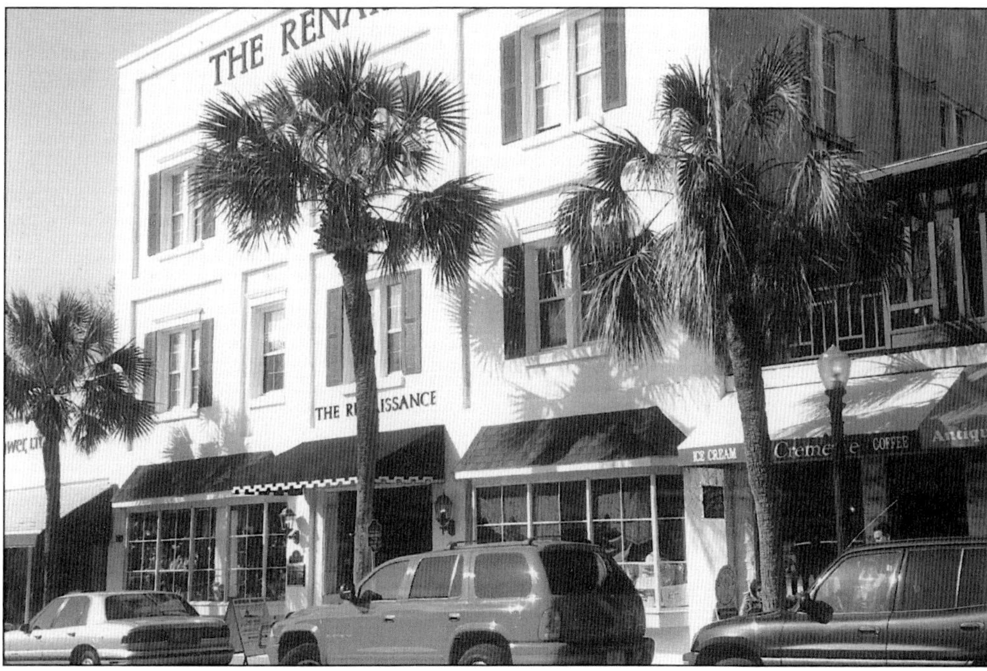

Much of Mount Dora's charm stems from its preservation and adaptive reuse of significant residential and commercial structures in the community. The former Mount Dora Hotel, 411 North Donnelly Street, has been renamed the Renaissance Building and has been converted into retail and office space. (Authors' collection.)

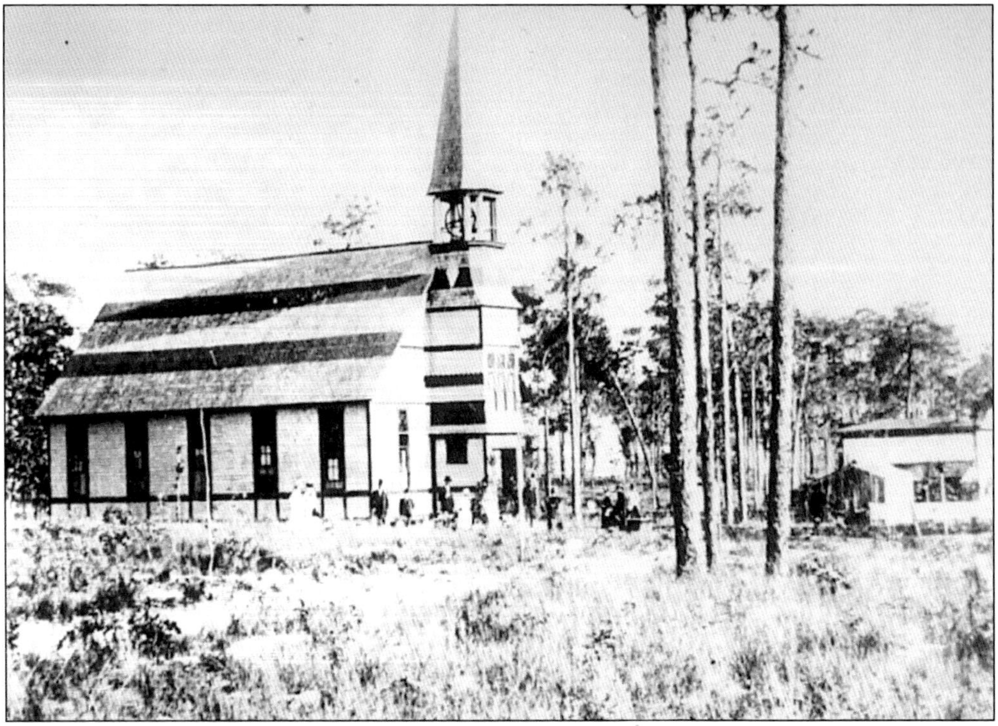

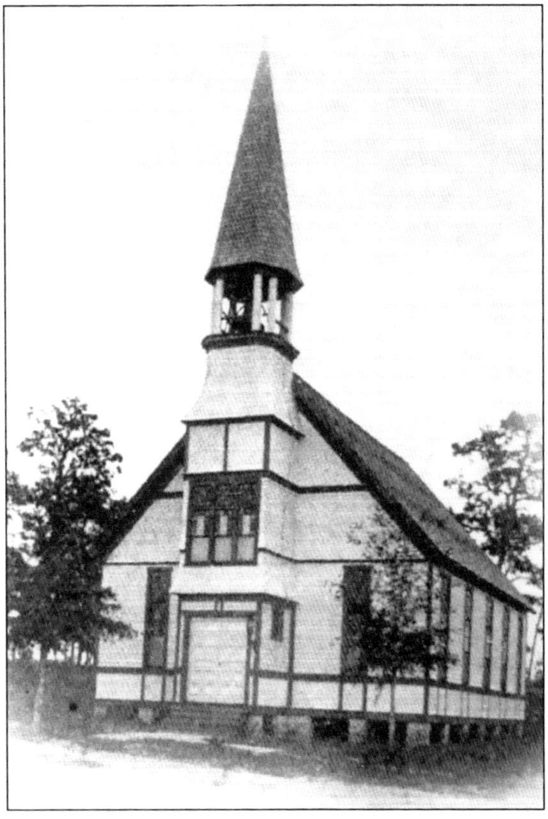

Less than four years after its founding in the home of one of its nine charter members, the new Congregational Church building opened for worship services in 1887. Built on land donated by J.P. Donnelly, the church was the second denomination in Mount Dora.

Until the 1920s, a succession of pastors, most of whom were winter visitors, conducted services at the Congregational Church. Except for Sunday school and prayer meetings, services were discontinued during the summer months. In 1929, the church was renamed the Community Congregational Church.

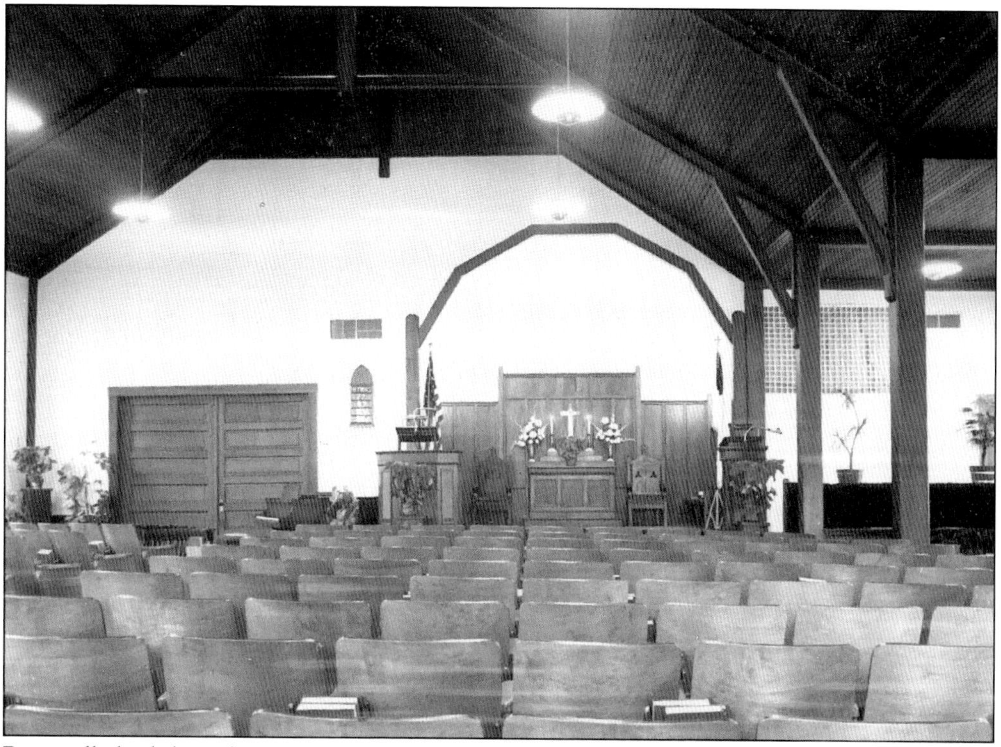

Reputedly built by a ship's carpenter from Philadelphia, the interior of the Community Congregational Church features a simplicity of style that gives credence to the idea. During the winter of 1929–30, former President and Mrs. Calvin Coolidge attended services.

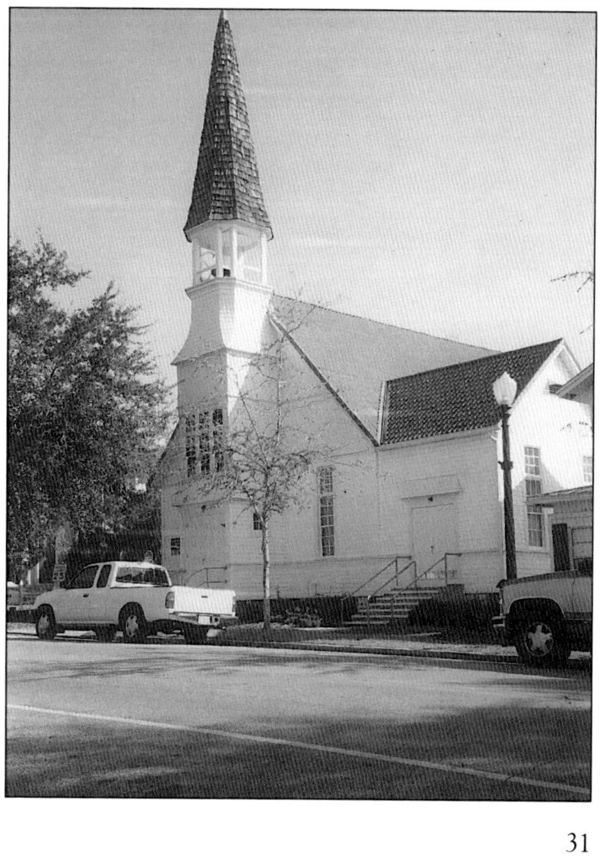

Located at 650 Donnelly Street, the Community Congregational Church is the oldest 19th-century church still in existence in Mount Dora. Despite some changes and additions, the present building bears a marked resemblance to the original. (Authors' collection.)

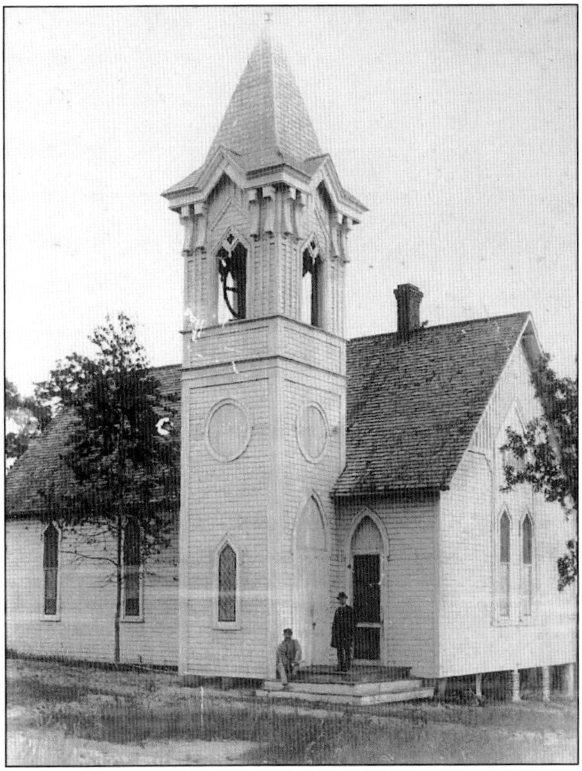

The First Methodist Church was organized in 1882 with the Reverend Henry Guller as pastor. Built at the corner of Baker Street and Fifth Avenue on land donated by J.P. Donnelly, the church was completed in 1885. According to church history, the congregation, in 1888, purchased a 40-inch bell; members contributed a reed organ. First Methodist Church had fewer than 50 members until 1920 and fewer than 200 until 1934.

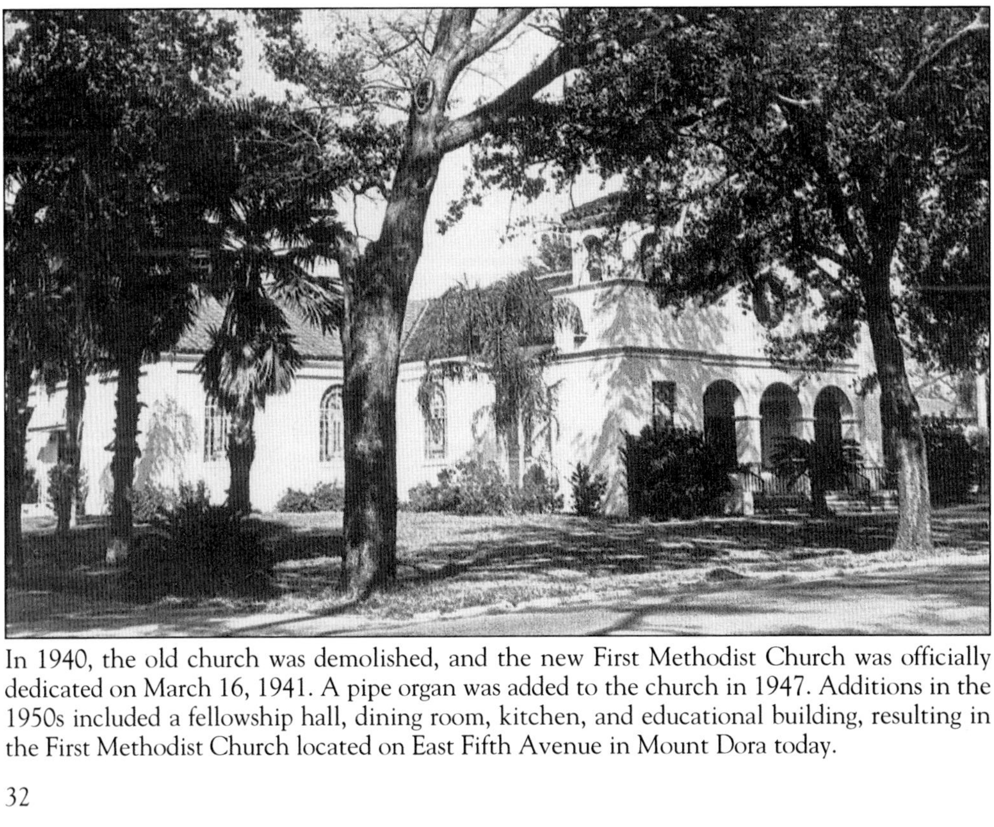

In 1940, the old church was demolished, and the new First Methodist Church was officially dedicated on March 16, 1941. A pipe organ was added to the church in 1947. Additions in the 1950s included a fellowship hall, dining room, kitchen, and educational building, resulting in the First Methodist Church located on East Fifth Avenue in Mount Dora today.

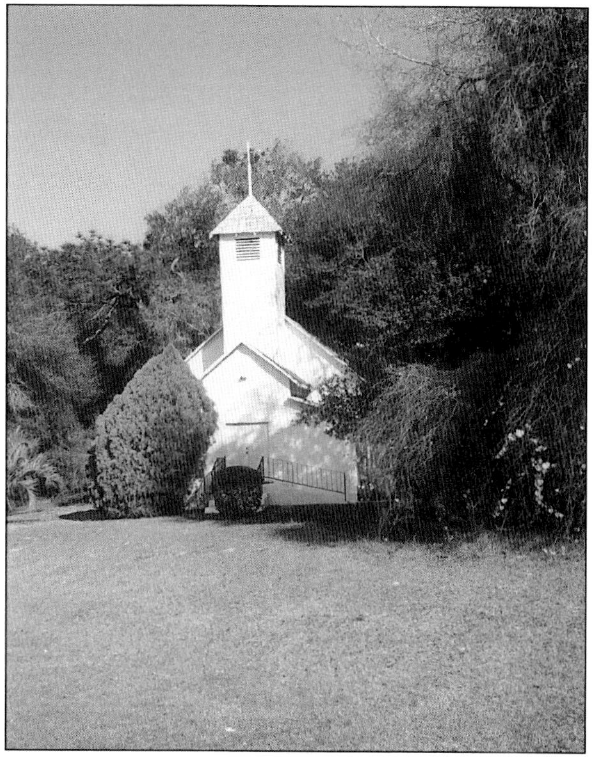

Situated between the modern U.S. Highway 441 and the dirt Harris Road on the outskirts of town, the Mount Zion Primitive Baptist Church seems caught between two time periods. The church itself is a modest frame structure with a tin roof; its only sign hangs from a canted wooden post in the side yard. Its simple style is typical of many early country churches of the era. (Authors' collection.)

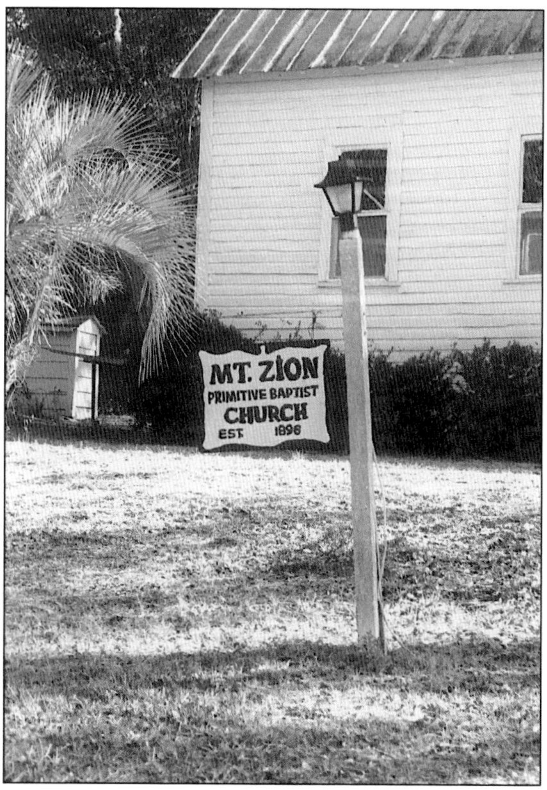

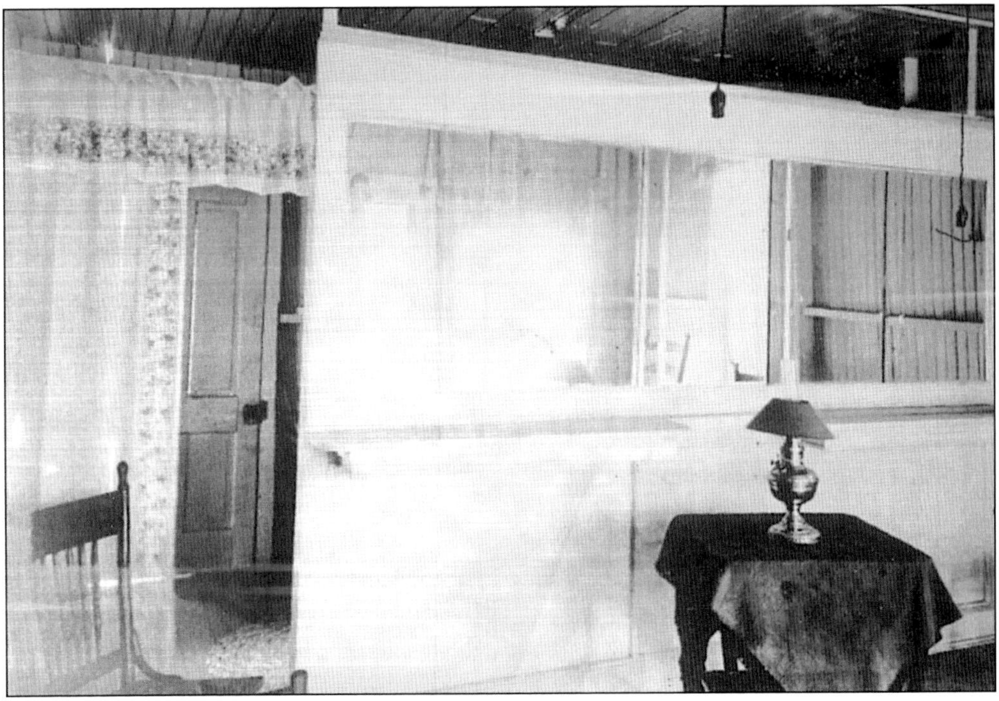

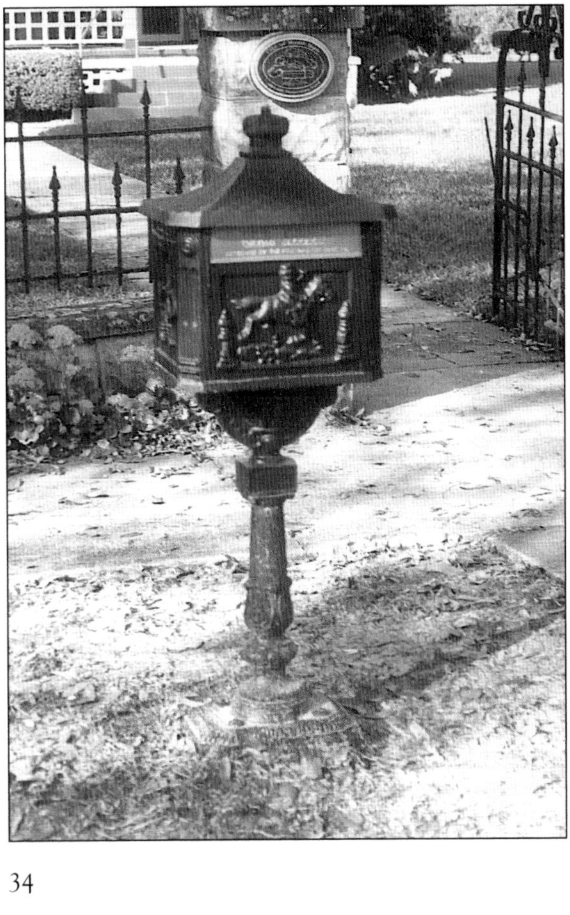

The location of the post office in Mount Dora depended upon the year in question. In some instances, the post office was housed in one corner of a business establishment; at other times, it was located in the home of the postmaster or postmistress. In 1918, this residential-type post office was photographed as part of a legal action against the city.

Whether a private residence, hollow tree, or bus, certainly the town's early postal facilities were more unusual than the current site. Today Mount Dora's post office, located on North Donnelly Street, is situated in a modern building devoted solely to postal purposes. Some Mount Dora citizens, however, prefer elaborate old-fashioned mailboxes, such as this, for the home delivery of their mail. (Authors' collection.)

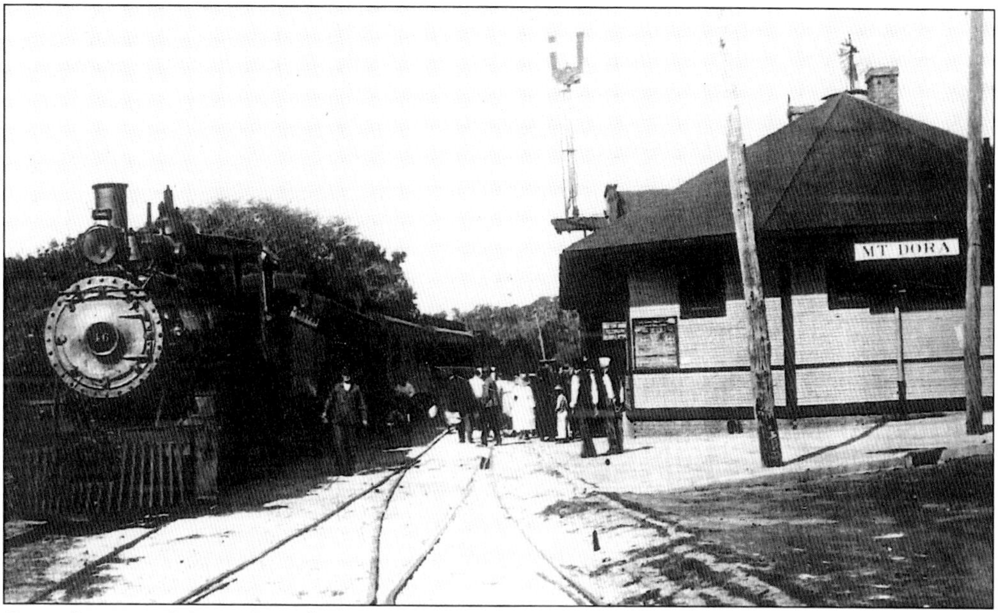

Over the years, Mount Dora has seen a succession of train depots. While the first two stations were similar in design, this depot, complete with locomotive and departing passengers, dates from 1915 and was constructed for a cost of $8,223.

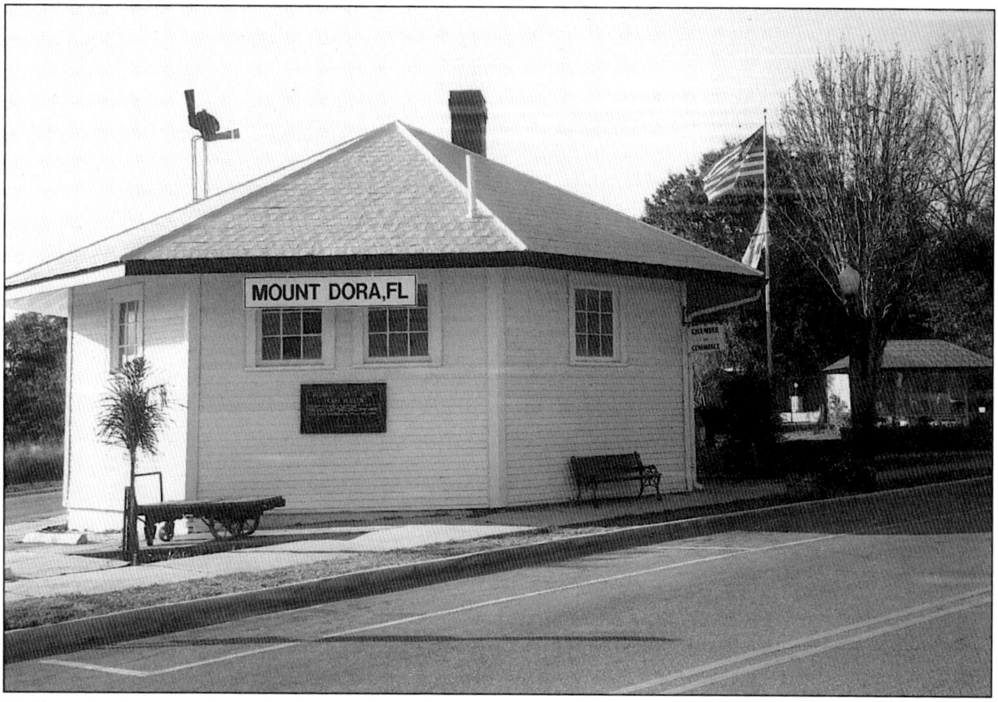

Today the former Atlantic Coast Line Railroad depot welcomes visitors arriving by different modes of transportation. The building housed the passenger station until 1950 and served as the freight depot until 1973, before being converted to the offices of the Mount Dora Chamber of Commerce. The depot is listed on the National Register of Historic Places. (Authors' collection.)

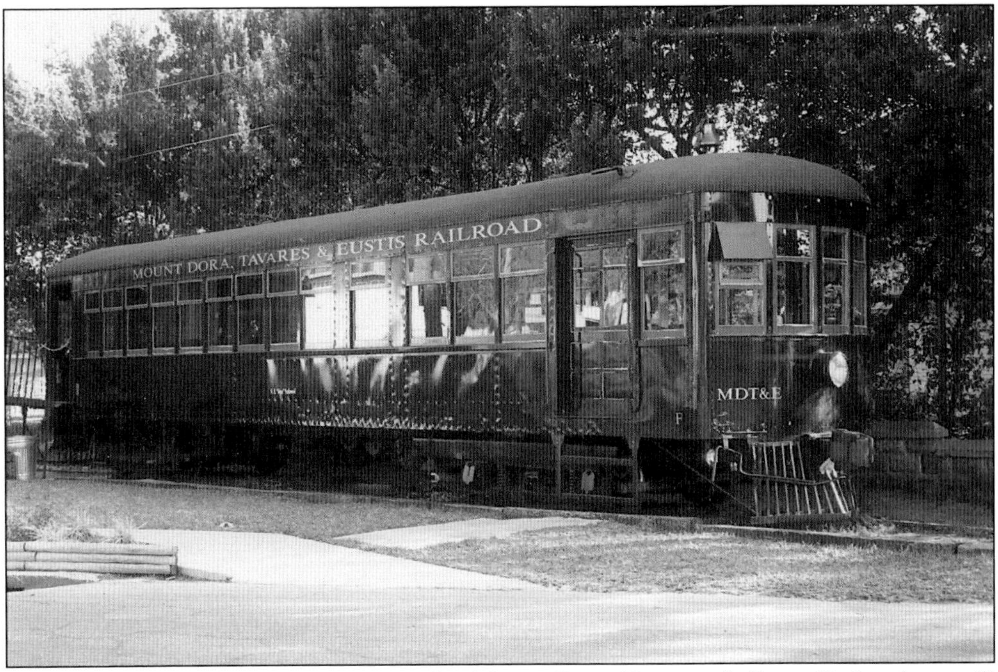

Just as it did more than 100 years ago, this Mount Dora, Tavares, & Eustis Railroad car still carries visitors to Mount Dora. Today, however, the passengers are tourists from all over the world who are enjoying a sightseeing excursion on the Mount Dora Scenic Railroad. (Authors' collection.)

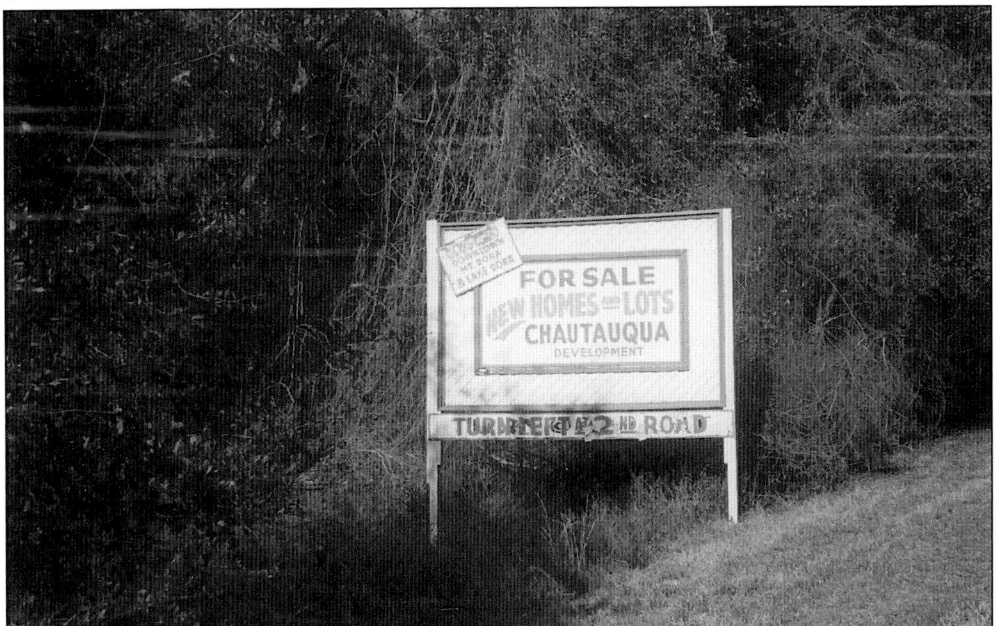

A booming real estate market awaits those visitors who decide to make their stay in the area a permanent one. Using a name that evokes one of the more significant cultural events in Mount Dora's history, this sign advertises the sale of lots and homes in the Chautauqua Development. (Authors' collection.)

Two

BEGINNINGS

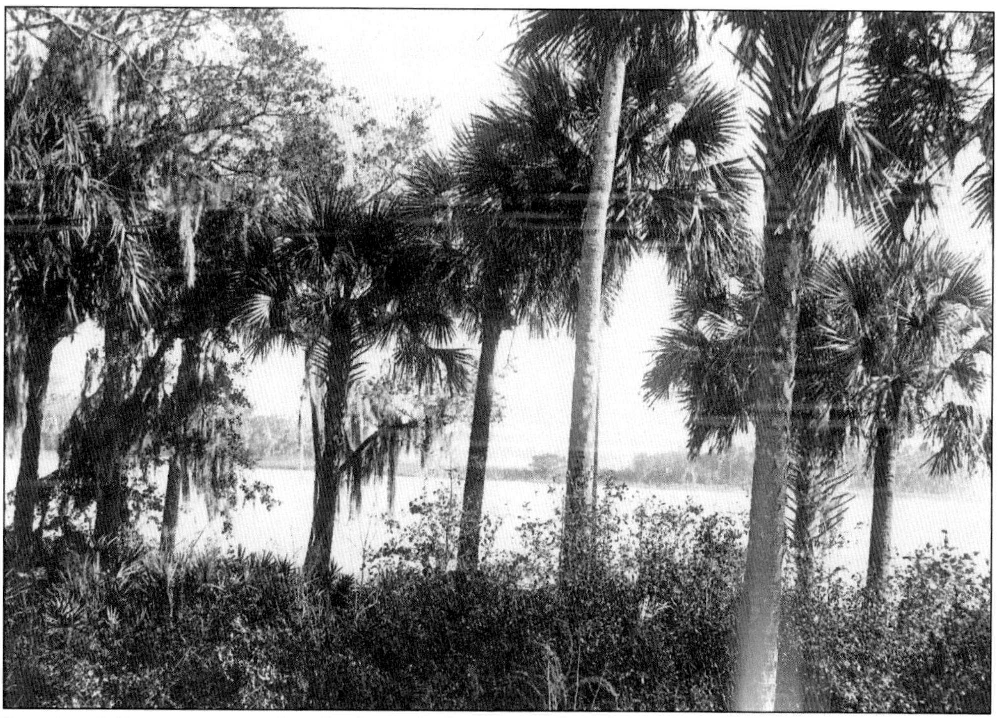

Imagine following a rutted path through dense woods only to come upon a shimmering body of water gleaming in the distance through the trees. Such was the experience of many of the first residents of the community that would come to be known as Mount Dora. When the first pieces of property were being homesteaded in the mid-1870s, the area had no official name. The acquisition of a post office in 1880 required an official designation, however. Popular local history states that the town was named after the postmaster's children—Roy, Ellen, and Louis Tremain. The spelling of the amalgamation varied, however, to include Royellou, Royallen, Royallien, Royalieu, and Royalview, to name just a few. Letter writing became somewhat simpler when the town officially became known as Mount Dora on February 12, 1883.

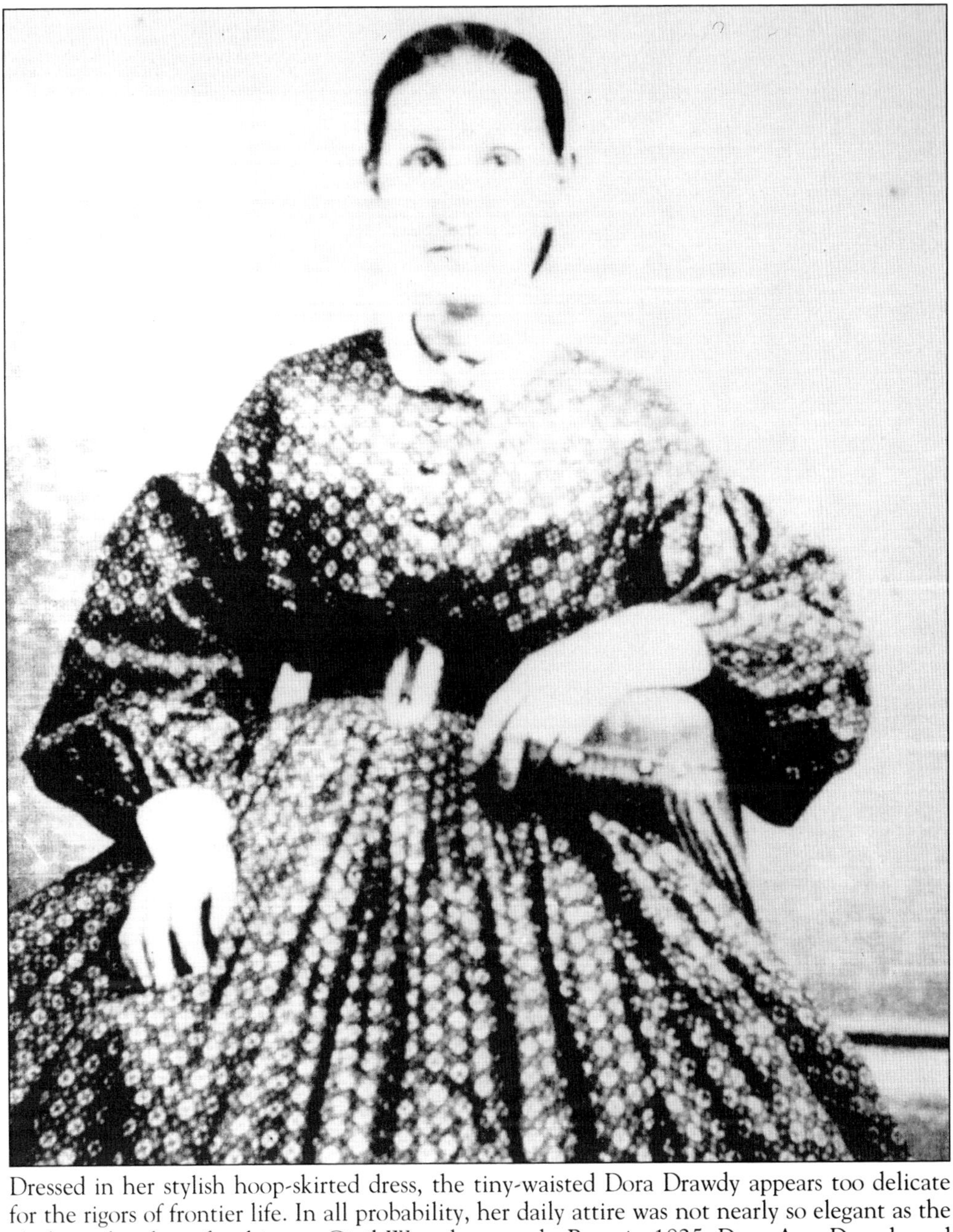

Dressed in her stylish hoop-skirted dress, the tiny-waisted Dora Drawdy appears too delicate for the rigors of frontier life. In all probability, her daily attire was not nearly so elegant as the clothing she chose for this pre–Civil War photograph. Born in 1825, Dora Ann Drawdy and her husband, Jim, moved to Florida in 1846 and established a squatter's homestead several miles south of Mount Dora. Family history states that in return for the Drawdys' hospitality, visiting U.S. surveyors offered to name the large lake just to the north in Dora's honor. Maps of 1848 indicate that the promise was kept. After Jim Drawdy left to serve in the Confederate Army during the Civil War, Dora and her six children moved to the security of the more densely populated community of Seneca, 10 miles to the northeast. When Jim Drawdy died in Richmond at the end of the war, Dora remained in Florida to raise her family. Upon her death in 1883, Dora Ann Drawdy was buried in the cemetery in Umatilla, FL.

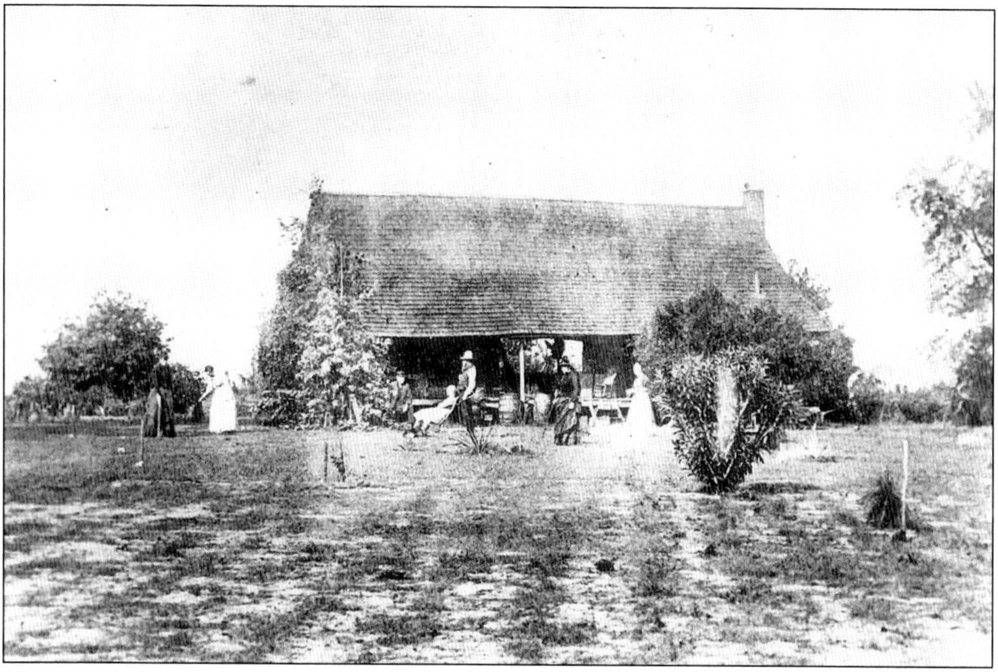

The Drawdy cabin was built on the eastern shore of what is now Lake Beauclair. Following the Drawdy family's move to Seneca, the house was vacant for several years. In 1878, Dudley Adams and his family stayed in the cabin until they could replace it with a larger two-story home.

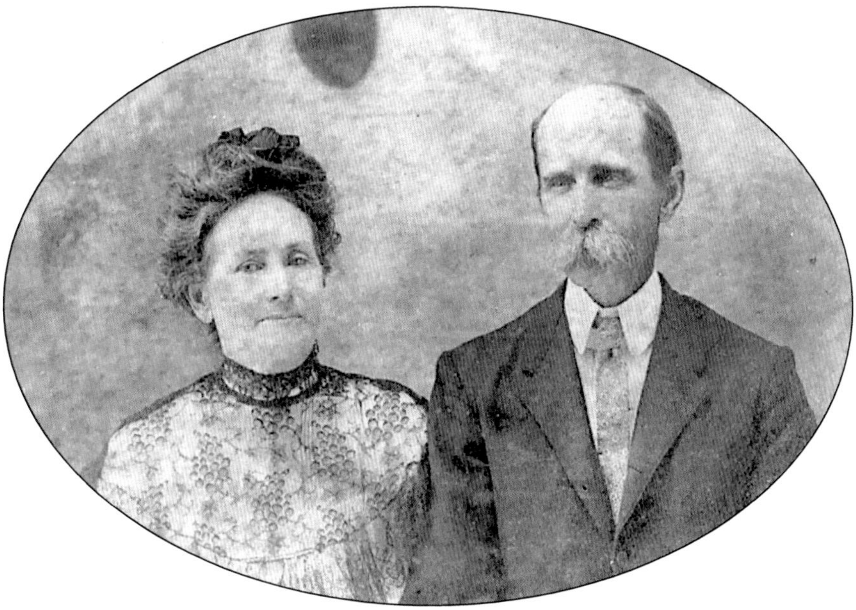

Officially recognized as the first homesteaders in Township #19, David M. and Mary Vann Simpson recorded the warranty deed for their 160-acre property on August 10, 1874. The following year, David's father, Milton, filed his claim to a similarly sized plot of land just to the southeast. In 1878, the Simpsons had a son, James, who was reported to be the first white male child born in the new community.

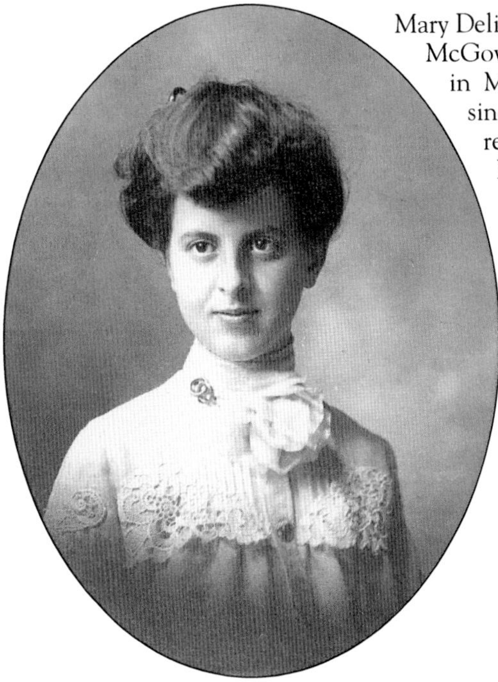

Mary Delilah McGowen, daughter of John E. and Delilah McGowen, was the first white female child to be born in Mount Dora. The racial qualifier is necessary since African-American births were not officially recorded in the community at the time. When Delilah McGowen died shortly after giving birth to her daughter on October 6, 1884, John and the infant returned to Malone, NY.

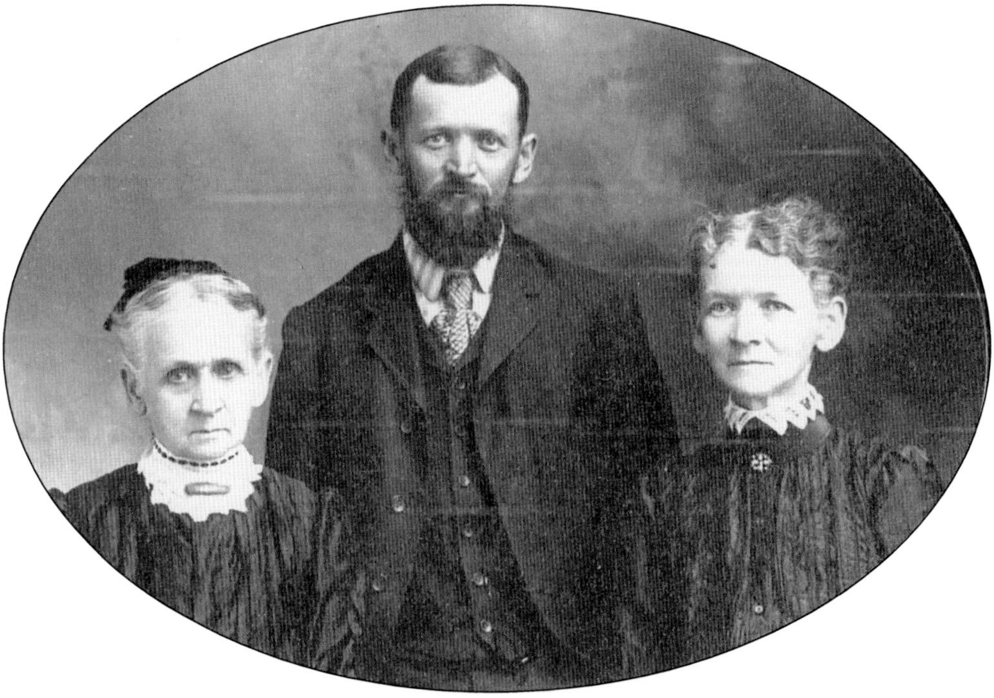

Even in the 1800s, many of Florida's residents were newcomers to the state. Then as now, most had moved to the area from the Northeast and Midwest; C.H. Longstreet and his family had moved to Mount Dora from New York. After three years as winter residents, the Longstreets became permanent inhabitants of the community in 1888, engaged in the citrus and beekeeping industry.

Dr. Orin W. Sadler, his wife, and children came to Mount Dora in 1884 in search of a winter home in a climate more temperate than that of their northern residence in Pittsburgh, PA. For a number of years, Dr. Sadler maintained his medical practice in Pittsburgh while his wife managed their Florida residence and citrus groves.

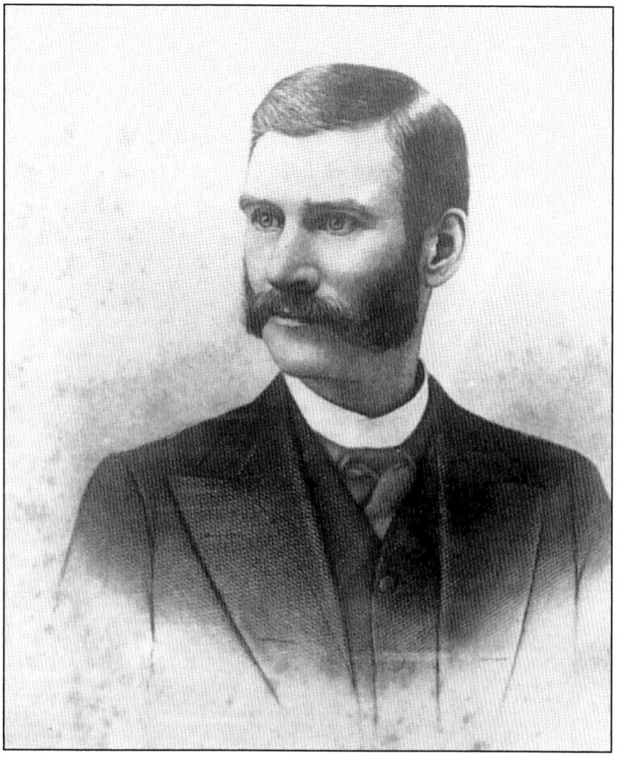

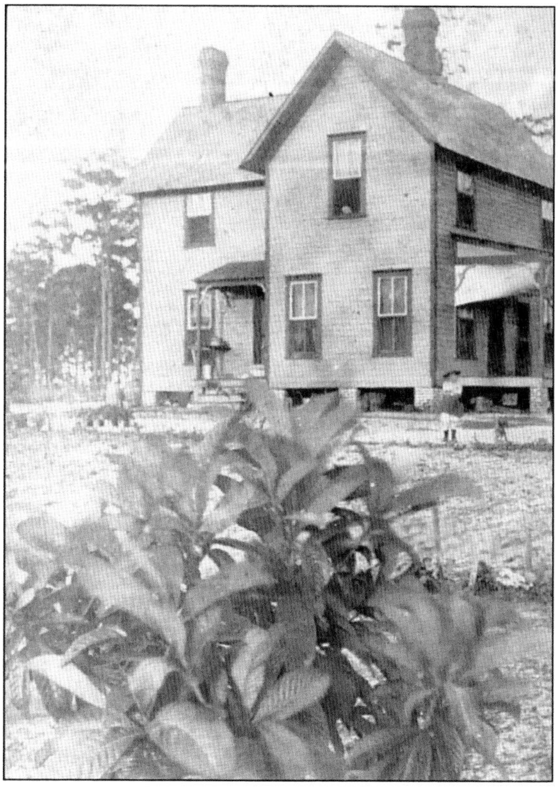

Built in 1885, the Sadler home was located on Highland Street on a 20-acre tract of land. After the "Big Freeze" of 1895, Dr. Sadler not only replanted his own citrus groves, but also purchased and replanted several hundred additional acres. Both Dr. and Mrs. Sadler were actively involved in community affairs, the Mount Dora Improvement Society, and the Chautauqua. Dr. Sadler served as mayor from 1917 until 1920.

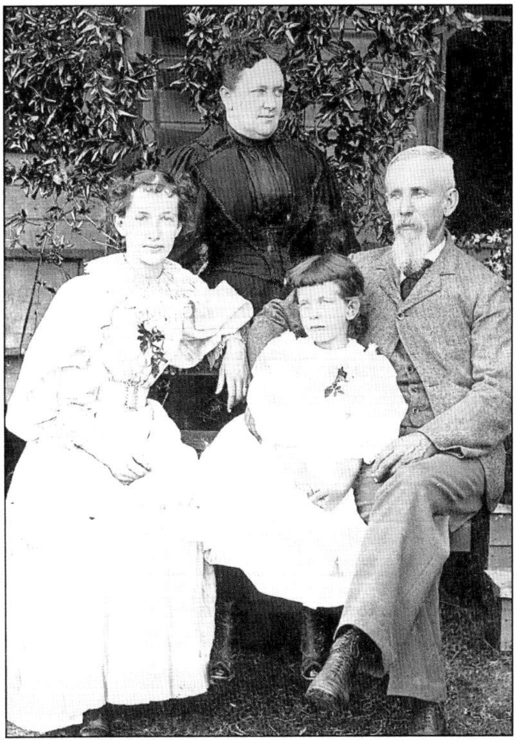

Russell True, his wife, Frances, and their daughters Carrie and Mary moved to Mount Dora in 1884 from Kansas. A Civil War veteran suffering from ill health, Mr. True was advised by his physician to relocate to a warmer climate. Apparently the prescription worked, since he lived in Mount Dora for another 20 years before his death.

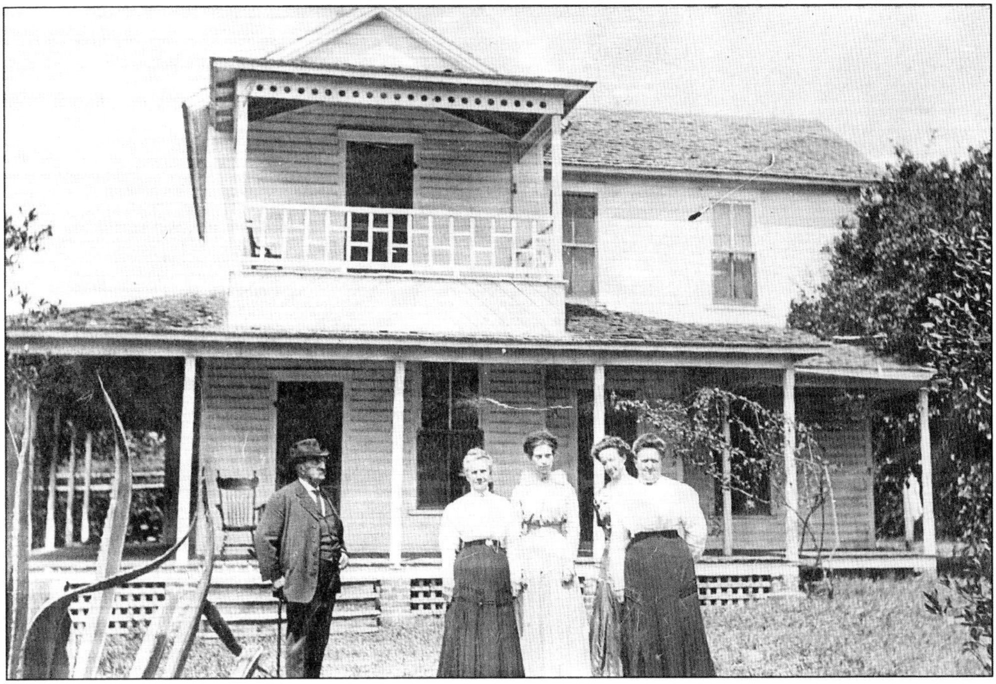

Members of the True family pose in front of their house on the corner of Fifth Avenue and Grandview Street. According to R.J. Longstreet's history of Mount Dora, Russell True first came to town alone, built a home, and then sent for his family. When they arrived in Fort Mason, he borrowed Ross Tremain's horse and wagon to travel to meet them.

Pictured at the time of her marriage to Will Rawson, Ida Eliza Hicks was the daughter of John Hicks, a wealthy winter resident. After the death of Rawson, she married William Bishop, a Michigan furniture dealer. Ida Hicks Rawson Bishop continued to winter in Mount Dora and remained active in community life until her death in 1949.

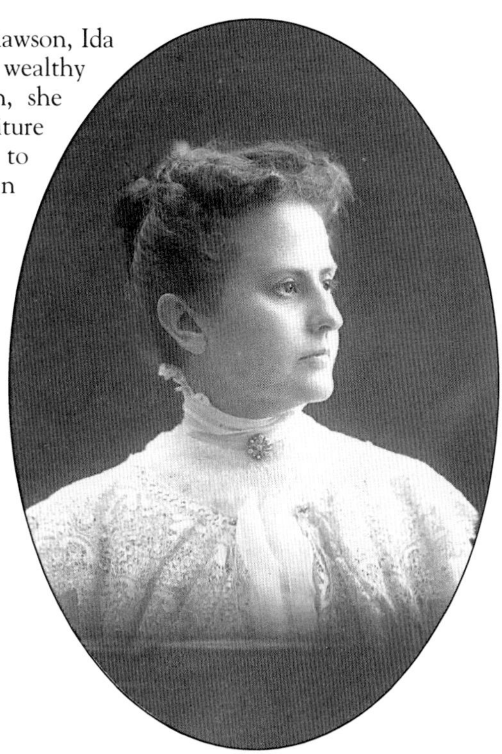

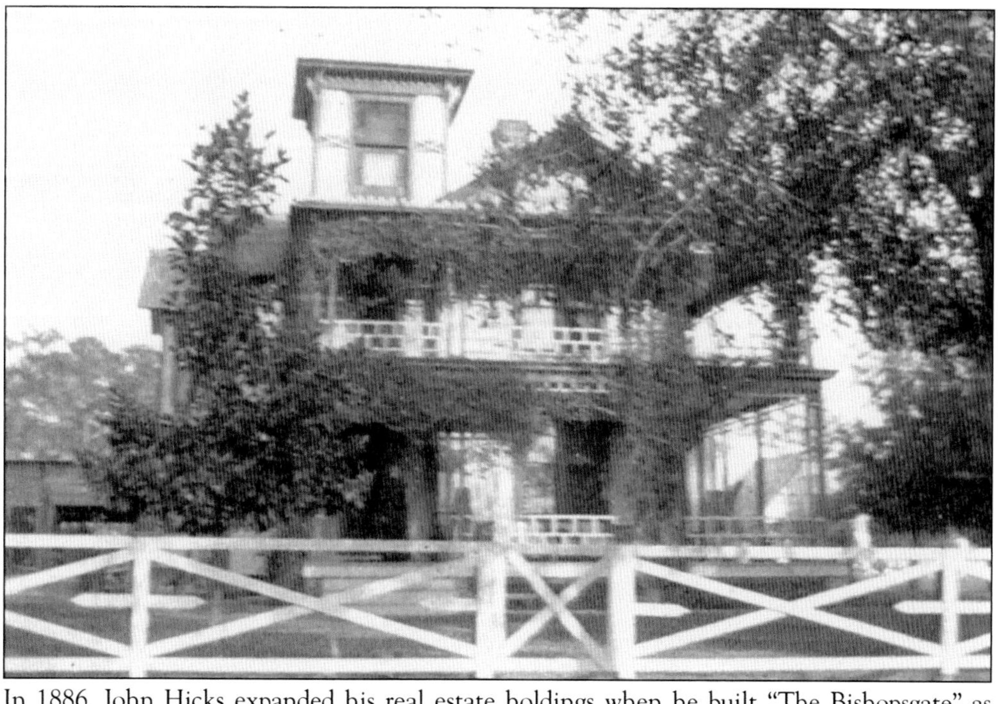

In 1886, John Hicks expanded his real estate holdings when he built "The Bishopsgate" as the family's new winter residence. Located on Seventh Avenue and Alexander Street, the house was constructed of yellow pine and cypress. J.P. Donnelly served as the contractor for the 14-room, one-and-a-half-bath residence.

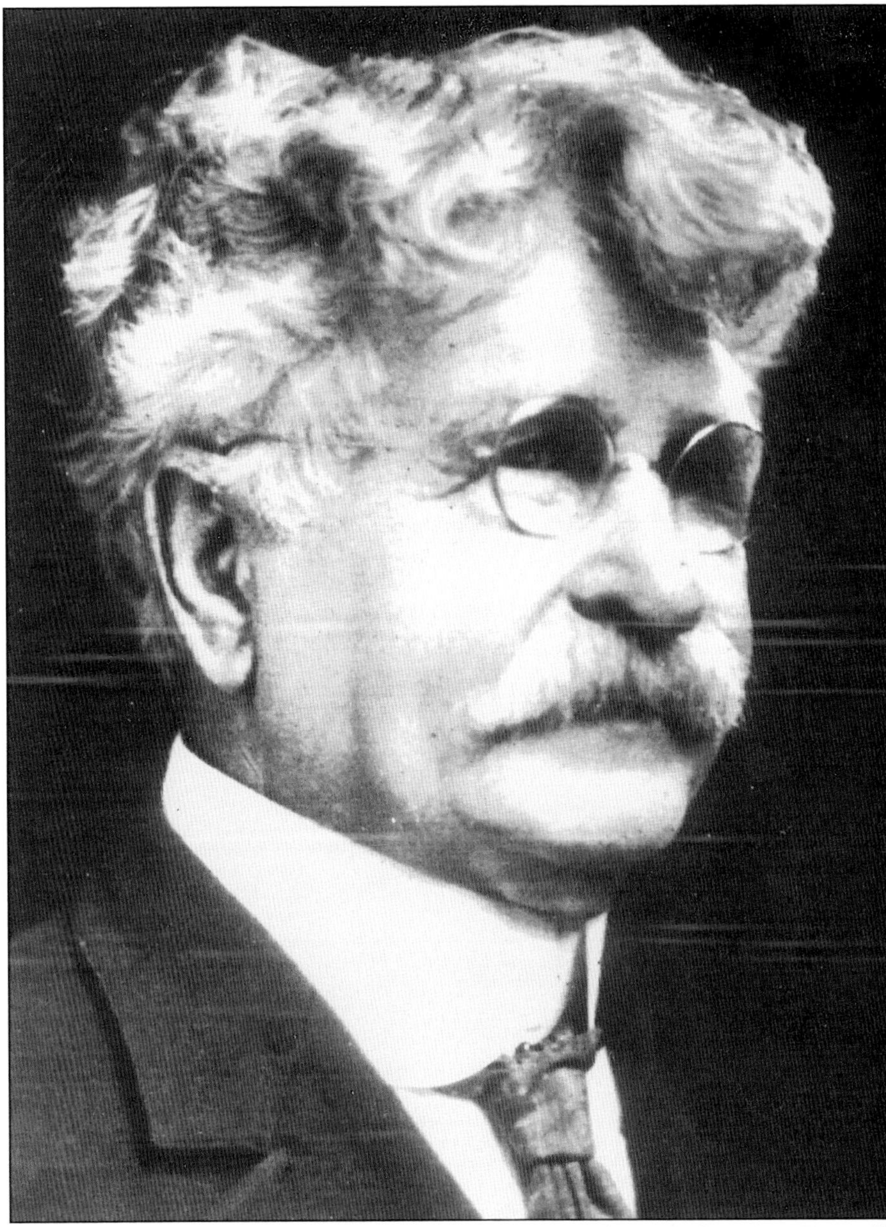

Despite the resemblance, the gentleman pictured in this photograph is J.P. Donnelly, not noted author Mark Twain. One of Mount Dora's best-known early residents, Donnelly arrived from Pittsburgh, PA, in 1879 and homesteaded property just north of that belonging to Annie McDonald Stone. When the two married in the early 1880s, their joint real estate holdings encompassed not only most of what would become downtown Mount Dora, but also all of the town's waterfront. Among the wealthiest of the town's citizens, the Donnellys provided generously for the new community, donating the land for the first two churches, a lot for the fire department, and a portion of the acreage for the cemetery. When Mount Dora was officially incorporated in 1910, J.P. Donnelly was elected as the first mayor, a position he continued to hold until 1913. He was also a member of the board of directors of the South Florida Chautauqua and one of the organizers of the Mount Dora Educational Society.

While J.P. Donnelly and his wife had no children of their own, Annie McDonald Stone had a daughter, Nellie, from a previous marriage. Nellie in turn had three children, including one son, pictured here with his grandfather, J.P. Donnelly.

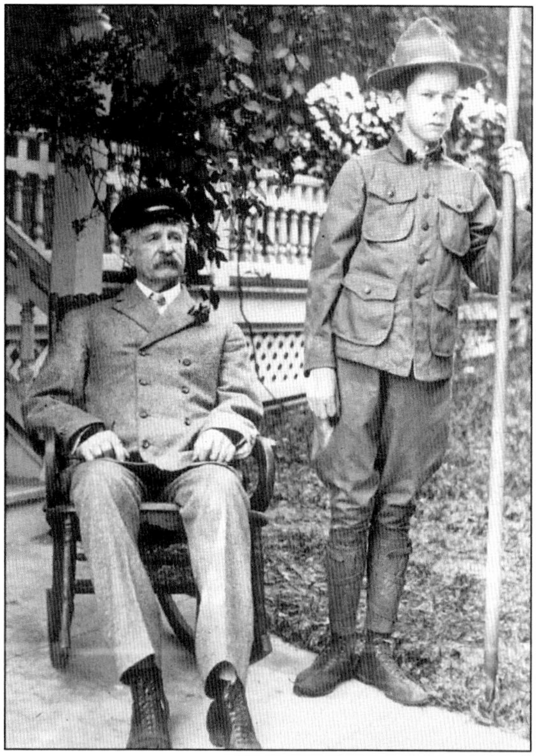

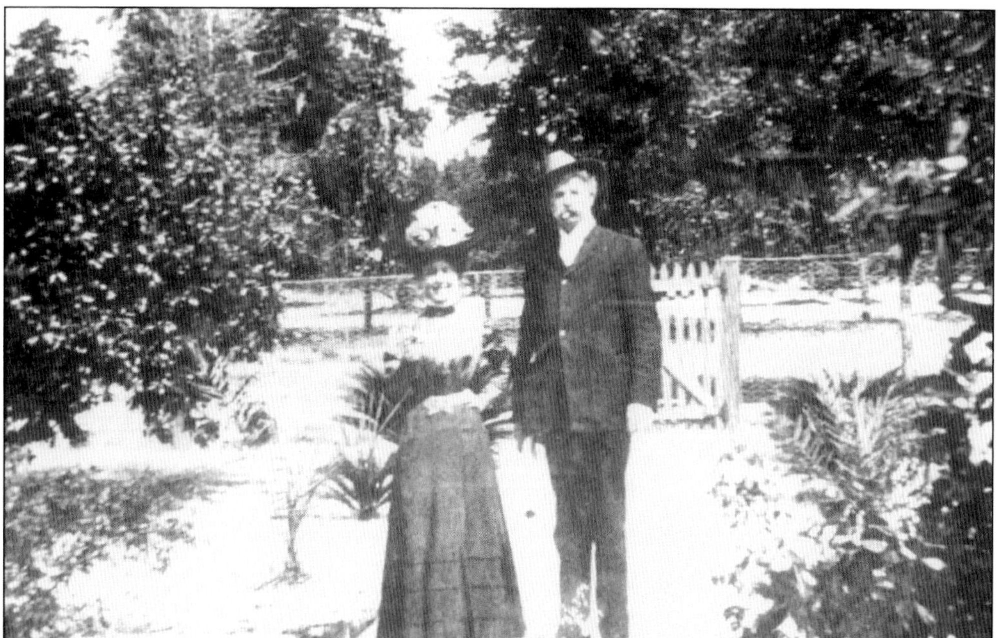

As might be expected, the Donnellys were actively involved in the social life of Mount Dora. In this photograph, J.P. Donnelly posed outdoors with Mrs. Watt, the wife of a fellow citrus grower. For his work with the development of the citrus industry, Donnelly was known locally as "the father of the tangerine."

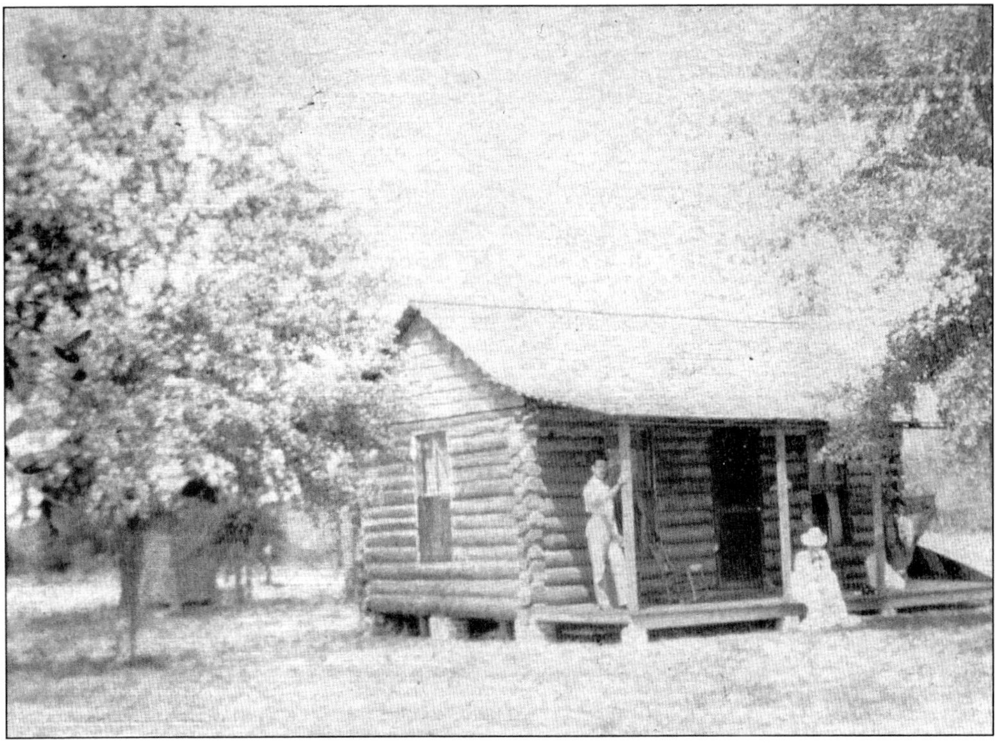

The first homes in the area were log cabins, such as this one that was located on Third Avenue. As evidenced by the small building in the backyard, indoor plumbing was an amenity not yet available.

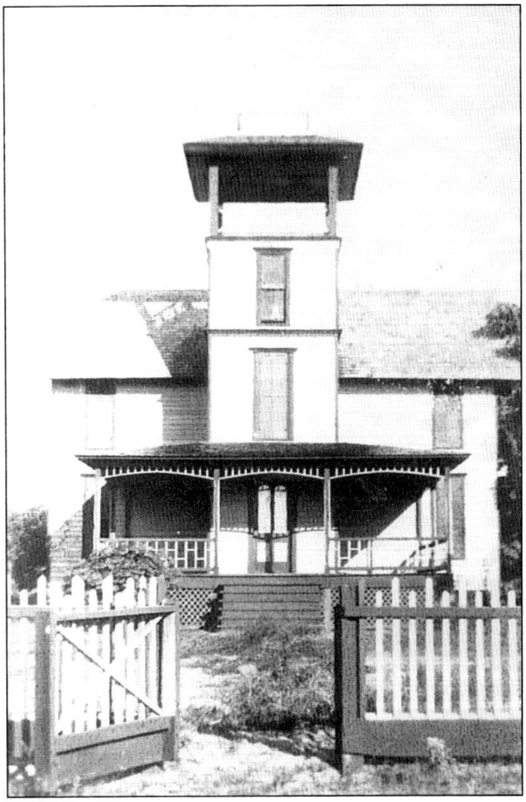

By the time Charles Javens's house was built in 1888, the styles of homes in Mount Dora had become considerably more elaborate. Architectural details included the latticework and ornamental trim on the front porch and the matching paint scheme on the house and picket fence.

Pictured on a 1911 postcard, the "Tower" could definitely be described as unusual. A windmill-powered water tank, located above the third floor of the residence, provided running water. Owned by Warren C. Butts, the house was located on South Donnelly Street between Third and Fourth Avenues.

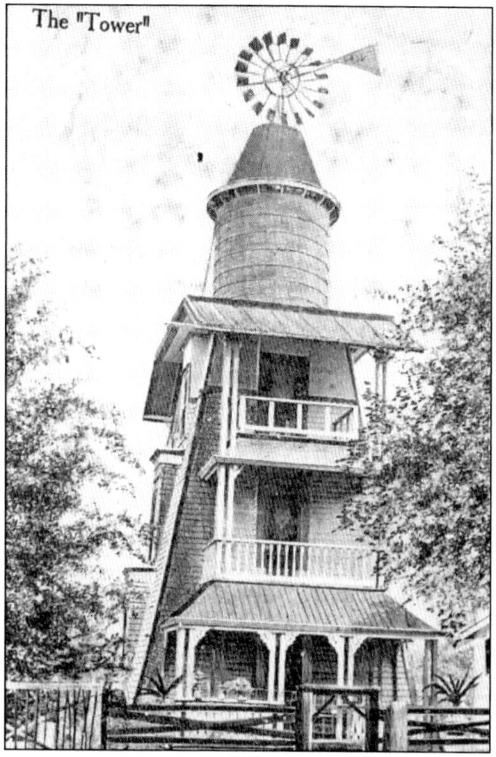

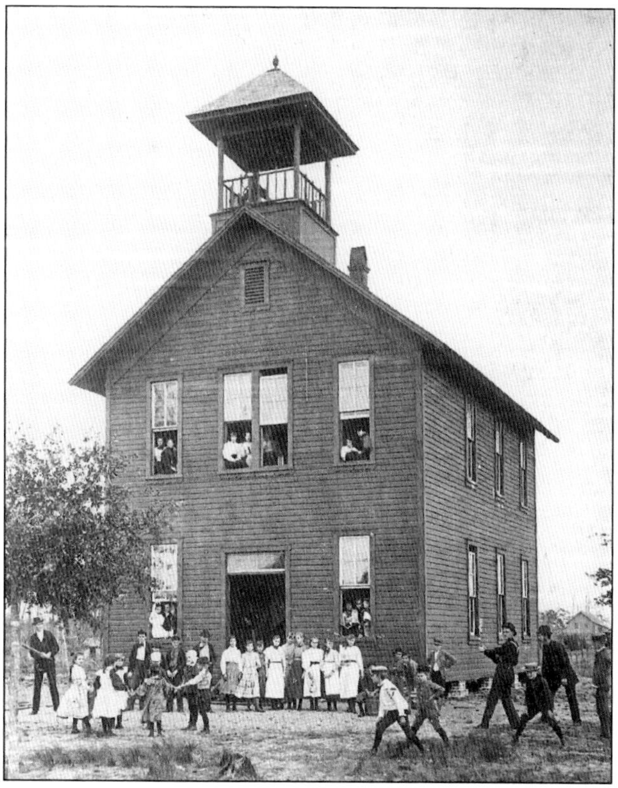

One of the most important buildings in any community is the school. In 1881, with the creation of a school district, public education in the town was established. As the community grew, so did the need for a larger schoolhouse. Built in 1895 on the corner of Seventh Avenue and Clayton Street, the new school was funded by $45 in public funds and the remainder in private contributions. The entire student body was comprised of 43 children—25 girls and 18 boys.

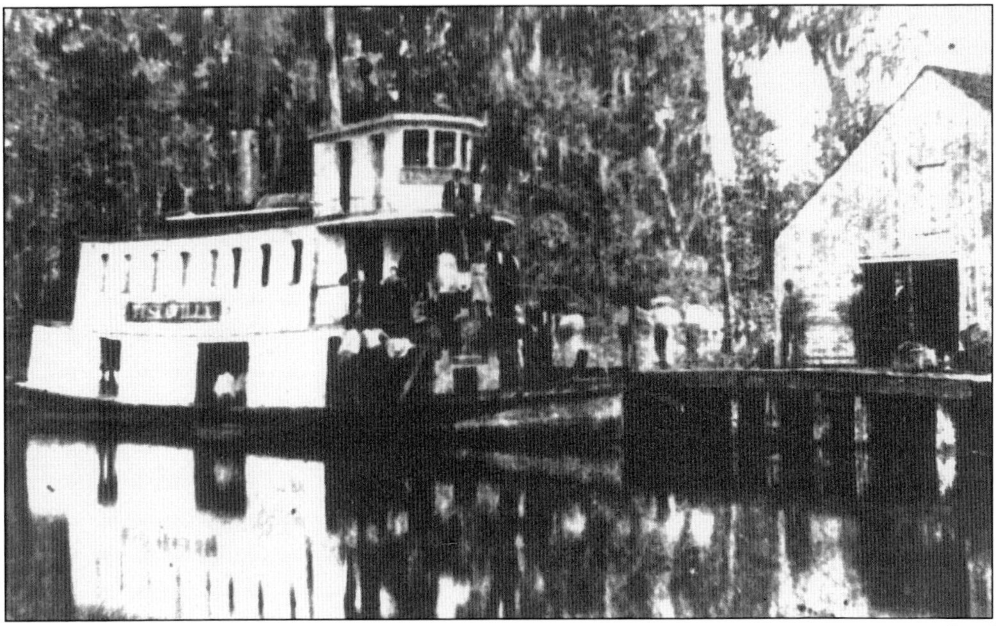

According to J.P. Donnelly, "the first steamboat ever brought into the lake was the *Tuscawilla* of the Hart Line on the Ocklawaha." Until the development of improved overland transportation, steamboats on the St. Johns and Ocklawaha Rivers brought most of the commercial goods into Mount Dora.

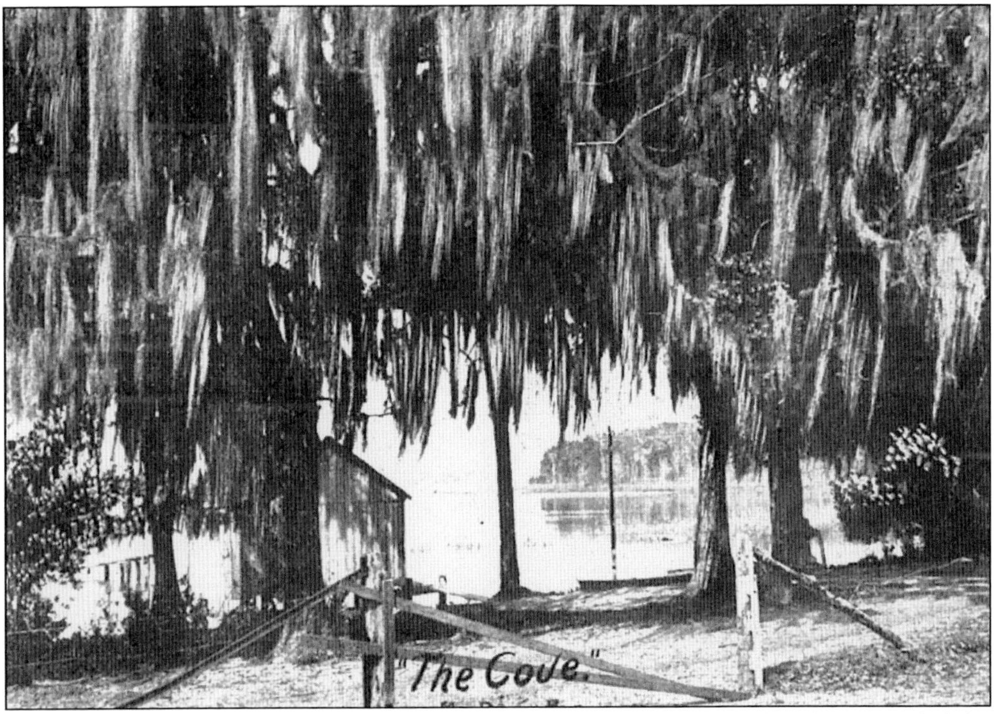

Known as "The Cove" or Gilbert's Cove, this portion of the Lake Dora shoreline provided the docking area for the *Dolphin* between trips to the Chautauqua. Belonging to Dr. C.R. Gilbert, the *Dolphin* hauled both passengers and freight on the lakes during the 1890s.

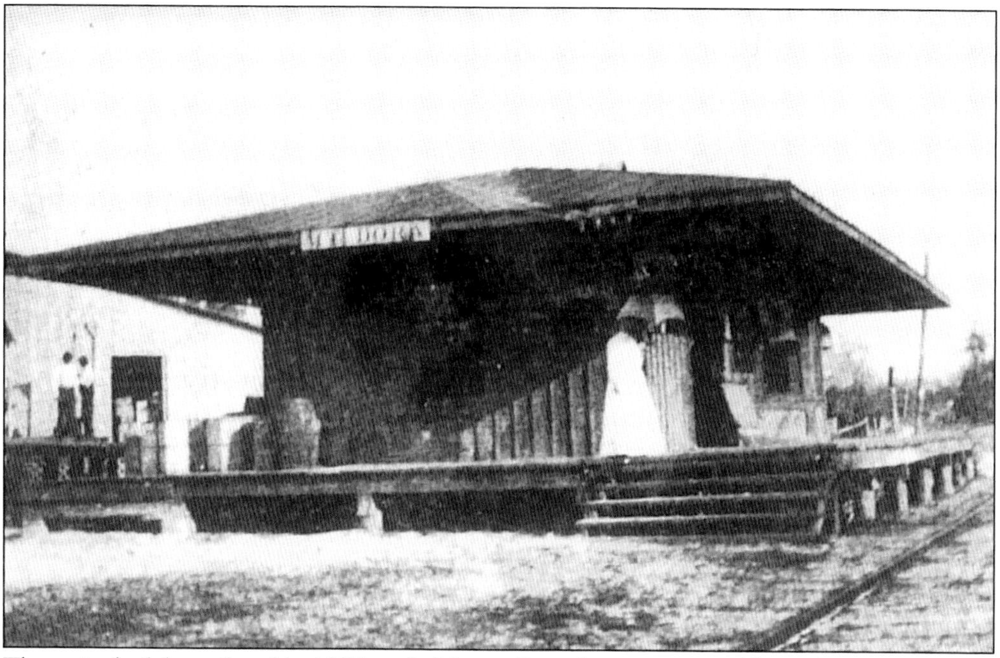

The arrival of the railroad in 1887 made Mount Dora far more accessible to the outside world. No longer dependent upon steamboats or wagons, merchants could receive goods more quickly. Running between Sanford and Tavares, the train made its easterly trip in the morning and its return trip each evening.

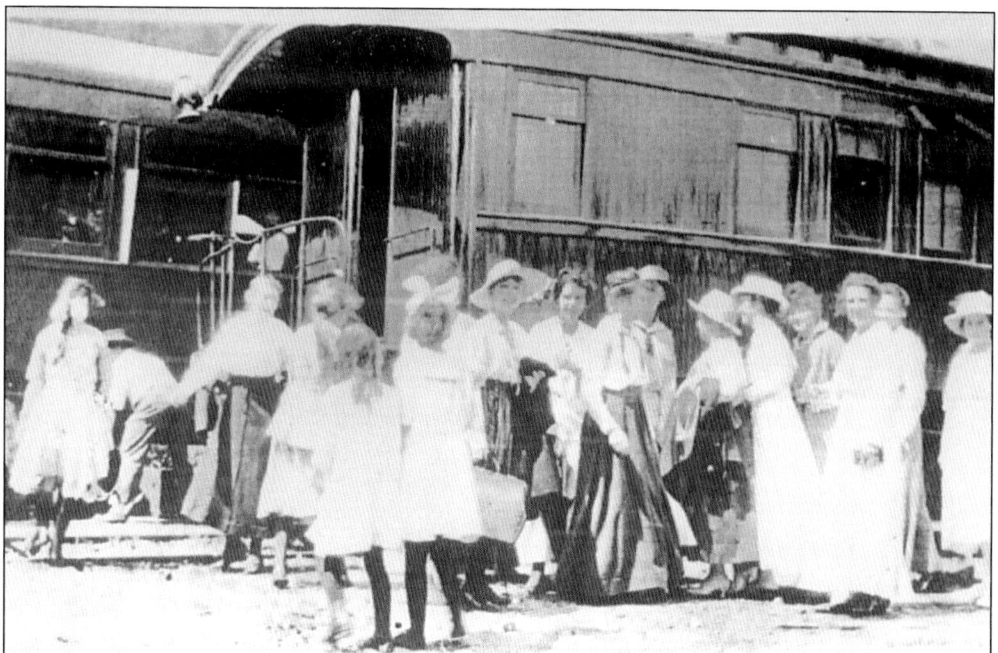

In the beginning, with only one train each day, the railroad carried freight, mail, and passengers. Later, separate passenger and freight trains were added to the schedule. This group of young ladies may have been taking part in an excursion to a Chautauqua program or a trip to Sanford.

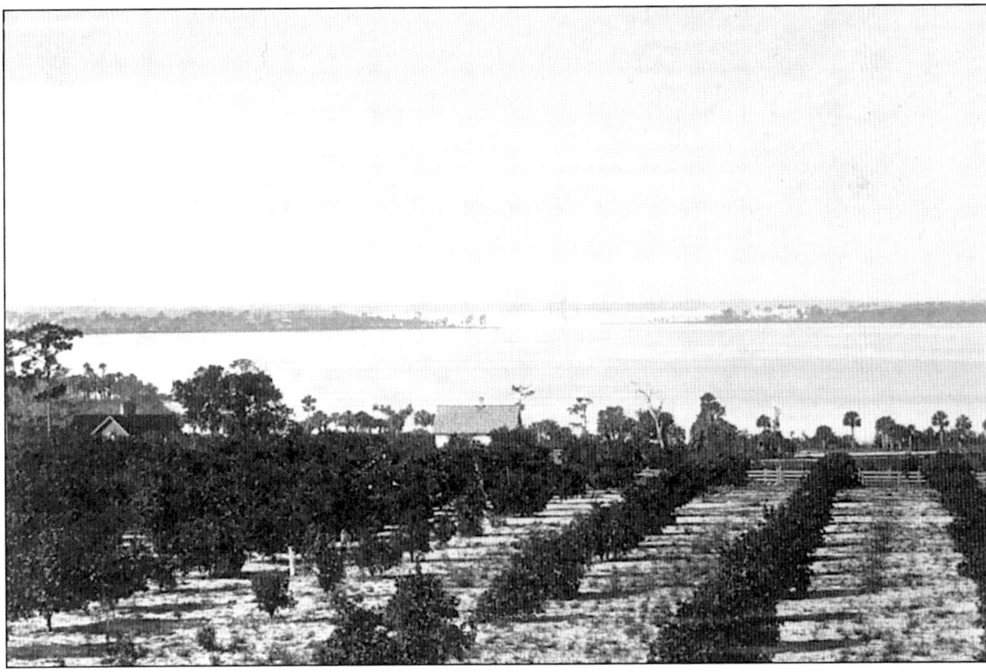

Mount Dora's early settlers quickly found that the region was ideally suited for growing citrus and planted hundreds of acres of groves. Since many of the newcomers were Northerners, the idea must have seemed especially appealing, exotic sounding, and synonymous with the tropical climate of Florida.

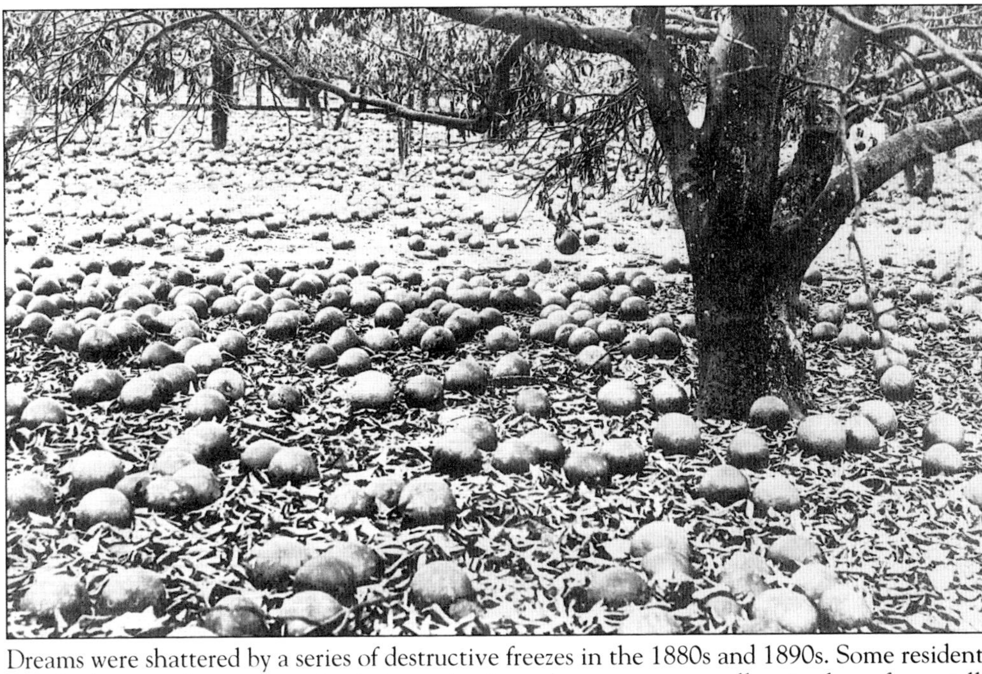

Dreams were shattered by a series of destructive freezes in the 1880s and 1890s. Some residents who had invested everything in their newly planted groves were totally wiped out financially and left the area permanently. Others sought alternative ways of making a living, while a few determined individuals replanted their devastated groves and started anew.

Although the plants were similarly susceptible to damage from cold weather, one experimental venture involved the planting of banana groves. Pineapple plantations were also attempted, although not with any great commercial success.

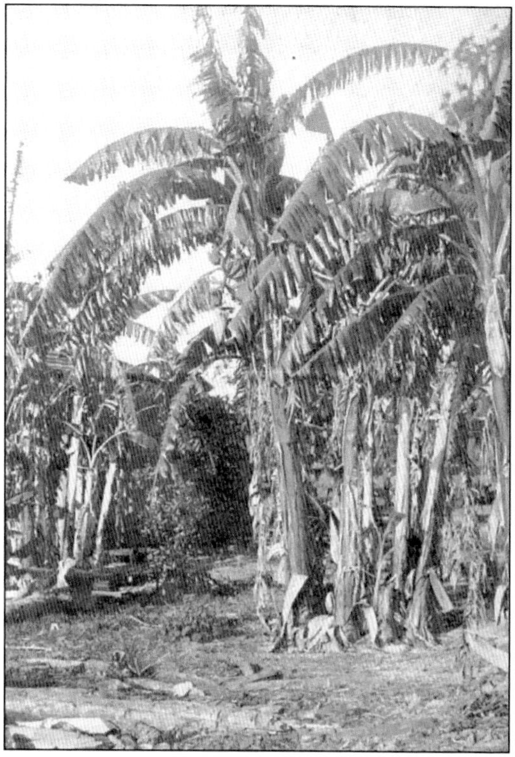

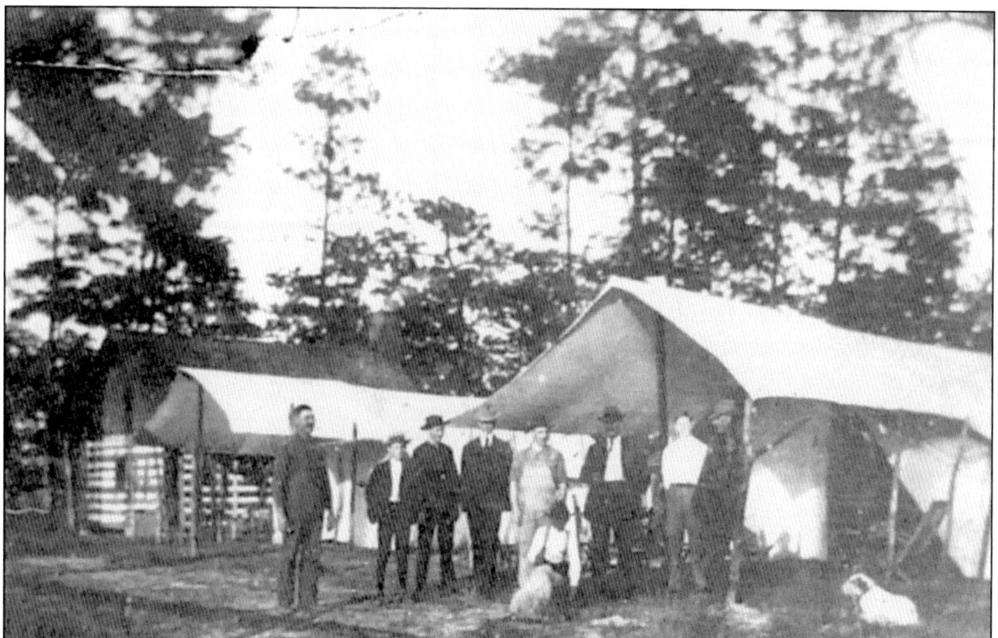

Although the freeze of 1894–95 discouraged his father's interest in the citrus industry, Jim Simpson remained an enthusiast. In 1900, he purchased equipment and began a grove maintenance business. His first citrus packing house was located in a tent across the street from his home on the corner of Donnelly Street and Eighth Avenue.

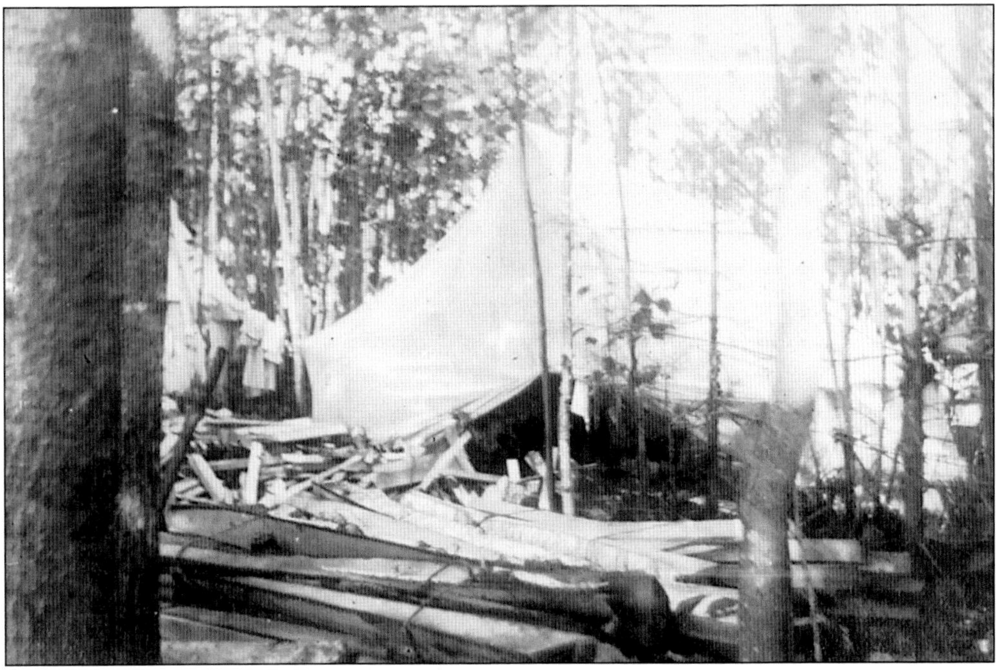

While most of the virgin timber in the area had already been harvested, a smaller scale lumbering industry still provided wood for the many frame homes being constructed in the early days of Mount Dora. Tents provided what shelter existed in the woods.

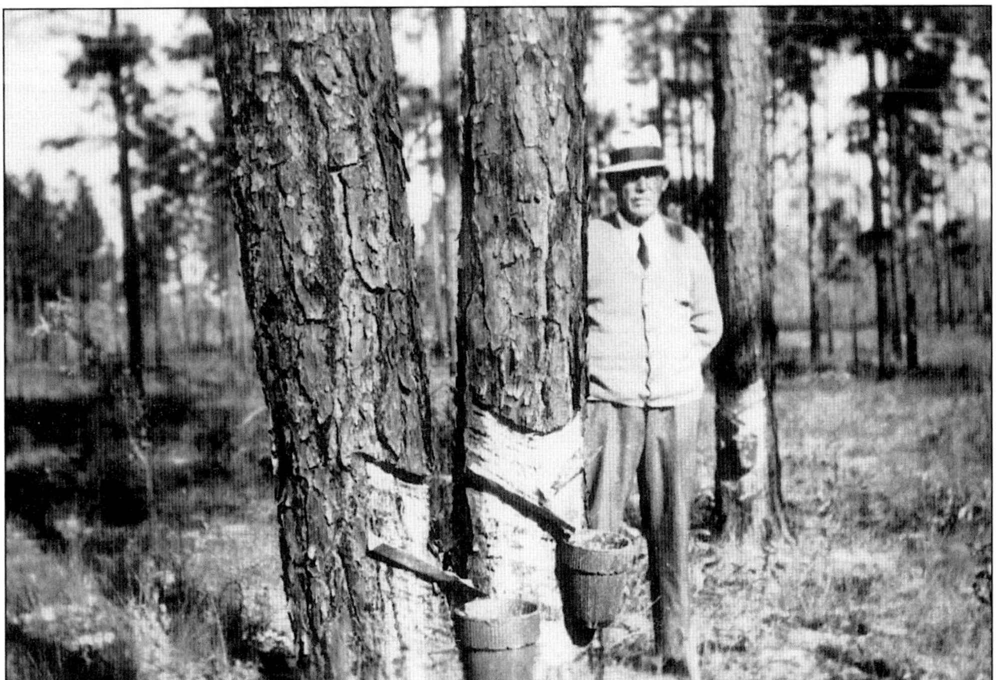

Sawmills had been part of the local economy since the founding of the community. Obtained from the local pine forests, naval stores including turpentine provided an additional source of revenue.

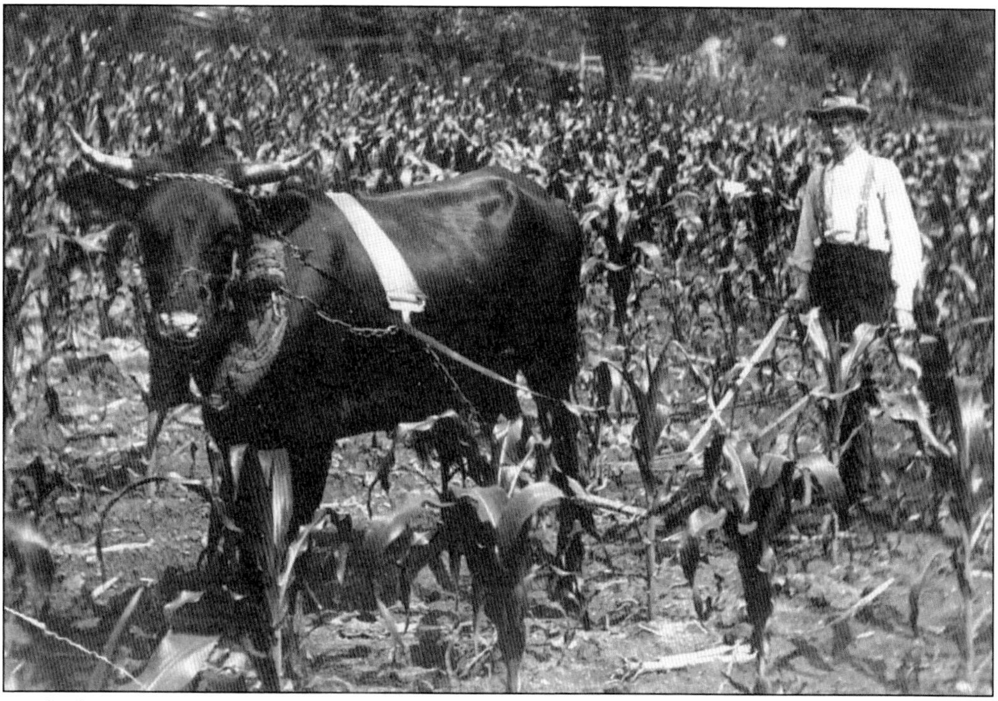

At the beginning of the 20th century, mechanized farm equipment was not available for Mount Dora's farmers. Rather than tilling the field by hand, this enterprising gentleman employed the laborsaving device of putting his ox to work in his cornfield.

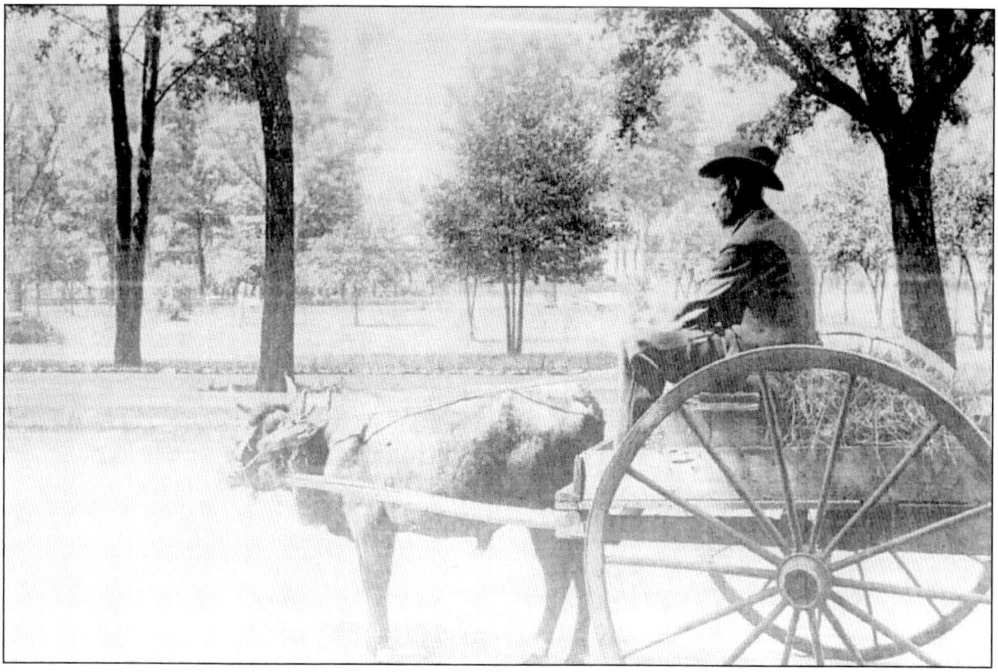

Oxen not only worked the fields, but also served as a means of transportation for early residents. This wagon, filled with straw, may have been on its way to a neighboring farm or destined for sale in Mount Dora.

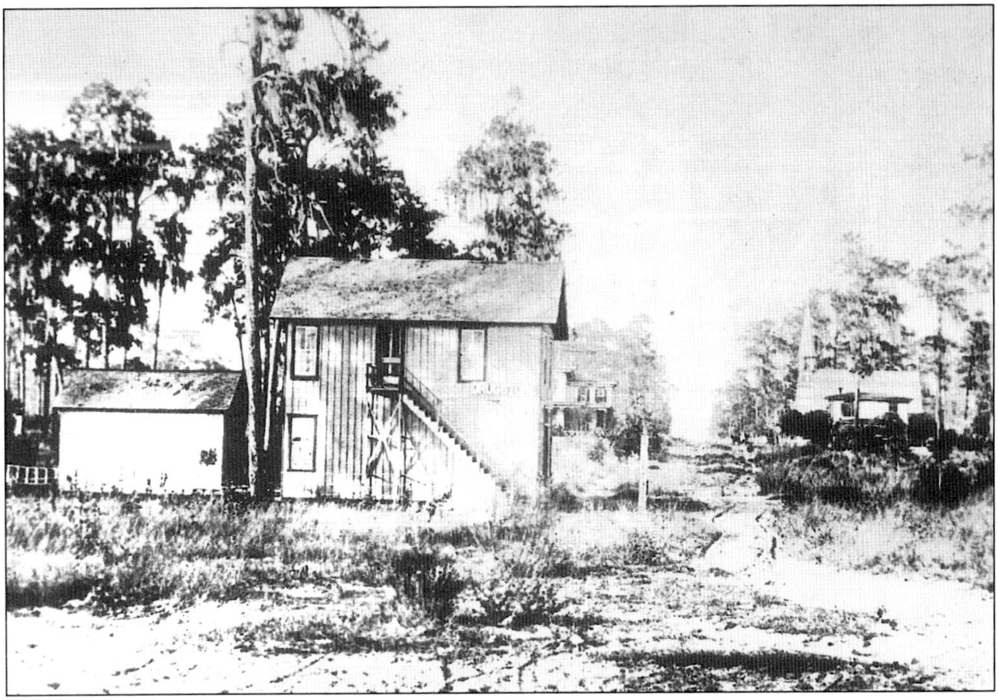

An early view of the business section of Donnelly Street revealed the presence of a drugstore sign on the building in the left foreground. In the distance on the right is the Congregational Church, the second oldest in Mount Dora.

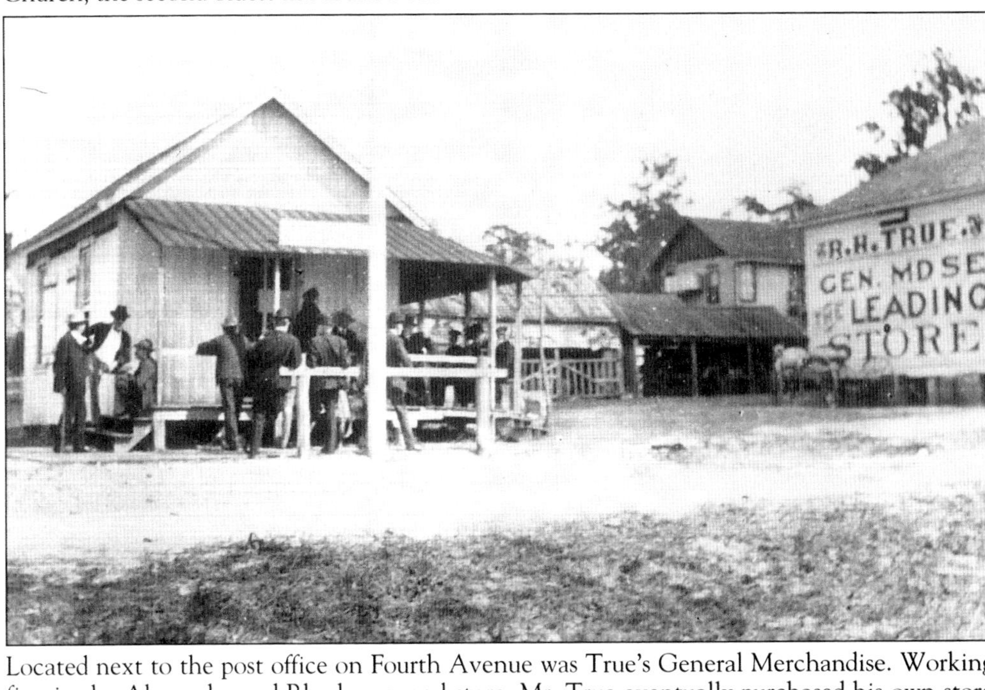

Located next to the post office on Fourth Avenue was True's General Merchandise. Working first in the Alexander and Rhodes general store, Mr. True eventually purchased his own store from C.M. Stowe after the "Big Freeze." Assisted by his daughter Carrie, he ran the general store until his death in 1904.

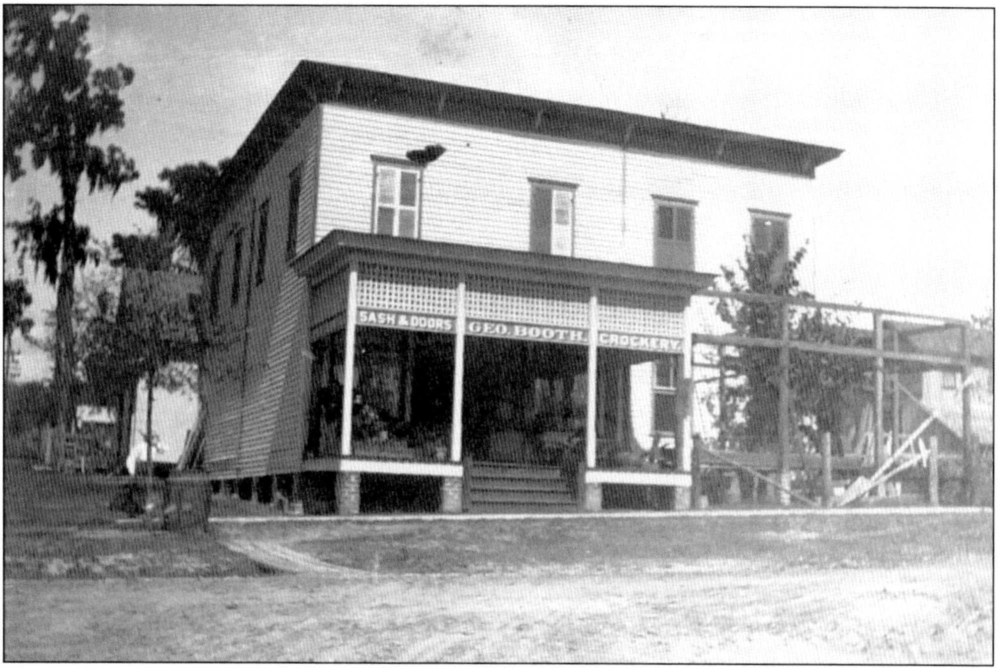

Originally from England, George Booth and his wife opened their hardware store in Mount Dora in the early 1880s. Although "sash and doors" and "crockery" were prominently advertised on the facade of the building, the store carried a wide variety of merchandise.

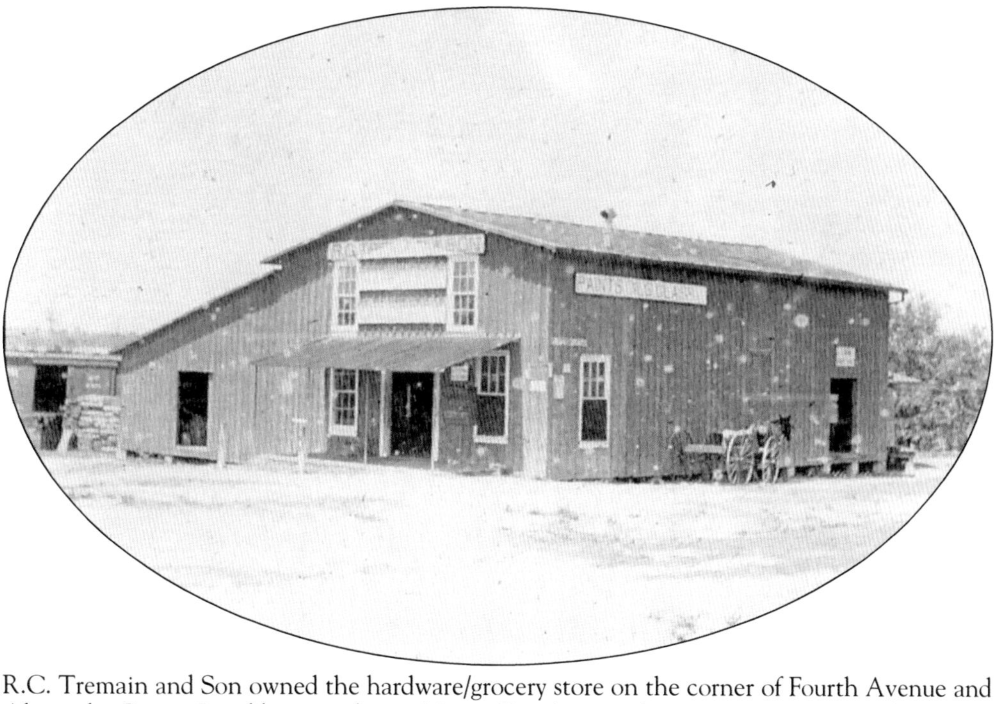

R.C. Tremain and Son owned the hardware/grocery store on the corner of Fourth Avenue and Alexander Street. In addition to being Mount Dora's second postmaster, Tremain also served on committees of the school board, the Chautauqua, the Congregational Church, and various local governmental entities.

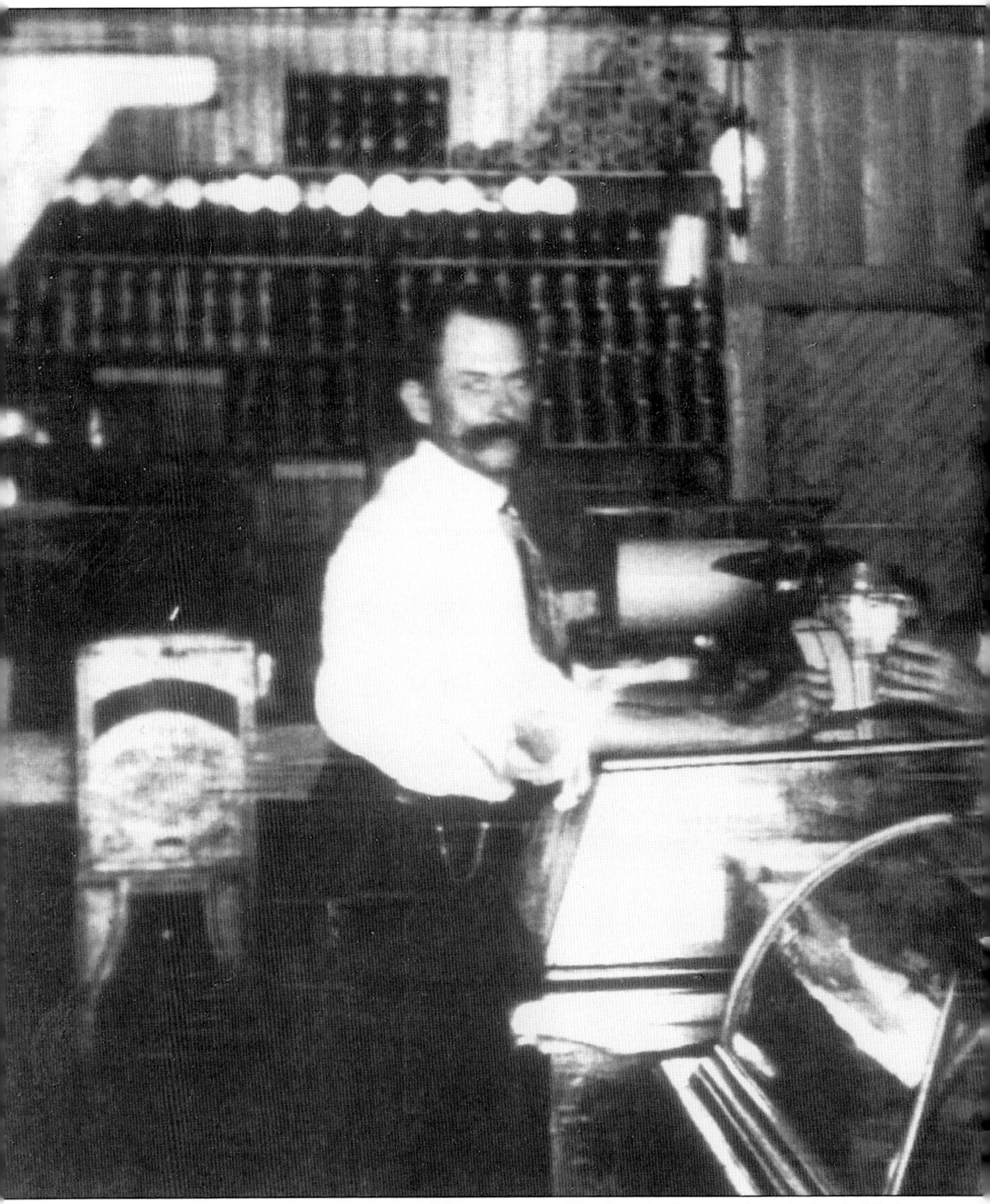

In 1905, Monroe Vann Simpson and his partner, Charles Little, purchased the R.H. True store, advertising it as "M.V. Simpson and Company, Leaders in General Merchandise." With Simpson taking the active role in the partnership, the enterprise quickly became known as Simpson's store. Comparable to today's department stores, albeit without the same quantity of merchandise, general stores in the early 1900s carried almost everything a shopper could

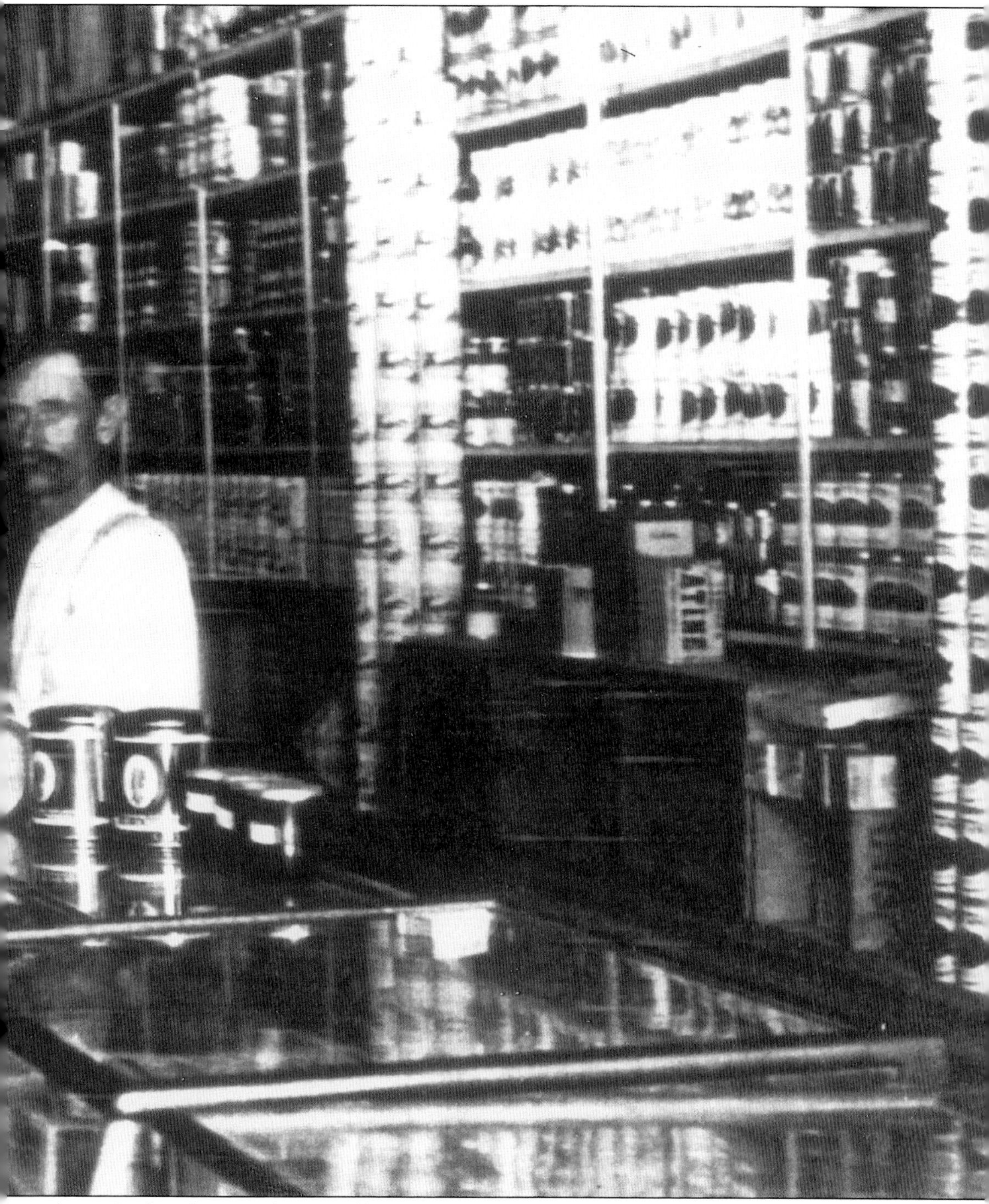

desire. In this photograph, rows of brightly colored labels on canned goods are reflected in the glass-topped display cases. A scale for measuring those purchases sold by weight rests upon the countertop just next to the big roll of paper used to wrap the newly acquired items. As a place to meet and converse with neighbors, the general store served a purpose almost as important as that of being a source of manufactured goods.

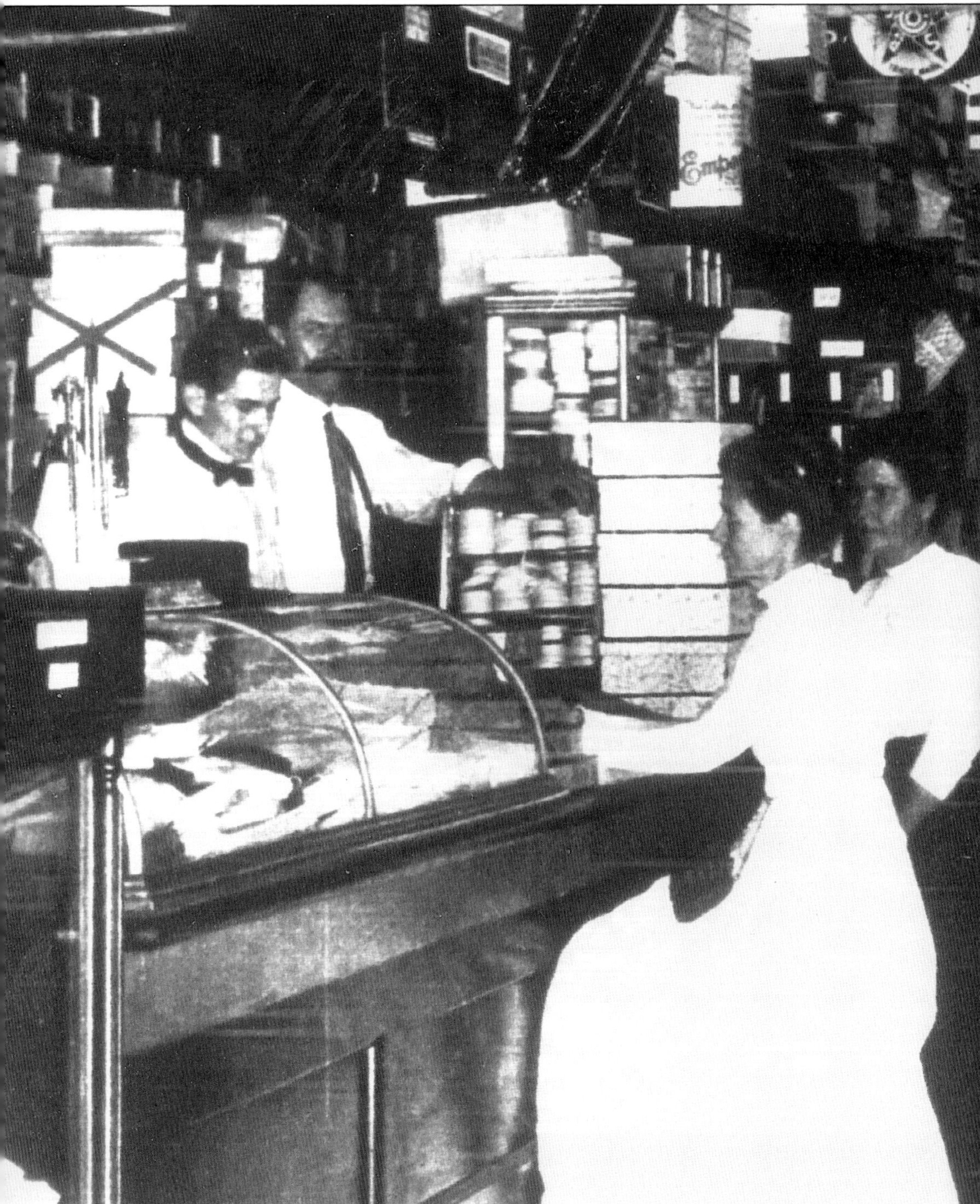

After the death of Charles Little in 1910, his wife and their son Robert purchased the Simpson store, changing the name to Little & Little. Assisted by her daughter, Emma Jane Tallant, Mrs. Little continued to run the store after Robert Little returned to New Hampshire. Groceries and penny candy, hardware and cooking pans, feed and fertilizer, clothing and other drygoods—all

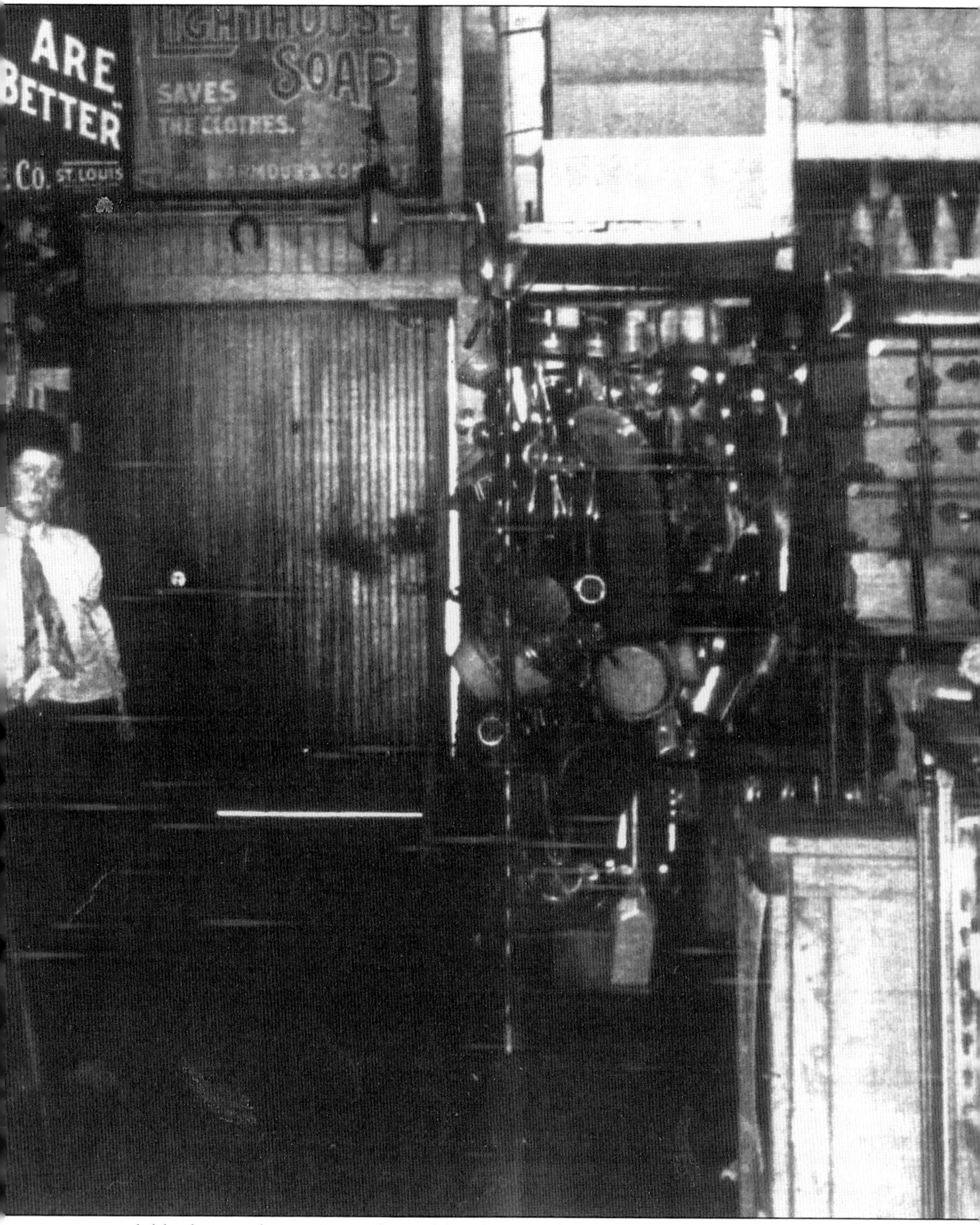

were available for purchase. As evidenced by the two female customers in this photograph, the store featured a variety of merchandise designed to appeal to patrons of both sexes. Signs advertising the wares of a St. Louis shoe company competed with a sales pitch for Lighthouse Soap that claimed, "It saves the clothes."

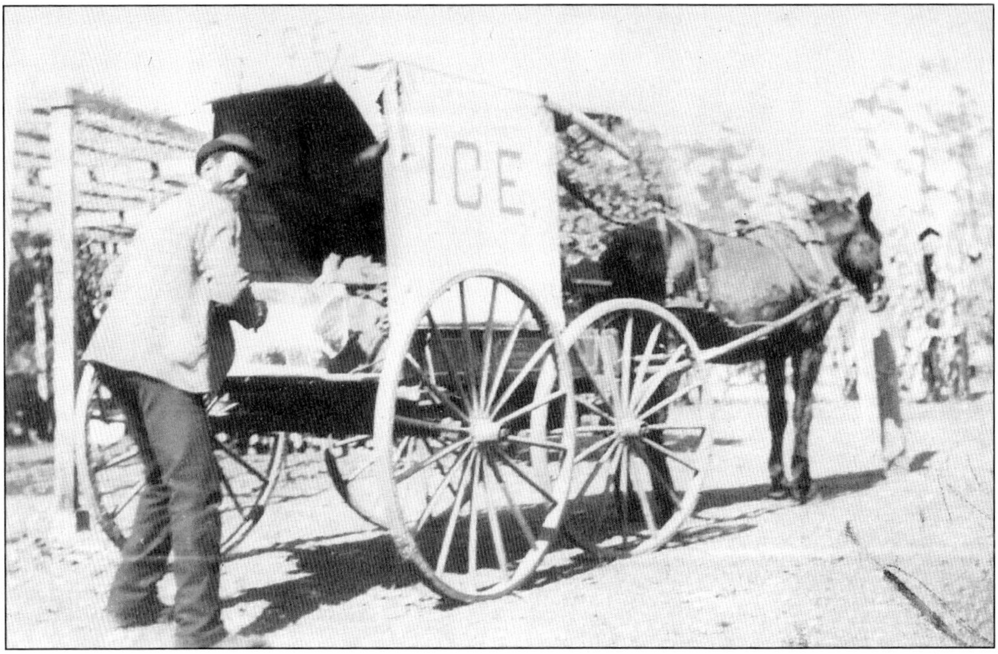

Built by James Simpson and George Patterson, Mount Dora's icehouse was located on Charles Street. In the days before the advent of electric refrigerators, a horse-drawn wagon driven by the "ice man" provided home delivery of the huge blocks of ice needed to keep food from spoiling in the Florida heat.

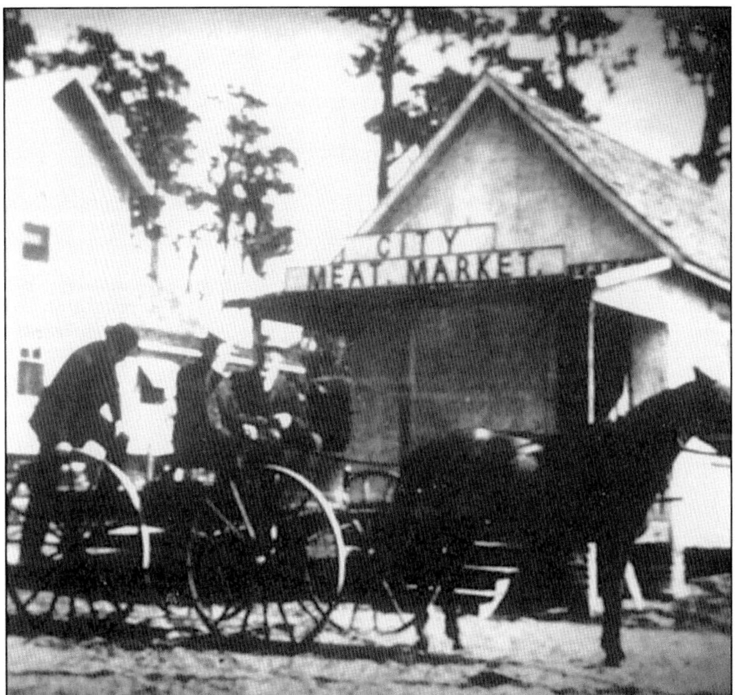

Although a far cry from today's modern grocery stores, complete with fancy coffee bars and deli counters, the City Meat Market still served the purpose. By the mid-1920s, Mount Dora had moved into the corporate world of retailing with the acquisition of an Atlantic & Pacific Tea Company (A&P) grocery store.

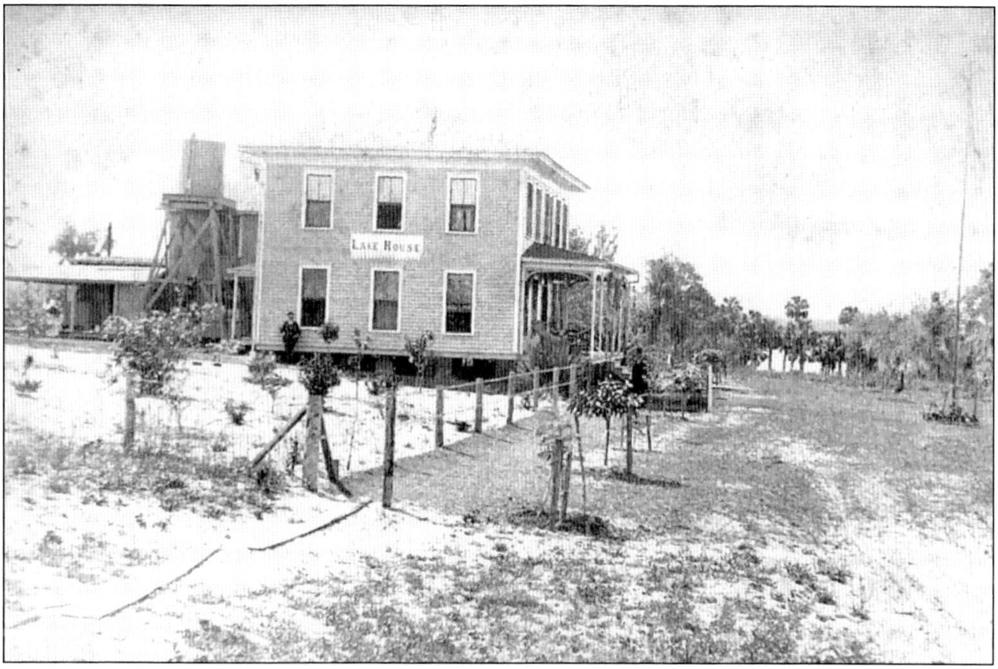

Long before Mount Dora was officially incorporated, visitors were a frequent sight in town, and, of course, they needed a place to stay. In 1882, a partnership of three area residents built a ten-room hotel known as the Alexander House. By 1895, the name of the hotel had been changed to the Lake House, the second step in the evolution to the Lakeside Inn of today.

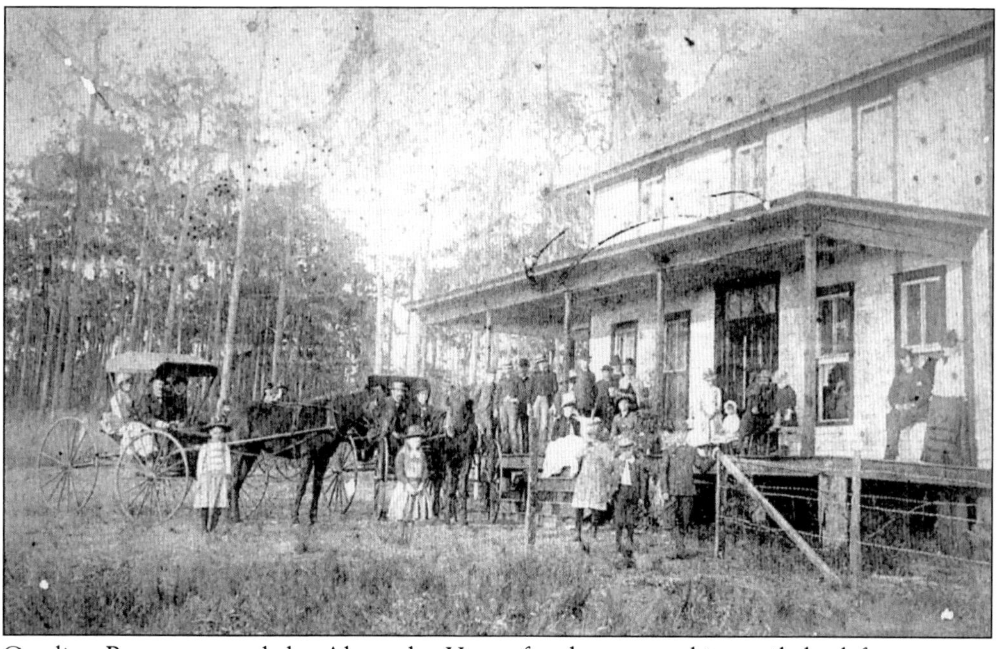

Caroline Bruce managed the Alexander House for the partnership until she left to operate her own hotel. Known as Bruce House, the hotel was located on Fifth Avenue and McDonald Street overlooking Lake Dora. Augmented by several additions, Bruce House subsequently became the Grandview Hotel.

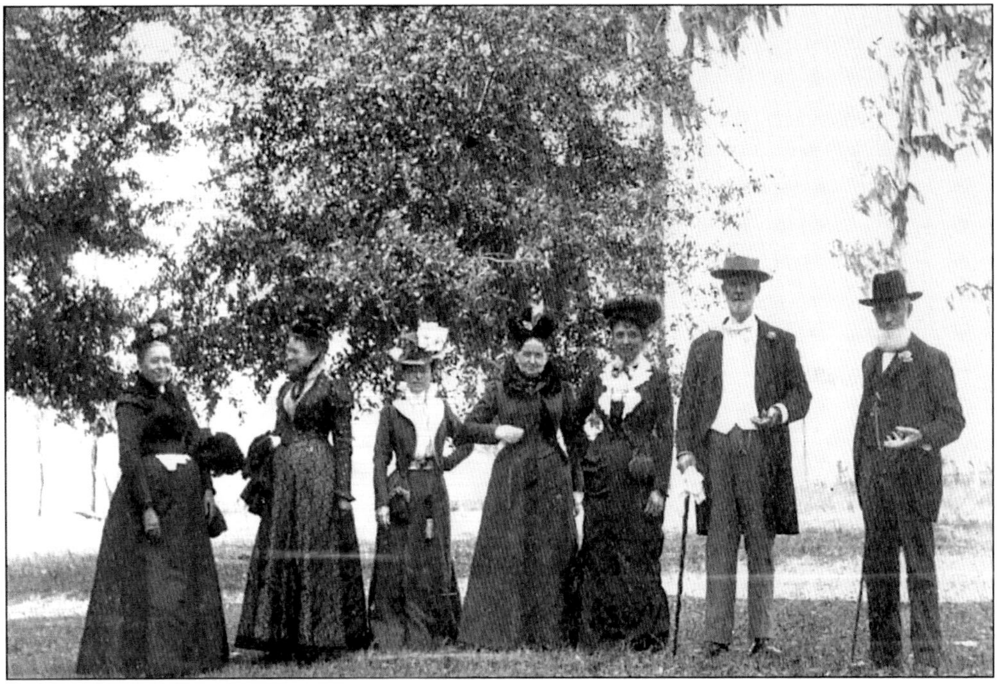

Life at the turn of the 20th century was not all work. In small towns such as Mount Dora, social life frequently revolved around religious and community-oriented activities. As evidenced by this group of men and women on their way to church, being attired in one's "Sunday best" was not just a figure of speech.

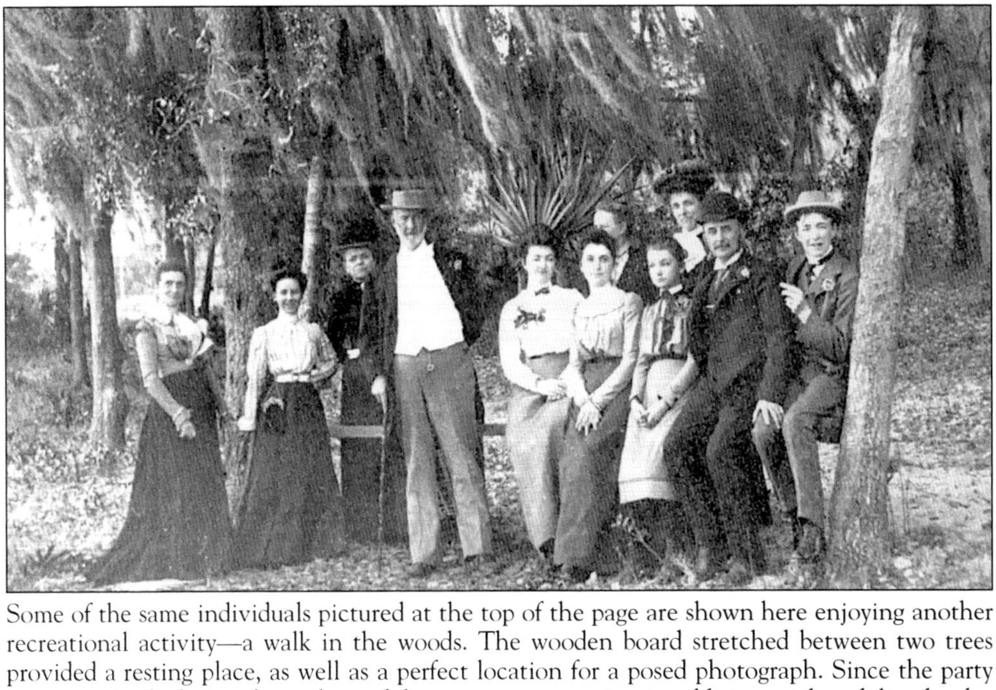

Some of the same individuals pictured at the top of the page are shown here enjoying another recreational activity—a walk in the woods. The wooden board stretched between two trees provided a resting place, as well as a perfect location for a posed photograph. Since the party was comprised of several members of the younger generation in addition to the adults, the day may also have included a picnic lunch out of doors.

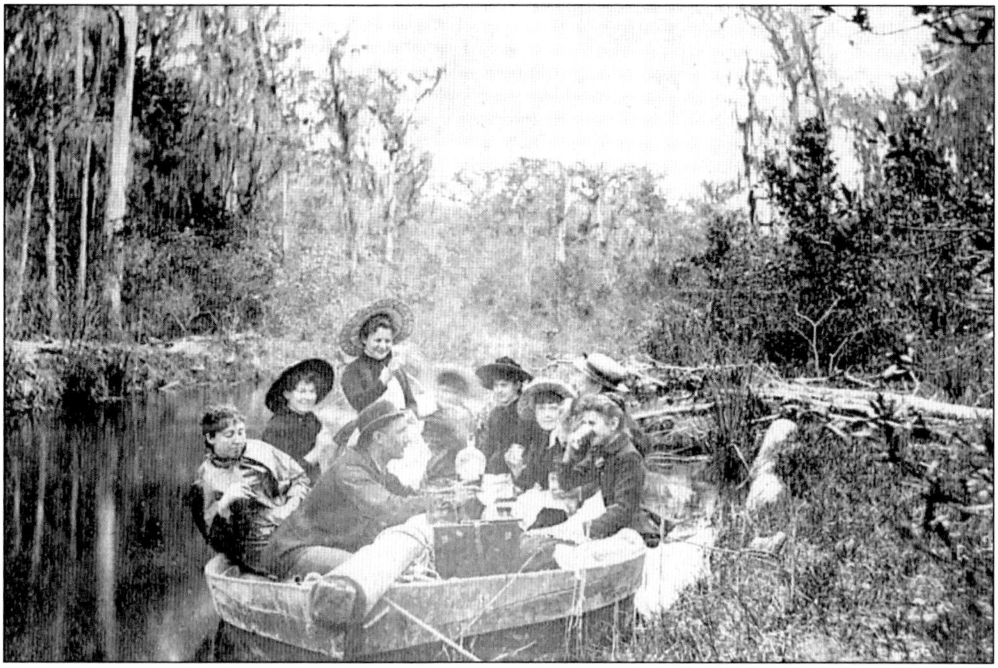

In this instance, it would seem that the picnic lunch is being enjoyed along one of the many streams in the area. With hundreds of lakes in the area surrounding Mount Dora, the photograph might have been taken almost anywhere in Lake County.

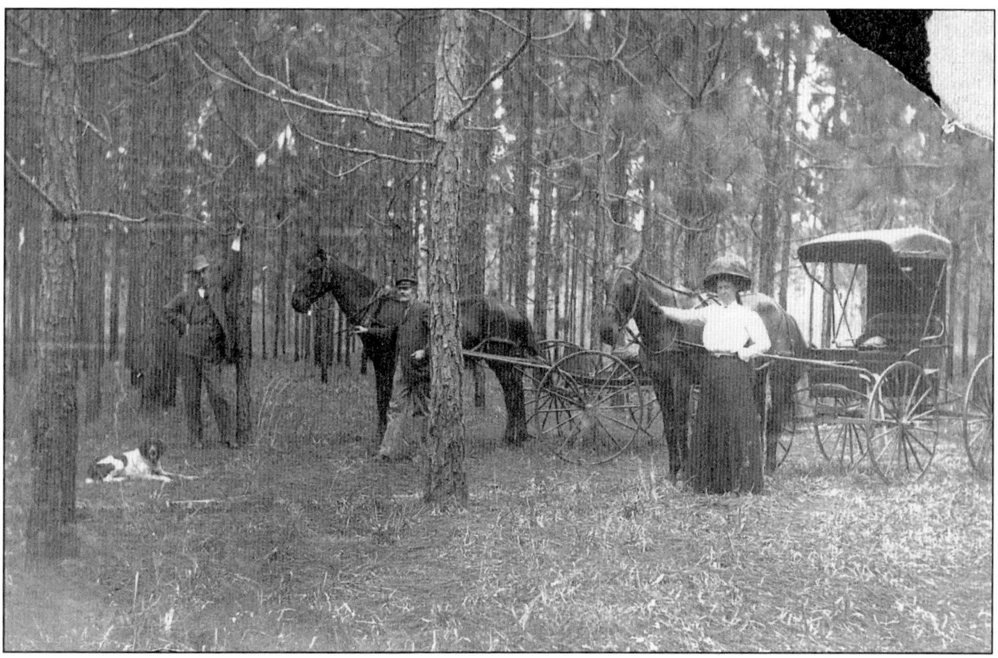

It is unknown whether the subjects of this photograph were local folks out for an afternoon jaunt in the woods or travelers passing through the area. Everyone, including the horses and the dog, seems to be posed for posterity, however.

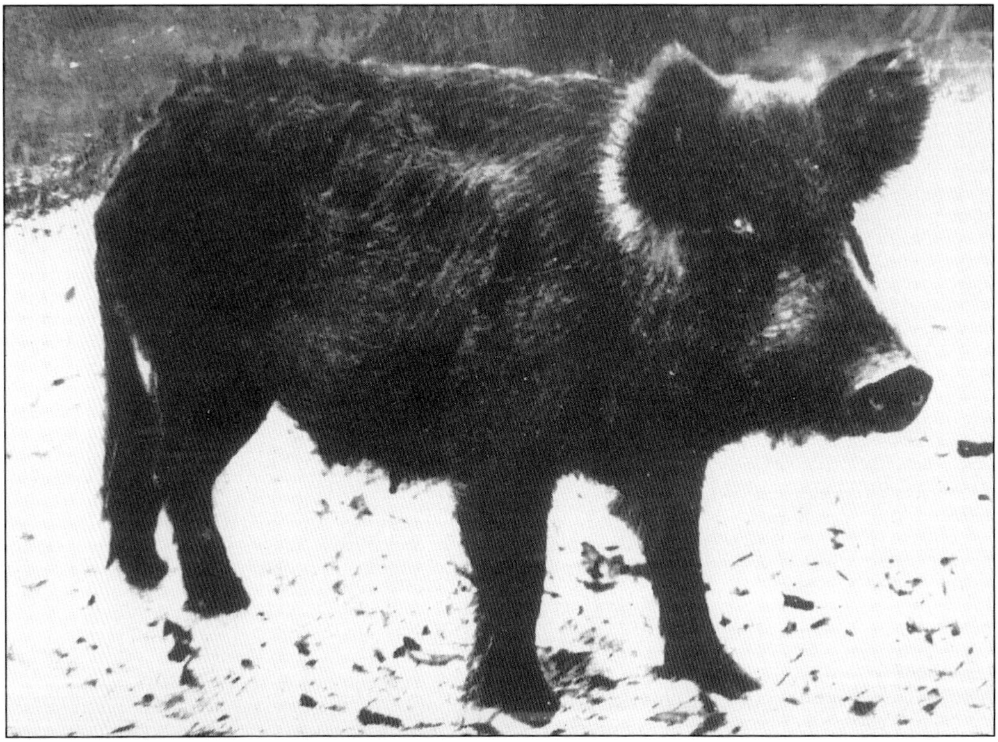

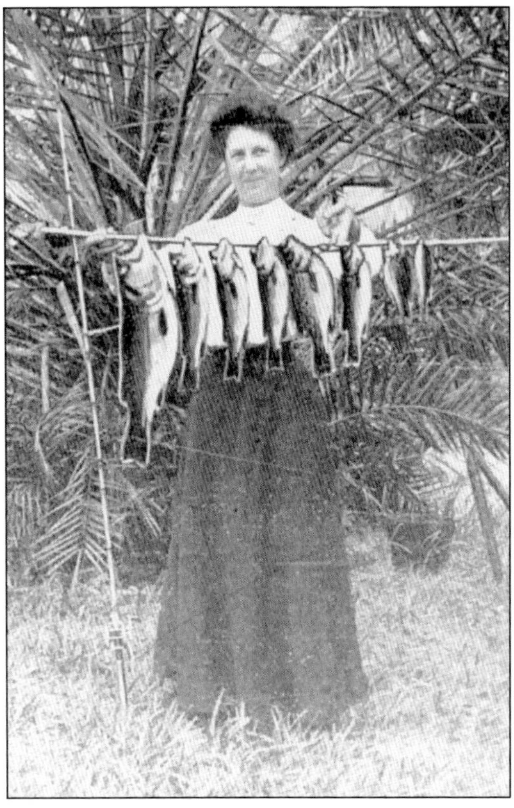

It does not require much imagination to envision the non-human inhabitants of this region. A source of both food and sport, waterfowl of all varieties, alligators, and wild hogs made their homes in the swamps and wooded areas surrounding the lakes.

This promotional image from the early 1900s touts the excellent fishing in the area's many lakes. While the fish that the woman is holding appear to be fake, in reality, such a good catch was not unusual. Before the lakes suffered the ravages of industrial and agricultural pollution, newspapers reported record catches on almost a daily basis.

Three

CHAUTAUQUA

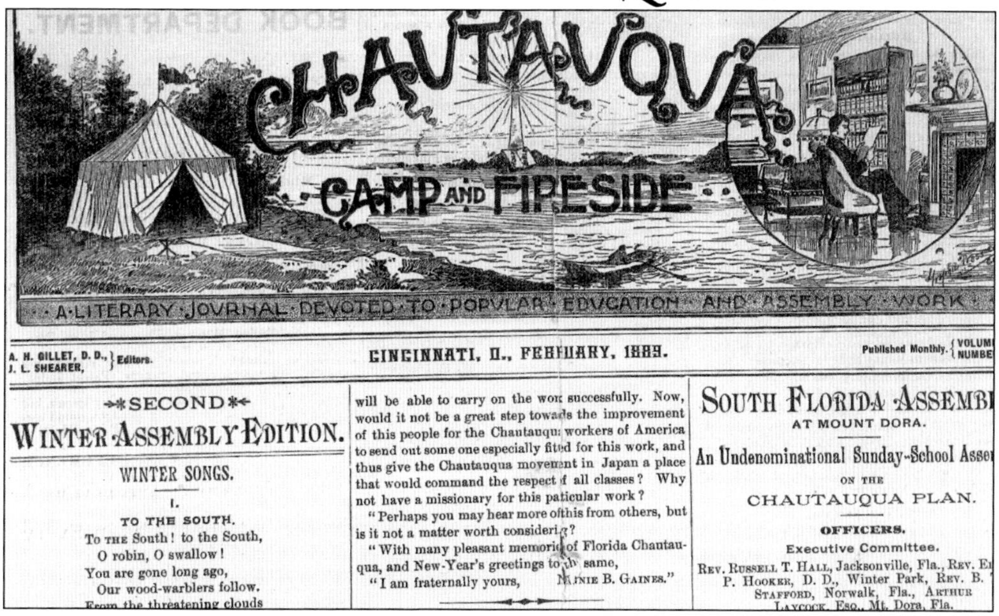
CHAUTAUQUA

CAMP AND FIRESIDE

A·LITERARY·JOURNAL·DEVOTED·TO·POPULAR·EDUCATION·AND·ASSEMBLY·WORK

A. H. GILLET, D. D., J. L. SHEARER, Editors.

CINCINNATI, O., FEBRUARY, 1889.

Published Monthly. { VOLUM NUMBE

SECOND

WINTER ASSEMBLY EDITION.

WINTER SONGS.

I.

TO THE SOUTH.

To THE South! to the South,
O robin, O swallow!
You are gone long ago,
Our wood-warblers follow.
From the threatening clouds

will be able to carry on the wor successfully. Now, would it not be a great step towards the improvement of this people for the Chautauqu workers of America to send out some one especially fitted for this work, and thus give the Chautauqua movement in Japan a place that would command the respect of all classes? Why not have a missionary for this paticular work?

"Perhaps you may hear more ofthis from others, but is it not a matter worth considering?

"With many pleasant memories of Florida Chautauqua, and New-Year's greetings to the same,

"I am fraternally yours, MINNIE B. GAINES."

SOUTH FLORIDA ASSEMB

AT MOUNT DORA.

An Undenominational Sunday-School Asse

ON THE

CHAUTAUQUA PLAN.

OFFICERS.

Executive Committee.

REV. RUSSELL T. HALL, Jacksonville, Fla., REV. E P. HOOKER, D. D., Winter Park, REV. B. STAFFORD, Norwalk, Fla., ARTHUR LAYCOCK, Esq., Mt. Dora, Fla.

The Chautauqua was a late 19th century spiritual and educational movement, originally taking life in 1874 at Lake Chautauqua in southwestern New York. Chautauqua was first conceived as a center to train New York Sunday school teachers, but quickly expanded. Founded by a pair of Ohioans, Lewis Miller and John Heyl Vincent, this renaissance fair of ideas could appropriately be termed a cross between a Bible-thumping, foot-stomping revival meeting and a county fair. Whether held indoors or beneath a white canvas tent, the Chautauqua movement offered rural America an eclectic assortment of religion, education, and entertainment. During a ten-day run, visitors could be treated to spirited lectures, music of all kinds, dramas, book discussions, opera, and general instruction in one of hundreds of subjects. The success of the New York Chautauqua led to several southern and Midwestern Chautauqua circuits. The Florida Chautauqua Winter Assembly first took root at DeFuniak Springs in February of 1885. As it grew in popularity, the movement spread throughout the state. Mount Dora was not left out; it became home to the South Florida Chautauqua in the spring of 1887.

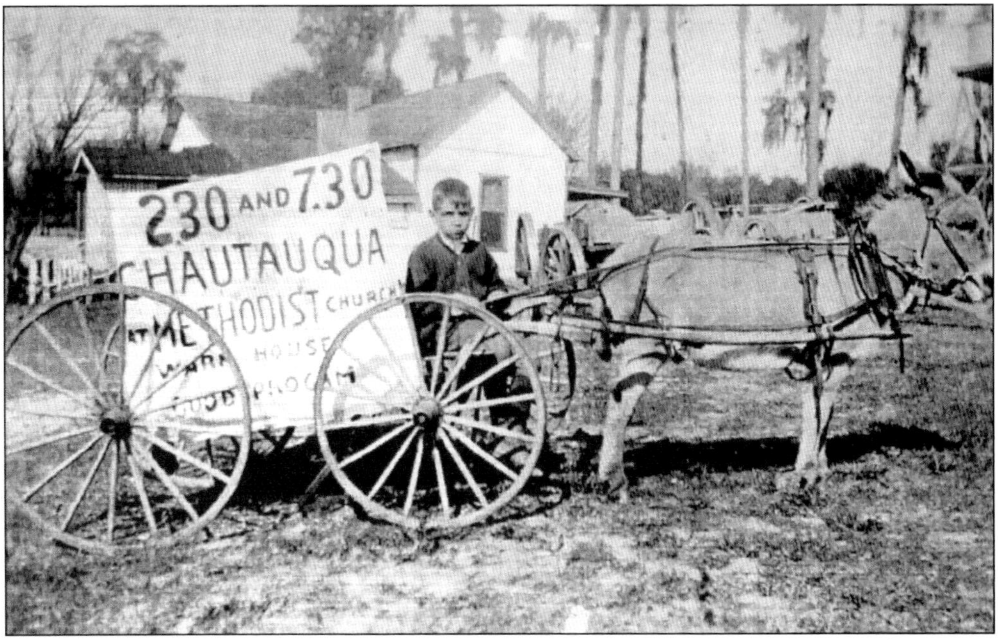

A local lad and his donkey cart were pressed into service to advertise the twice-daily Chautauqua meetings. The first Mount Dora assembly was held from April 5 to April 14, 1887. Early settler J.P. Donnelly had big hopes for the influence of the Chautauqua movement in Mount Dora, promising that it would "bring 5,000 to 10,000 people each winter."

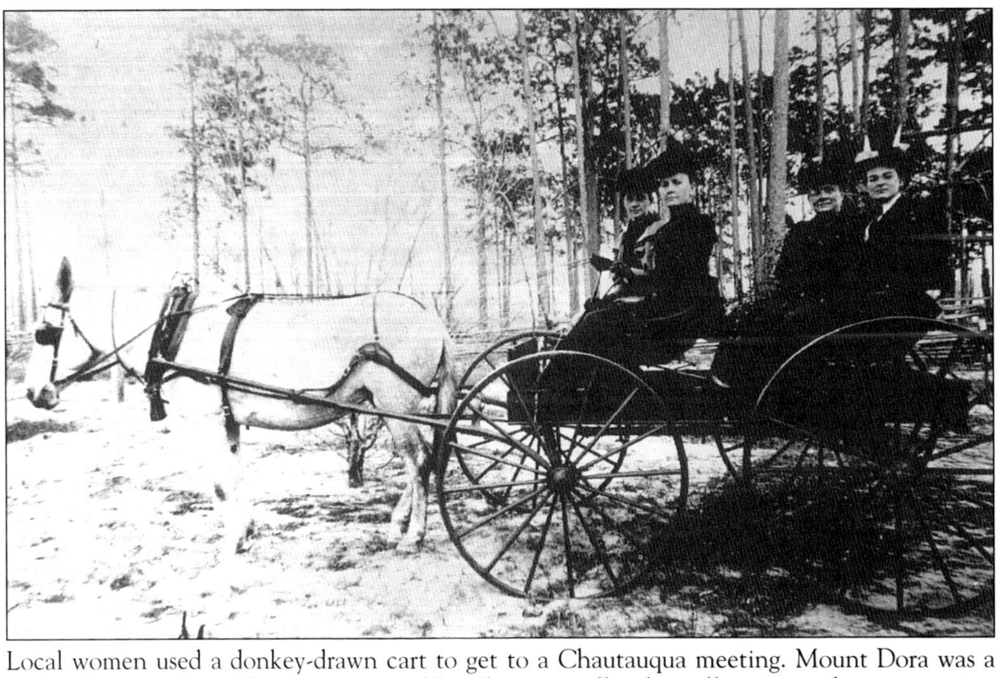

Local women used a donkey-drawn cart to get to a Chautauqua meeting. Mount Dora was a perfect location for a Chautauqua assembly. The town offered a well-connected transportation system with which to bring people. There was regularly scheduled train and steamer service. In an effort to attract people to the assembly, the railroads offered half-price excursion tickets.

A big pine along the Chautauqua path served as a familiar landmark to all visitors to Mount Dora's Chautauqua assembly. Advising visitors of the assembly location, an eight-page pamphlet printed for the 1888 South Florida Chautauqua stated that "the grounds of 16 acres are located on Lake Dora 24 miles from Sanford, on the main line of the J.T. & K.W. Railroad."

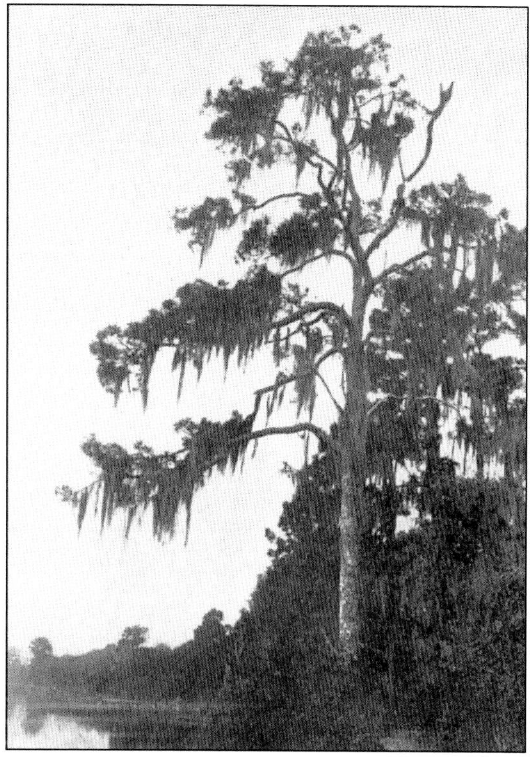

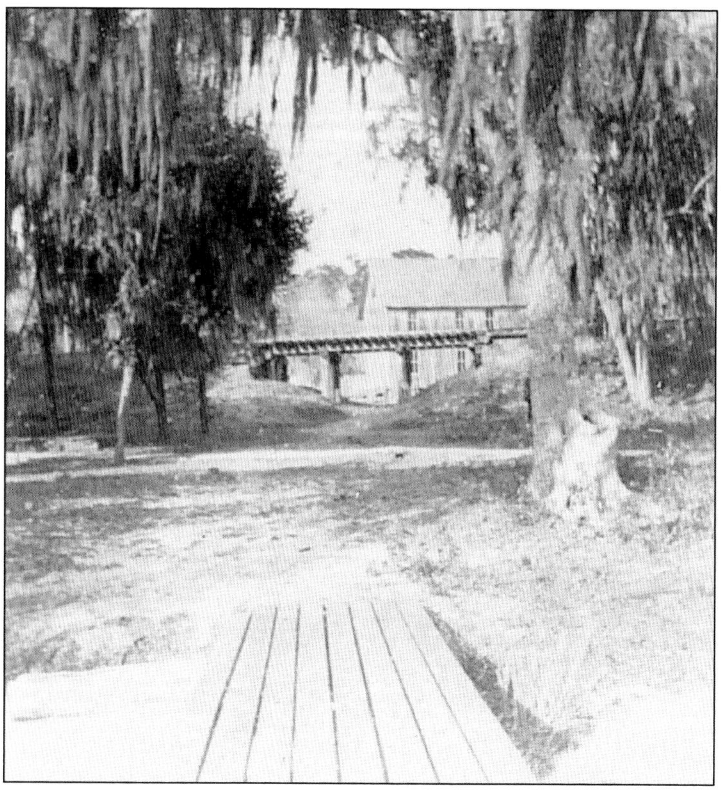

A panoramic view from the Lake Dora boat landing offered many attendees their first sight of the Chautauqua grounds, with the railroad trestle and the Chautauqua Hotel in the background. The assembly was held under a tent the first year. By the second year, the Chautauqua Hotel and an auditorium had been built.

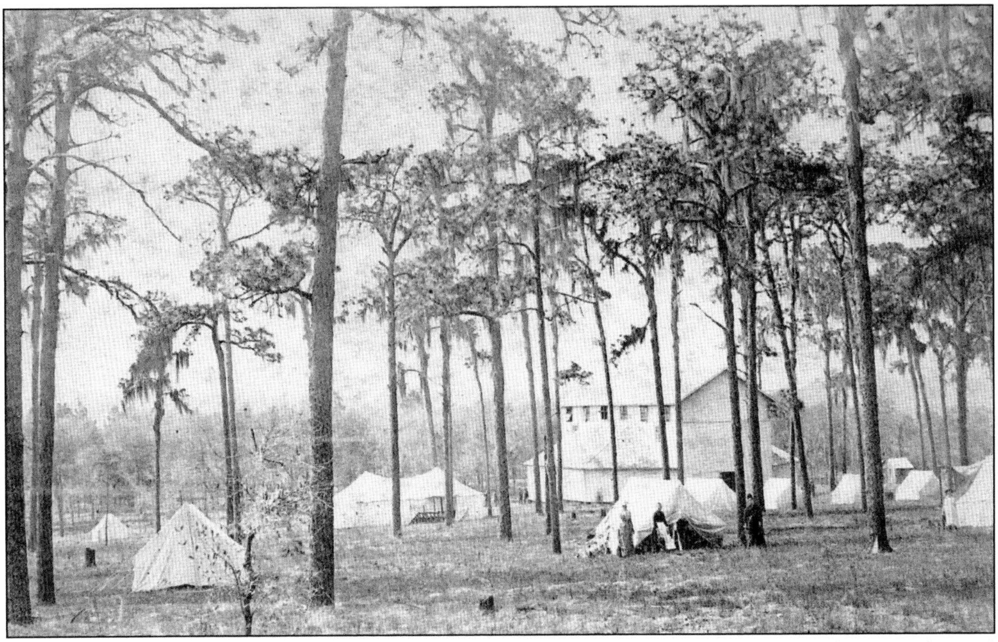

A view of the Chautauqua Hotel and tents on the assembly grounds in March 1889 showed the accommodations available. Visitors looking for a place to stay could rent tents on a daily or seasonal basis. The session, which ran from March 19 to 28, included lectures on such far ranging topics as "Womanhood in Shakespeare," "Alaska," and "The Farmers of Palestine." In a spirit of almost unheard-of equality, lecturers were both men and women.

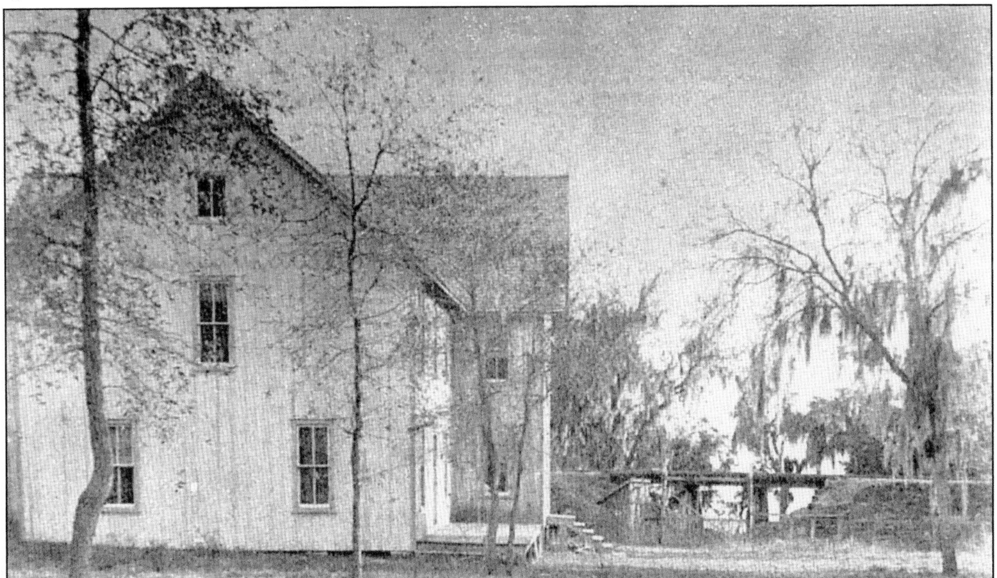

While some opted for the rigors of camping in tents, other, probably more affluent, visitors chose to be guests at the Chautauqua Hotel. The two-story farmhouse style of construction offered a lower level used for a communal dining hall. Food was prepared in the attached kitchen. Sleeping accommodations were located on the second floor and in the attic. Guests could rent rooms at the hotel for $6 per week.

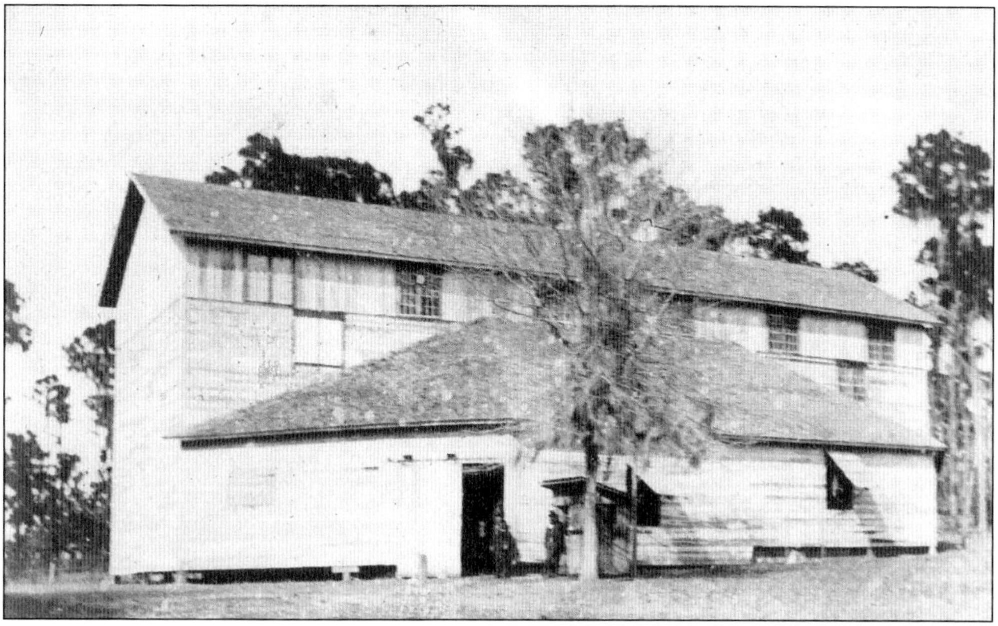

Realizing that the Mount Dora Chautauqua site needed an auditorium, the board of directors sold building lots to pay for the construction of the hall. Centrally located on the grounds, the auditorium was built on a north central section site. In addition to the auditorium, a large tent was erected to house smaller gatherings.

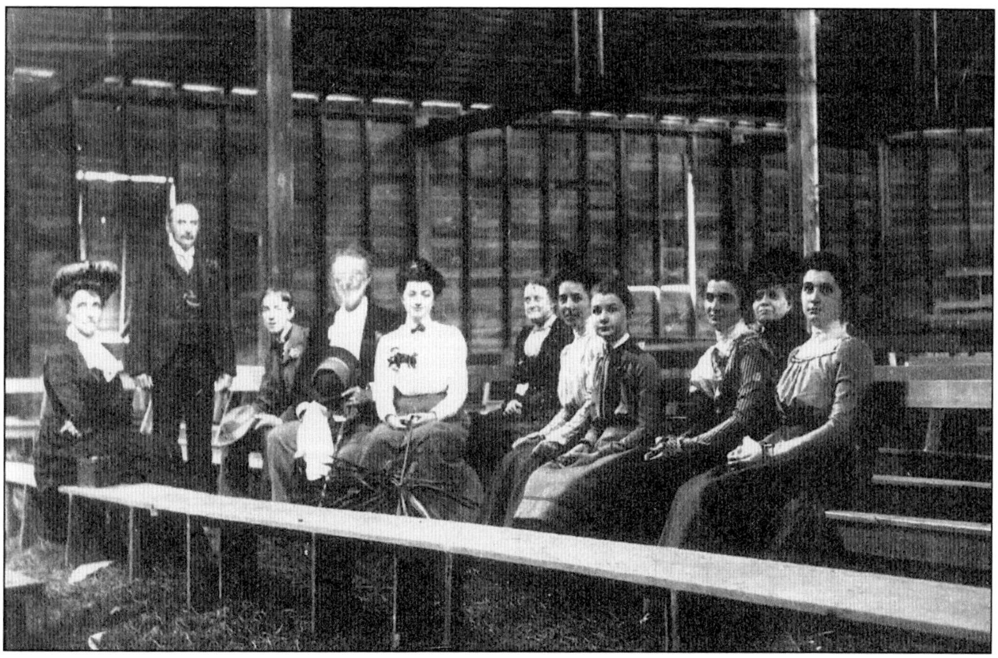

Although somewhat crude in appearance, the Chautauqua auditorium was really a grand structure for its time and place. The building boasted a seating capacity of 1,500 people. Seating accommodations were rudimentary; rows of wooden benches were placed upon a floor of packed dirt. Across the front of the building was a large stage. The building lacked heat and was lighted by carbide lamps.

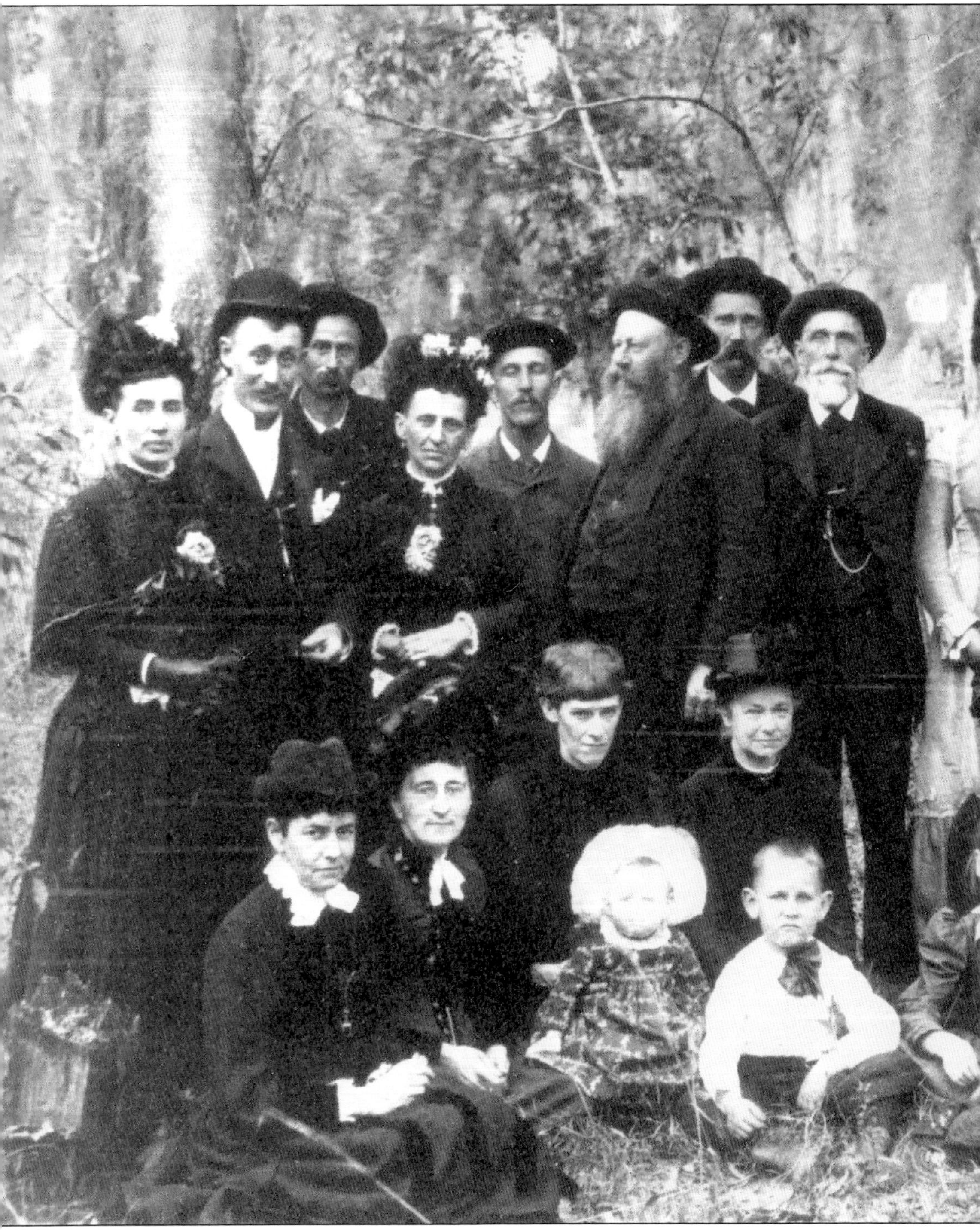

Visitors to the Chautauqua grounds pose for a photograph to record their visit to the assembly. A day at the Mount Dora Chautauqua was a day to remember for everyone in the family, young or old. For the children, there were daily boys' and girls' classes and Bible study. If a child was on his or her best behavior, the reward might be a piece of freshly baked cake or pie from the

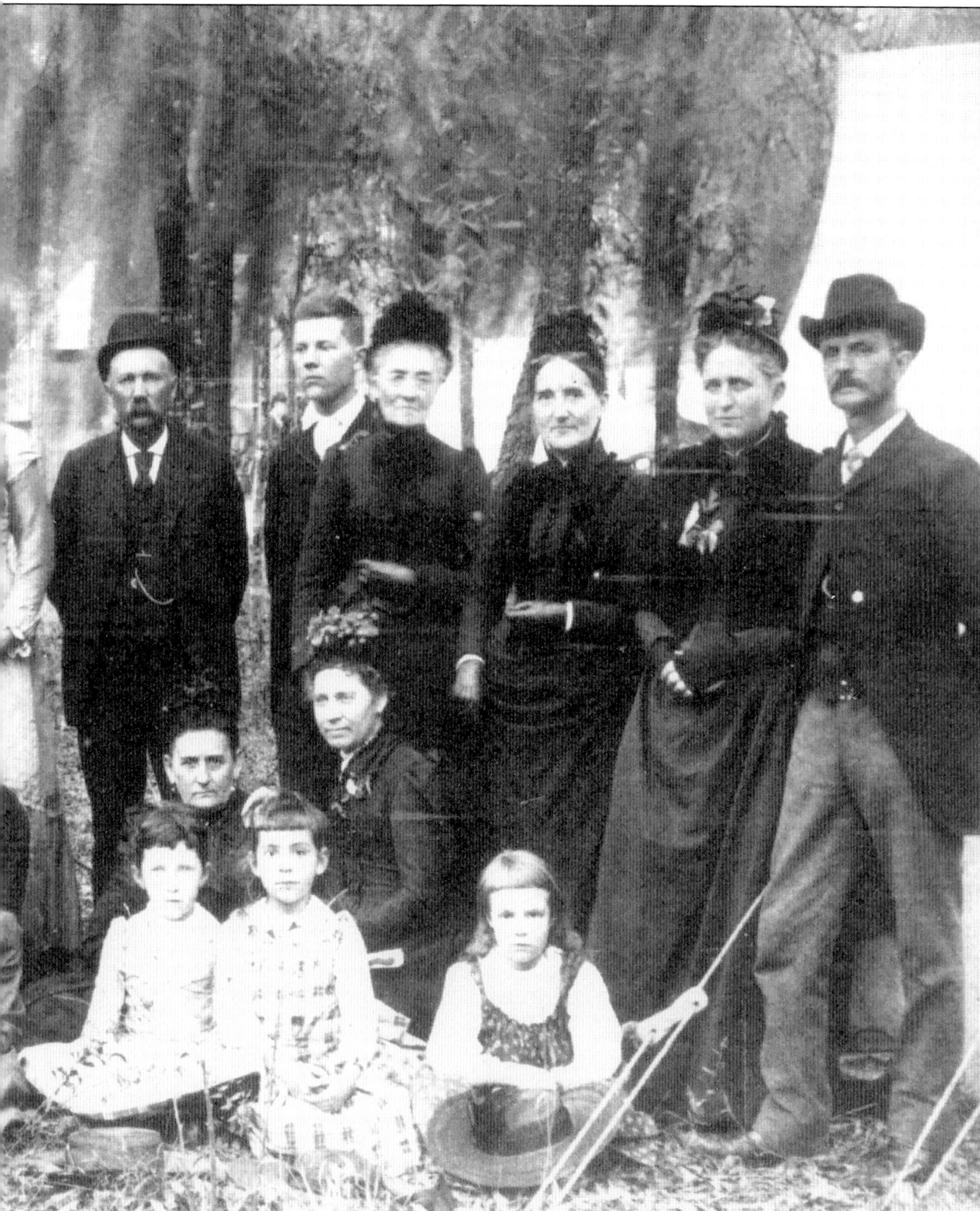

refreshment stand. For teenagers and young men and women, a walk along the lake with a member of the opposite sex was comparable to the modern meeting at the mall. For adults, there was an opportunity to renew old acquaintances, acquire a little culture, and spend a day in the fresh air.

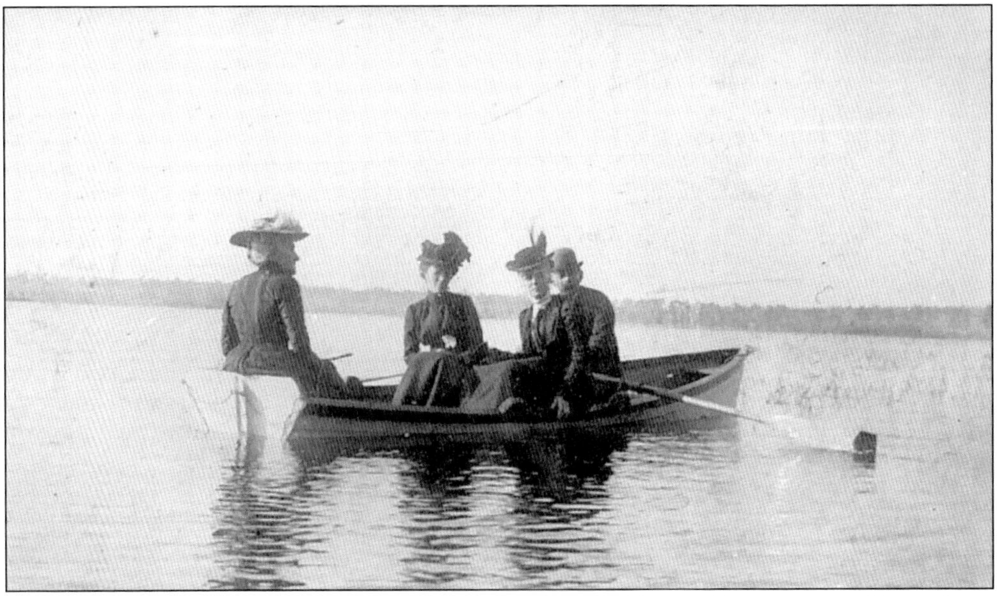

A day on the lake was as much a part of attending the South Florida Chautauqua in Mount Dora as listening to a lecture on such enlightening subjects as "The Irish Potato" or "The Geology of Florida." After an illustrated lecture on "1,000 Miles Up the Congo River," children and their parents could rent a rowboat for a ride on Lake Dora and conjure up visions of poisonous snakes and deadly insects.

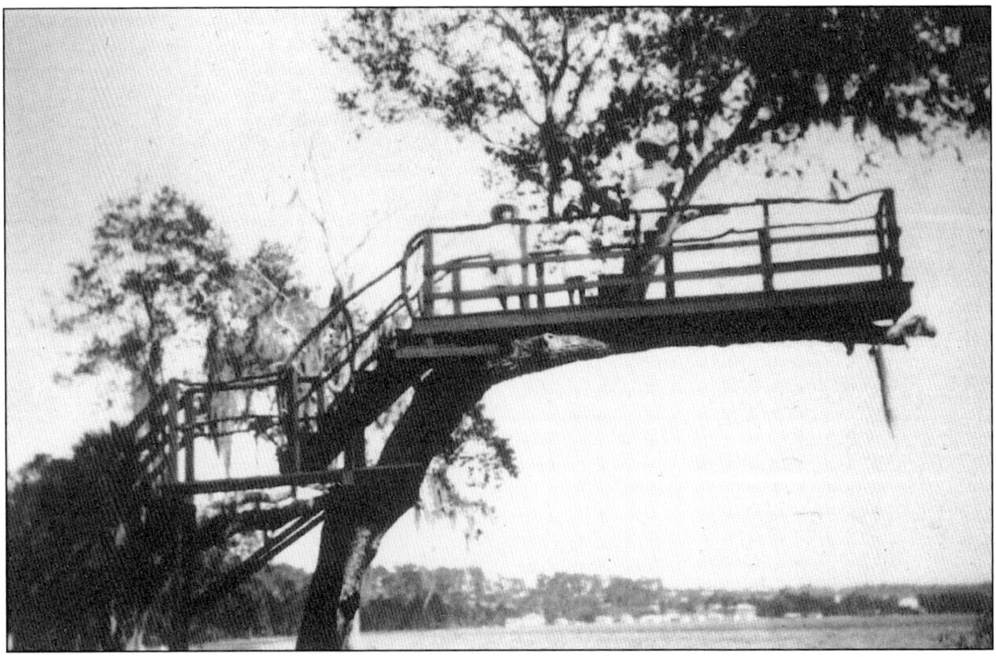

A tree house on the Chautauqua grounds overlooks Lake Dora. A special treat for youngsters visiting Chautauqua was a trip across the lake on the steamer *Dolphin*. The Chautauqua auditorium was destroyed in a fire in 1905; supporters in Mount Dora struggled to keep the movement alive but with little success. The Great Depression, America's neophyte film industry, radio, and the automobile all contributed to the end of the Chautauqua.

Four

A Community Grows

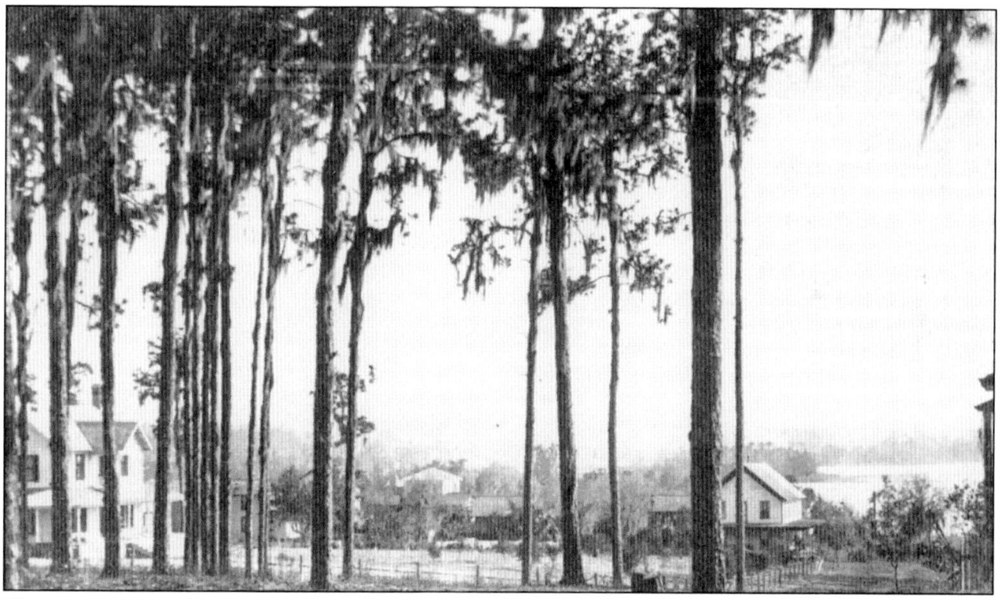

This panoramic 1906 view from the intersection of Seventh Avenue and McDonald Street shows, from left to right, the L.I. Todd homestead, the Lake House, the Bruce House, and the edge of the Smith home. Progress was coming to Mount Dora. The Lake House would become the Lakeside Inn; the Bruce House, the Grandview Hotel; and the Ed Smith home, the Villa Dora Hotel. In 1910, Gertrude Thorne, originally a native of Toronto, purchased Edward Smith's house, added several rooms and a lounge, and christened her purchase the Villa Dora Hotel. The Bruce House and the Lake House had long been offering their hospitality to visitors to Mount Dora. The Bruce House had been constructed in 1884. The Alexander House, dating to 1882, evolved into the Lake House. All of the properties on Seventh Avenue and McDonald Street offered unparalleled views of Mount Dora's premier attraction, the beautiful Lake Dora.

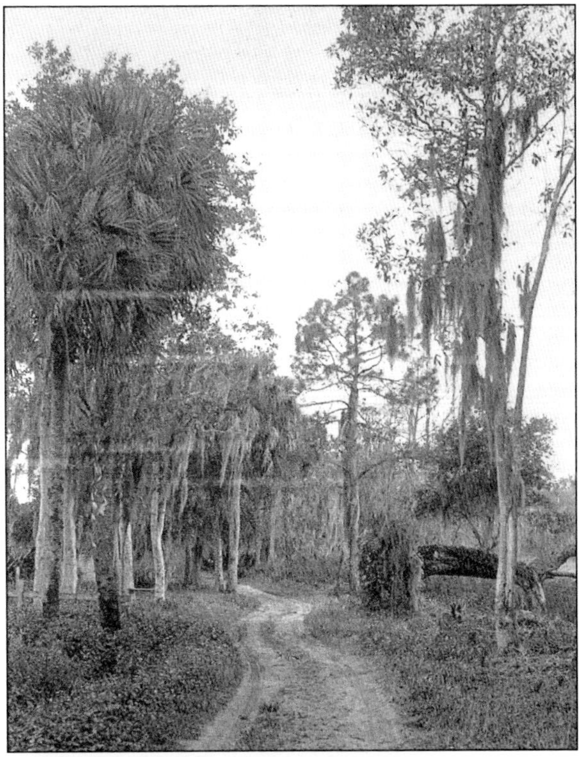

The chamber of commerce proclaimed, "Mount Dora, by virtue of its delightful all-year climate, its wonderful scenic beauties, its remarkable variety of charms and advantages is one of the leading tourist communities in central Florida." Tennis, volleyball, horseshoes, shuffleboard, cards, lawn bowling, boating, golf, fishing, and hunting were all attractive activities for visiting tourists. Many visitors wanted only the quiet of a walk along a country road and the beauty of the lake.

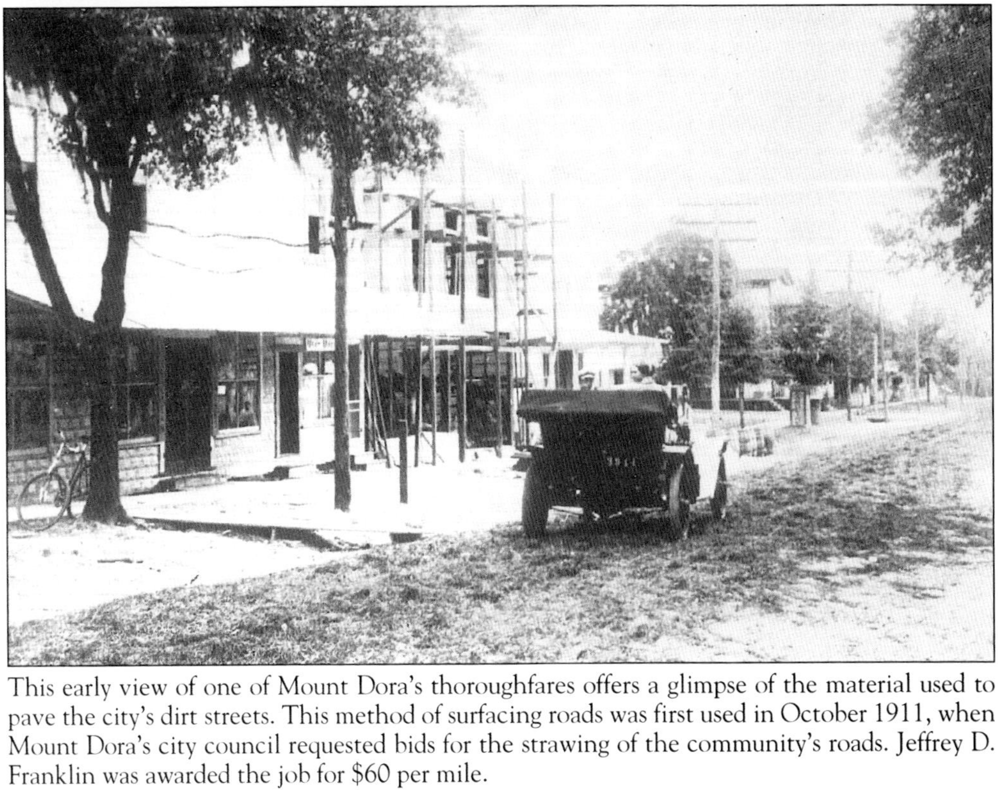

This early view of one of Mount Dora's thoroughfares offers a glimpse of the material used to pave the city's dirt streets. This method of surfacing roads was first used in October 1911, when Mount Dora's city council requested bids for the strawing of the community's roads. Jeffrey D. Franklin was awarded the job for $60 per mile.

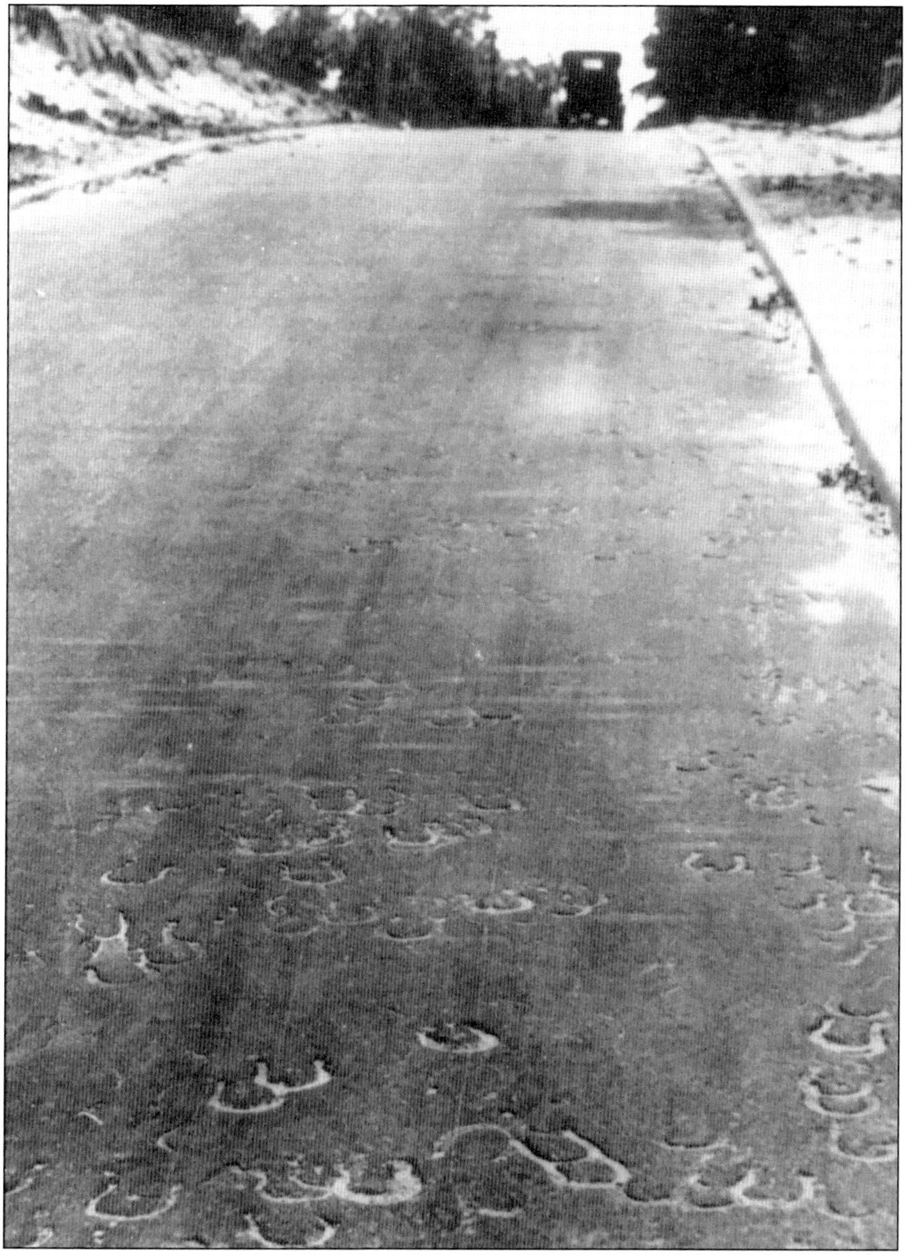

Sand asphalt eventually replaced pine straw as a material used to pave the roads of Mount Dora. Three miles out of Mount Dora, on the road to Sanford, hoof prints in the pavement are obvious. In June 1914, the council appointed Councilman James Simpson to study the feasibility of paving the city's roadways with a mixture of oil and sand. After spending several weeks in the rural communities of Cape Cod, MA, observing firsthand the success of the paving material, Simpson recommended that it be applied to the roads of Mount Dora at a cost of 65¢ per square yard. City council received his report with enthusiasm and awarded the project to Simpson, who supervised the street paving. Shared by horses and cars, Mount Dora's roadways were soon a combination of pine straw and oil and sand paving. City council set the city's speed limit at 15 miles per hour, "except in the business district and around corners."

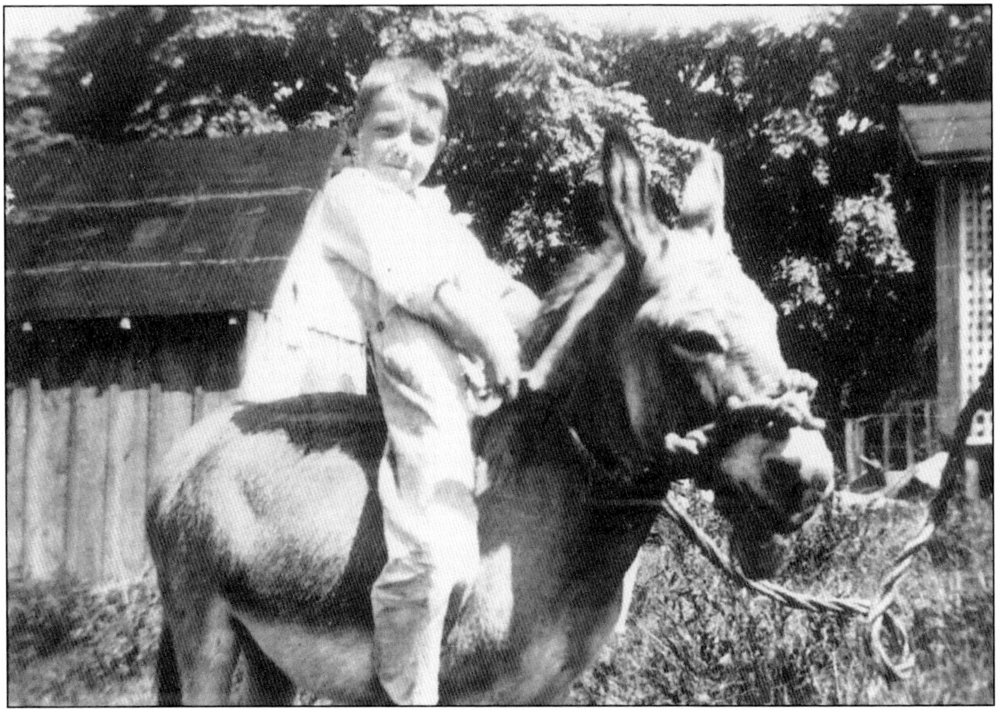

Clayton Tremain, grandson of one of Mount Dora's early citizens, Ross C. Tremain, proudly sat on his donkey. The name Tremain in Mount Dora boasted a proud and long lineage. The accomplishments of many founders of Mount Dora have been immortalized by the honor of having a street named after them—in this case, Tremain Street.

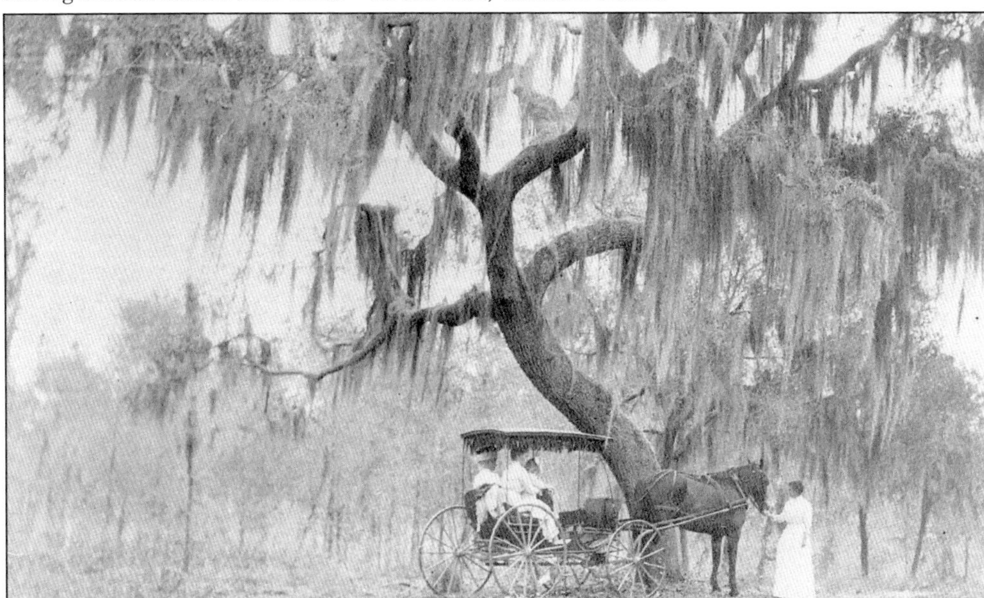

Life moved at a slower pace at the turn of the 20th century. One of the joys of a Sunday afternoon was a leisurely surrey ride around Lake Dora. Picnic lunches and strolls along country paths were also part of a Sunday afternoon's recreation.

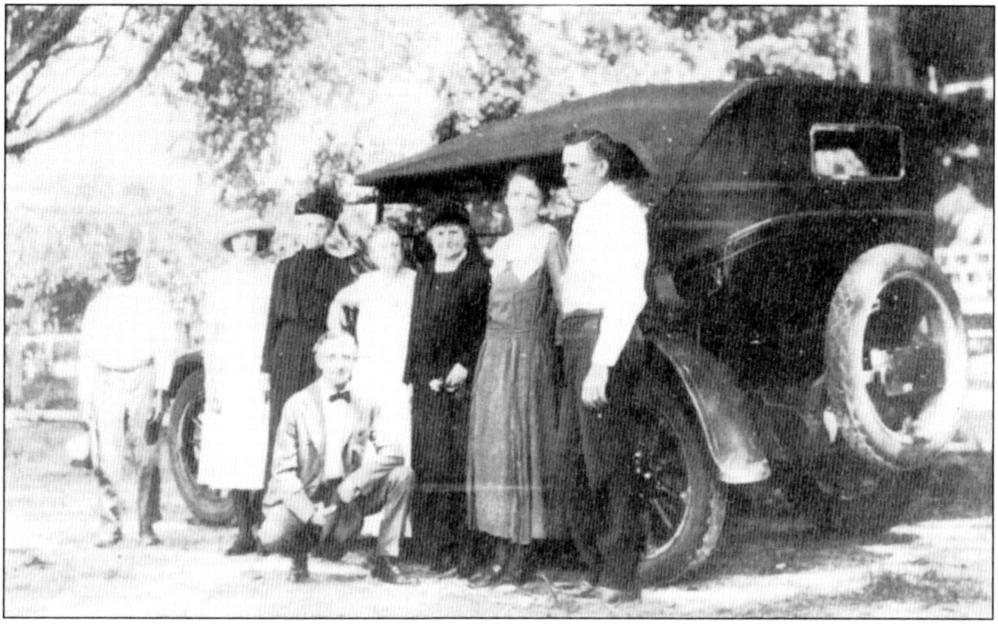

James Simpson and his friends proudly pose in front of Simpson's seven-passenger Buick touring car. As did many of Mount Dora's well-to-do families, the Simpsons employed African Americans from Mount Dora's "East Town" in the role of domestic workers. The black man on the left served as the Simpsons' chauffeur.

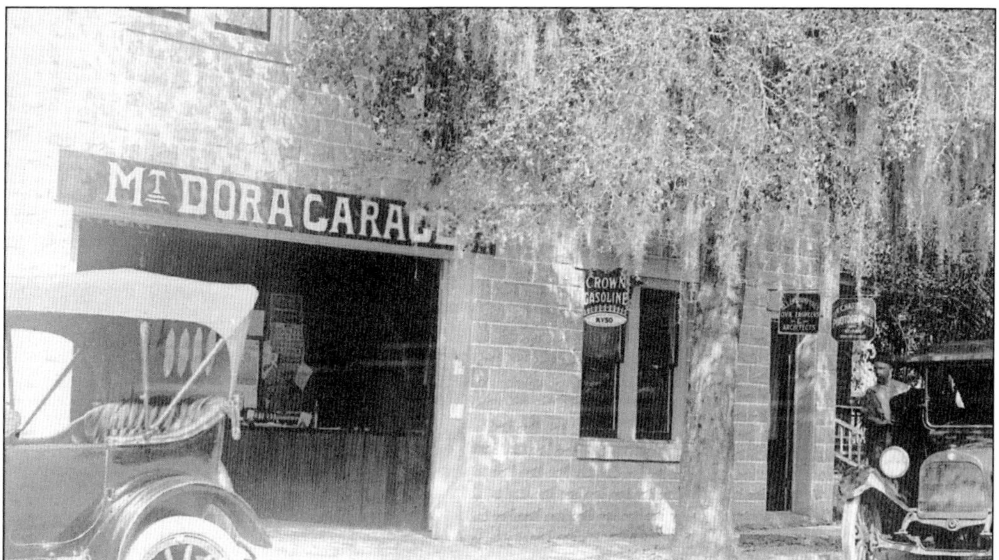

Around 1918, the Mount Dora Garage was owned by Jerome George LaDue. Like most Mount Dora families, the LaDues were not native Floridians but had relocated from Minnesota. LaDue's business interests were varied. Among other ventures, he was a principal in the Mount Dora Development Corporation and a director of the Cooperative Citrus Culture Association. LaDue Street was named in his honor.

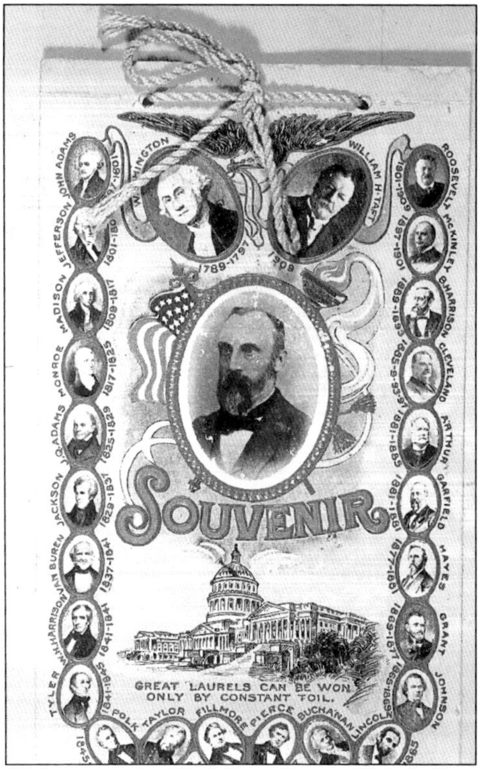

During the 1908–09 school year, Mount Dora students were awarded a souvenir for good scholarship and citizenship. Joseph Henry Crane, the school's bearded teacher, is prominently featured in the center of the six-page pamphlet's light blue cover. Page three of the booklet listed the school's students and trustees.

Mt. Dora Public School
Mt. Dora, Florida
Lake County
1909-10

J. H. CRANE, Teacher

Pupils

Maurice Pike	Boochie Pike
Alfred Lane	Cestie Vrooman
Ernest Bostick	Eva Shallenberg
Edward Jaques	Dorothy Shallenberg
Walter Shallenberg	Edda Shallenberg
Devoux Vrooman	Mae Orton
Philip Vrooman	Leo Hudson
Everett Hudson	Christine Stokley
Fletcher Crane	Doris Lane
Lee Silas	Effie Simpson
Otto Simpson	Maud Bostick
Charles D. Griffeth	Ruby Merritt
George Kimball	Elizabeth Harold
Howard Chamberlain	Ruth Setzer
Paul Stokley	Ruth Bostick
Ralph Cooper	Martie Bostick
Dewey Setzer	Ruth Butts
Harry Wellesford	Eleanor Slifer
Roland Fish	Ruth Slifer
Darragh Javens	Blanche Simpson
Rollin Javens	Helen Lewis
Richard Saunders	Pearl Watkins
Burgess Thayer	

Trustees

Arthur Orton James Simpson Thomas Bostick

Prof. Wm. T. Kennedy, County Supt.

Each year, at the end of the school term, teacher J.H. Crane gave his students a remembrance. For school year 1909–10, Crane wrote, "With compliments of your teacher, this gift is presented to you believing that it will grow in value as the years glide by."

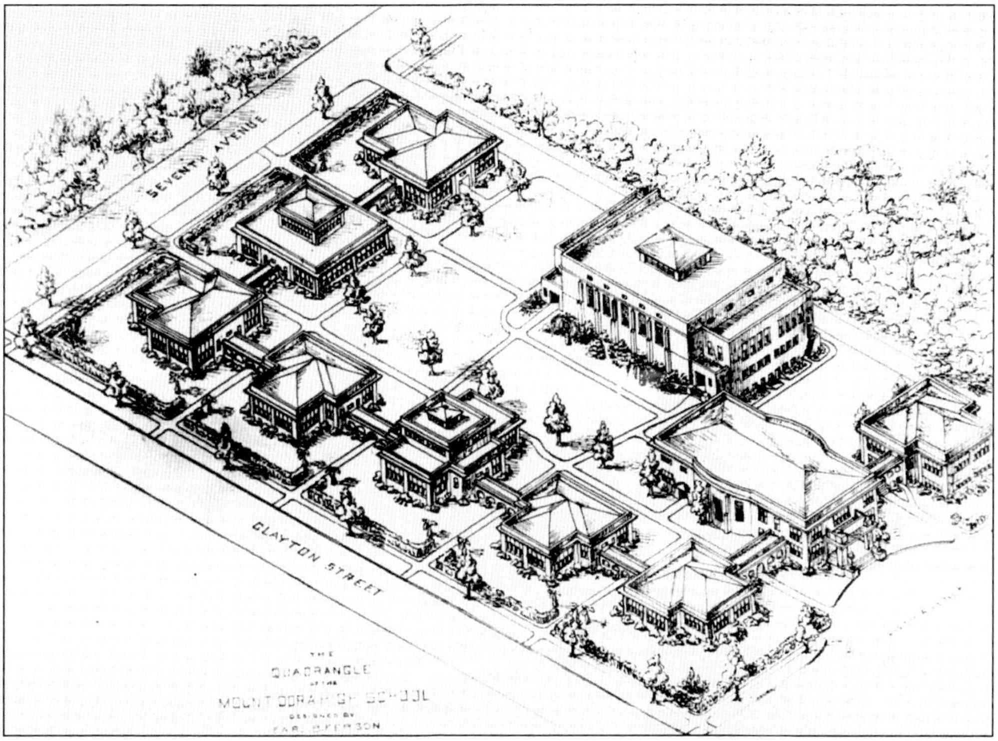

Designed by Earl B. Ferson, an overhead drawing depicted the Mount Dora High School in the 1920s. The purchase price of the land located between Seventh Avenue, Clayton Street, and Fifth Avenue was $3,350. As Mount Dora moves into the 21st century, this complex still exists but is scheduled for demolition. Preservationists, however, are waging a battle in the courts against the destruction of the complex.

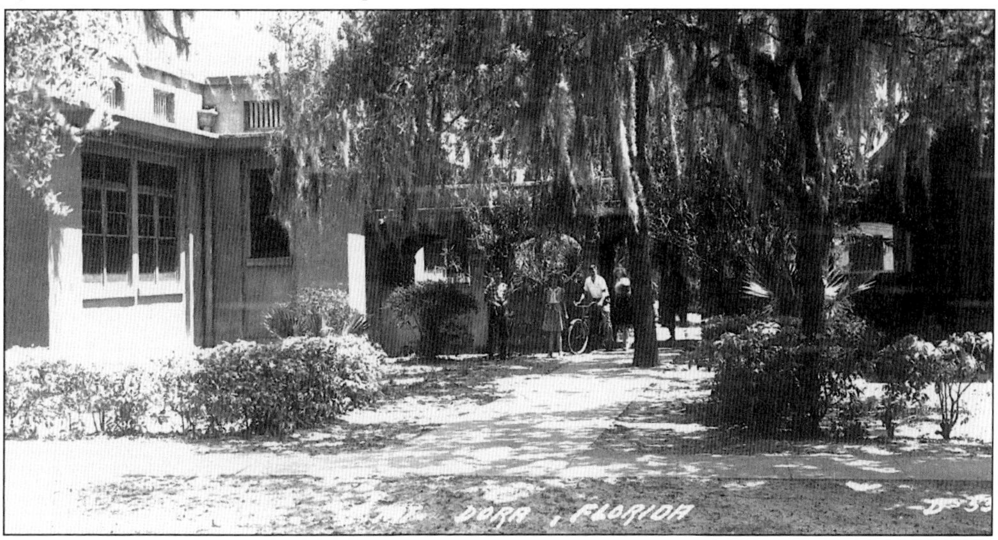

On opening day in September 1922, the new Mount Dora school boasted only 5 teachers and 105 pupils. Within 10 years, the school's population had doubled, as had the number of teachers on staff. Due to the rural setting, children from all parts of town rode their bicycles to school each day.

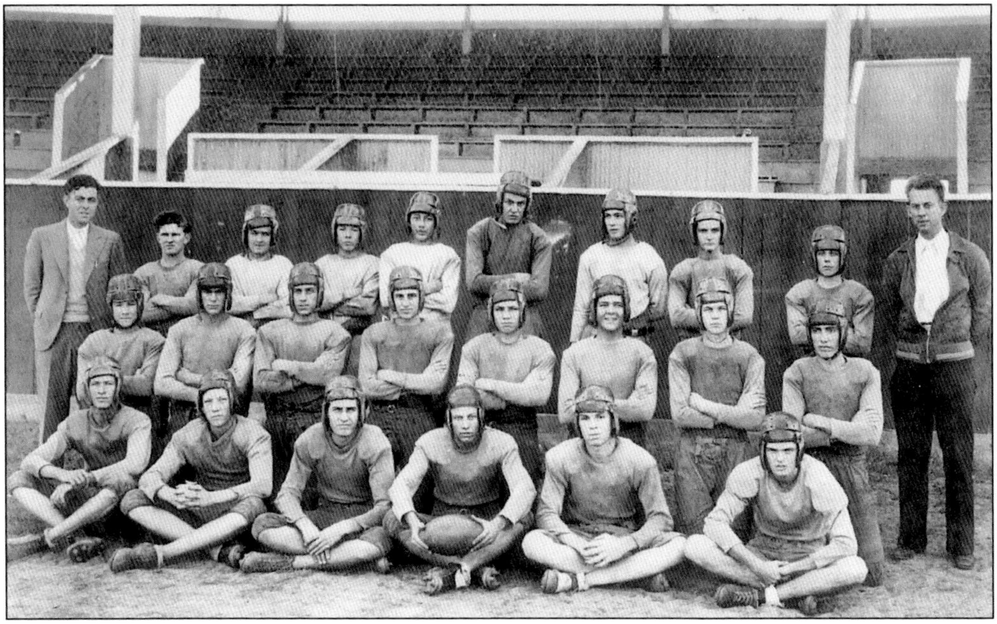

Like most small town or large city school systems, in 1933, Mount Dora fielded a football team. As were other American cities in that year, Mount Dora was still in the midst of recovery from the Great Depression. Even though teacher salaries had been reduced approximately 20 percent and many property owners struggled to pay their taxes, enough money was found to equip the school's sports teams.

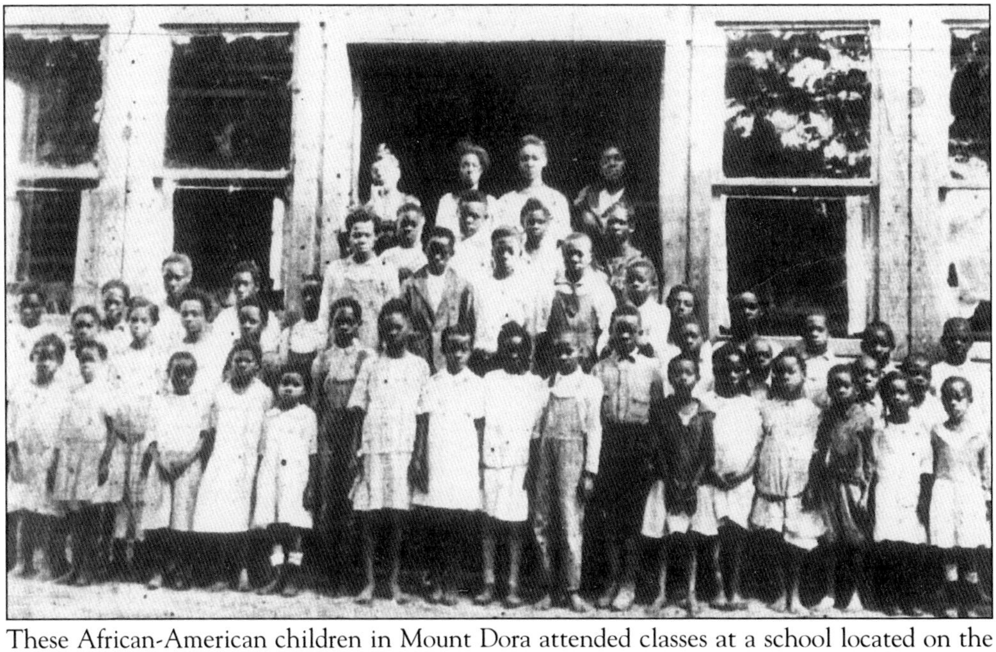

These African-American children in Mount Dora attended classes at a school located on the first floor of the Witherspoon Lodge, home to the Prince Hall Masons, on the corner of Jackson and Clayton Streets. Later, Duncan Milner worked with the Julius Rosenwald Foundation to build a more modern school for Mount Dora's black students. The Milner-Rosenwald Academy also offered night school for adults.

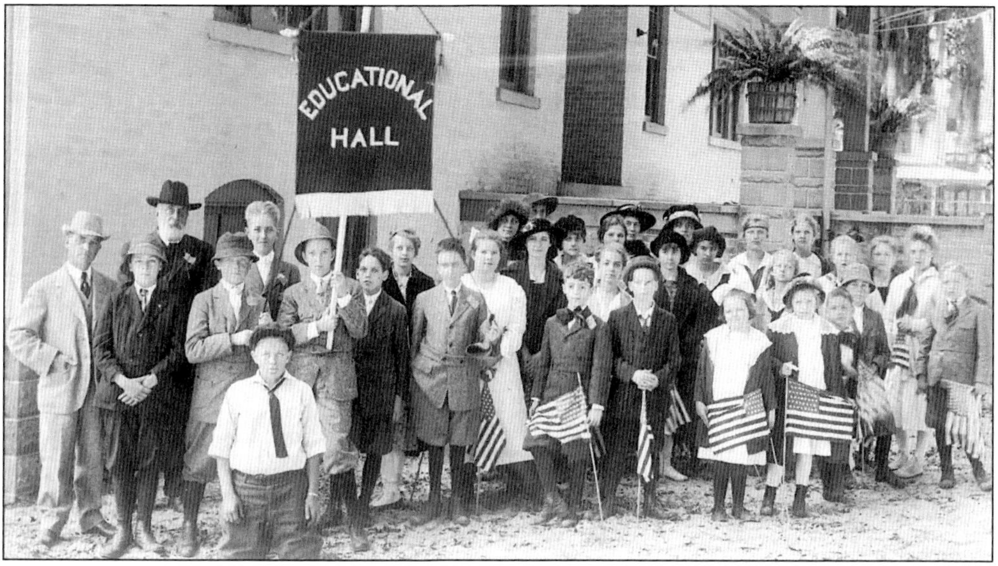

Students and headmaster J.H. Crane pose in front of Educational Hall on the opening day of school on September 15, 1913. When the town's leading citizens, including John P. Donnelly, James Simpson, and Carl Risley, became dissatisfied with the public school, private funds were raised to construct Educational Hall. Serving both local residents and the children of winter visitors, the school continued to function until 1923.

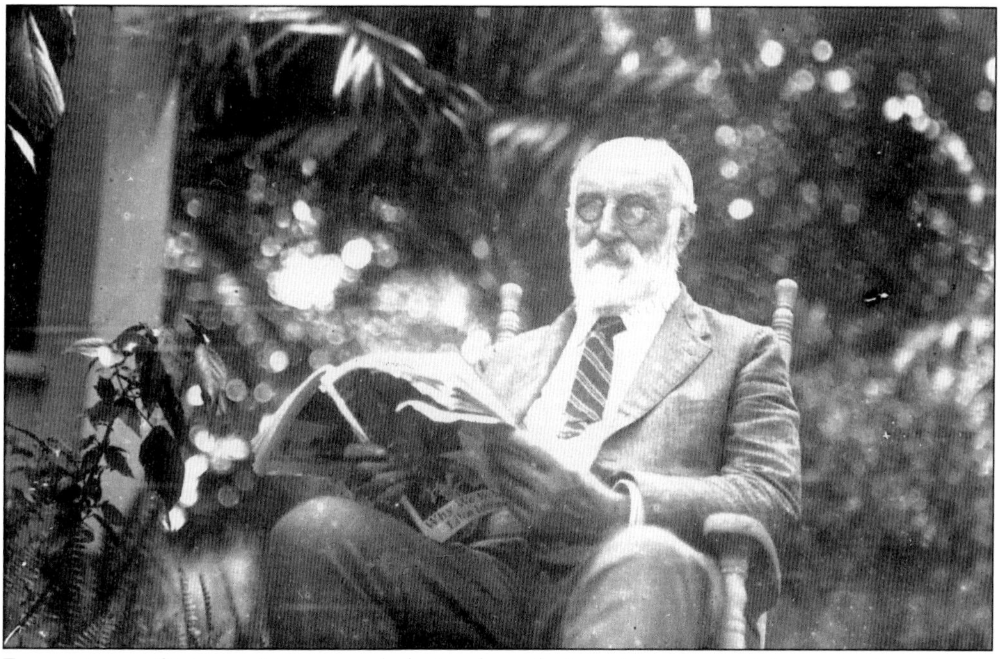

Few citizens of Mount Dora served their adopted city with more public spirit than Joseph H. Crane. Originally a teacher in the public school system of New York, Crane first started teaching in Mount Dora in 1908 for the princely sum of $50 per month. He remained in the public school system until 1913, when he became headmaster of the private Educational Hall. In addition to his teaching duties, Crane served several terms as a city councilman, clerk, and treasurer, and was elected mayor of Mount Dora in 1915 and 1916.

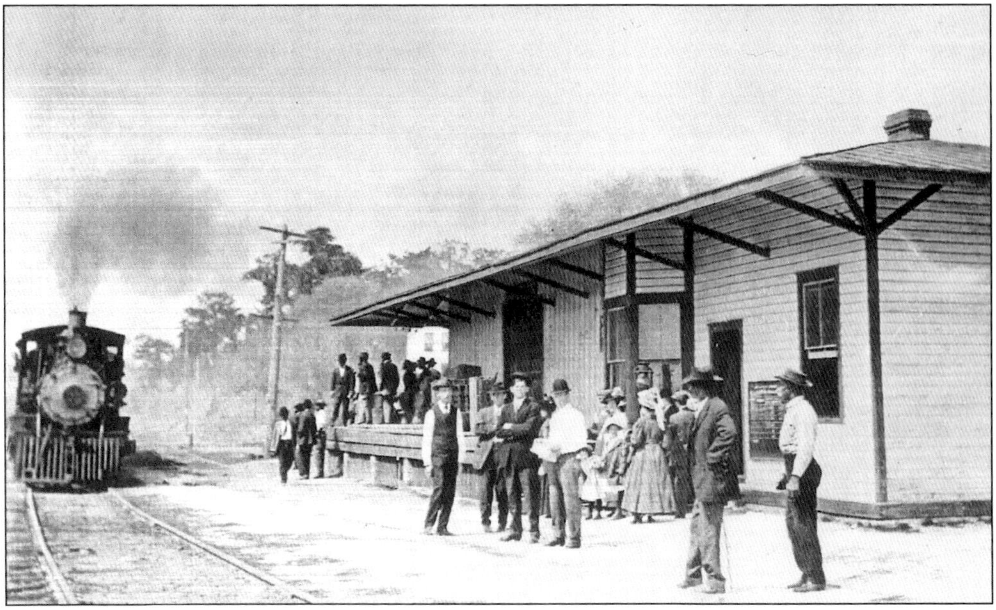

The Mount Dora train station was a busy place in 1916. The "official" town census of that year reflected the fact that fewer than 1,000 people lived in Mount Dora on a year-round basis. During the winter, the population nearly tripled as hundreds of tourists from the Midwest and Northeast arrived each day on one of the Atlantic Coast Line's trains.

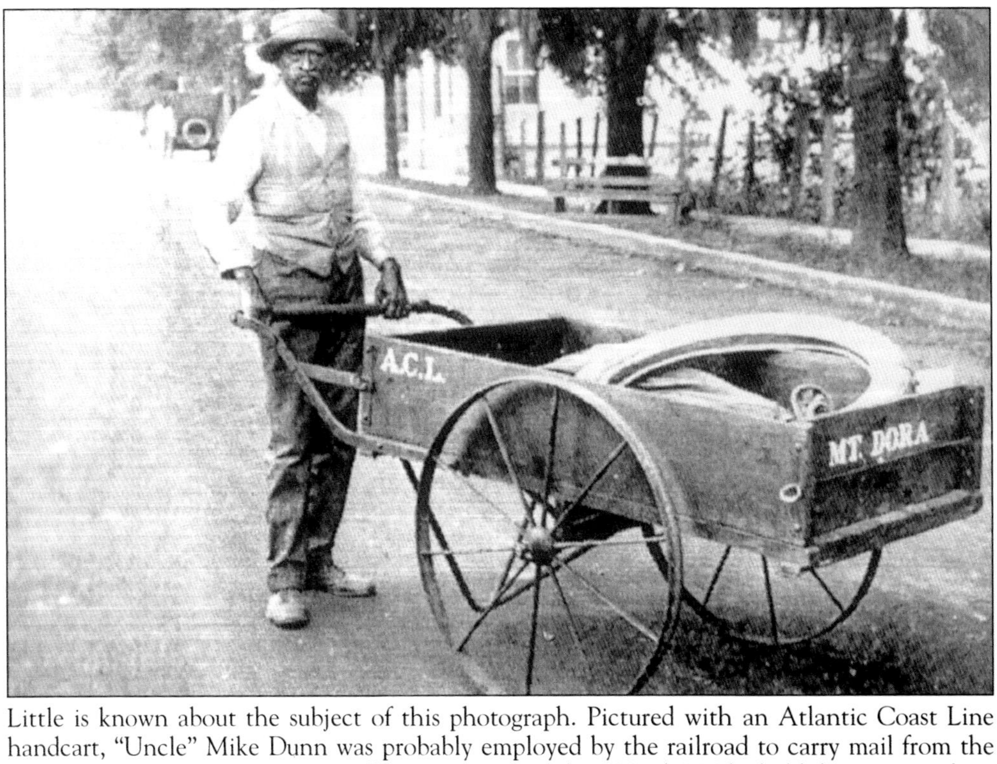

Little is known about the subject of this photograph. Pictured with an Atlantic Coast Line handcart, "Uncle" Mike Dunn was probably employed by the railroad to carry mail from the train depot to Mount Dora's post office. It is reported that "Uncle" Mike held this position from 1915 to 1935.

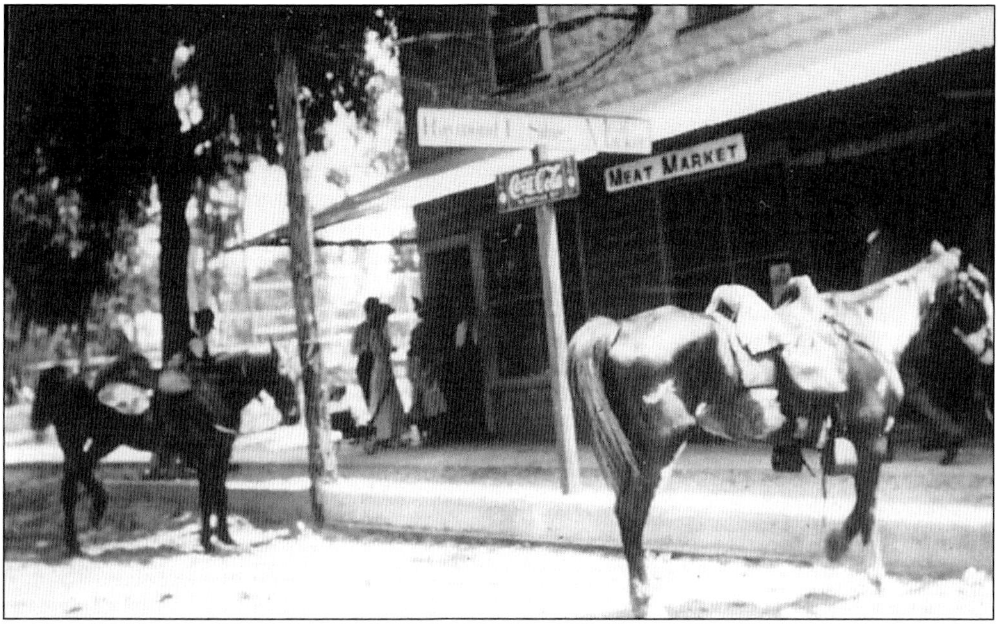

Taken not many years after the turn of the 20th century, this photograph of one of Mount Dora's main streets evokes a strong image of the Old West. Dirt streets and horses tied to hitching posts would lead one to believe that the town offered few amenities. This was not, however, the case. Raymond L. Silas's butcher shop offered not only tender cuts of meat, but also cold Coca-Colas for the thirsty. Silas, one of the founders of the Mount Dora Yacht Club, operated the meat market until some time in the 1920s.

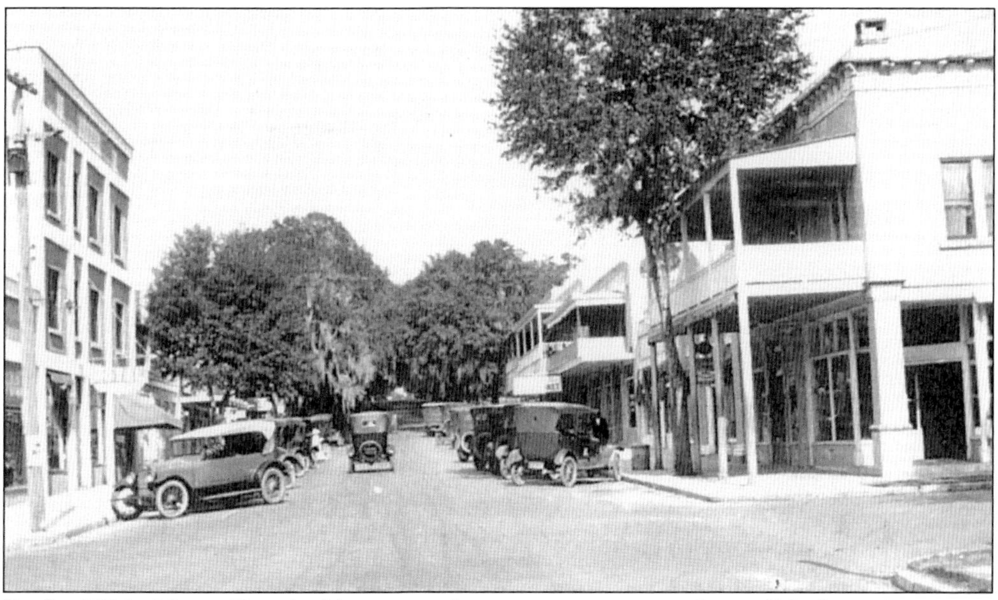

By the 1920s, Mount Dora had become a thriving community with a well laid-out downtown. The keystone building on this block was the Mount Dora Hotel, constructed in 1922. Streets were paved, and speed limits were posted. In September 1926, mail delivery was inaugurated. Carrier service was offered to all houses on paved streets in Mount Dora, affecting about 300 residents. One carrier made two daily deliveries.

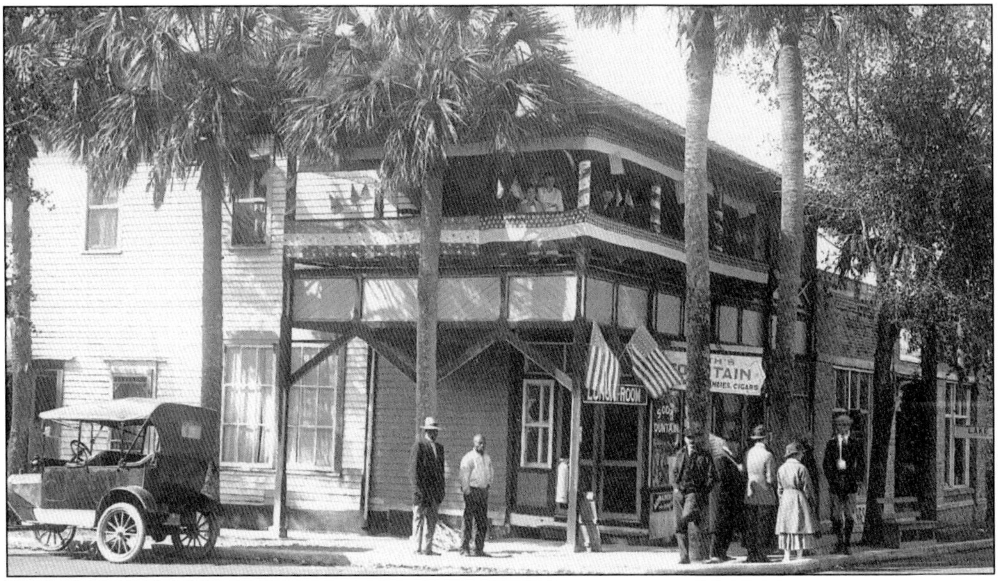

The Butts Building was located on the corner of West Fourth Avenue and Donnelly Street. Although not an original settler of Mount Dora, Warren C. Butts was one of the community's elder statesmen, having arrived in 1896 from nearby Sorrento, FL. Butts was elected as a city councilman in 1910 and tax collector in 1911. Like many other prominent citizens of Mount Dora, Butts was credited with assisting in the construction of the town hall in 1904.

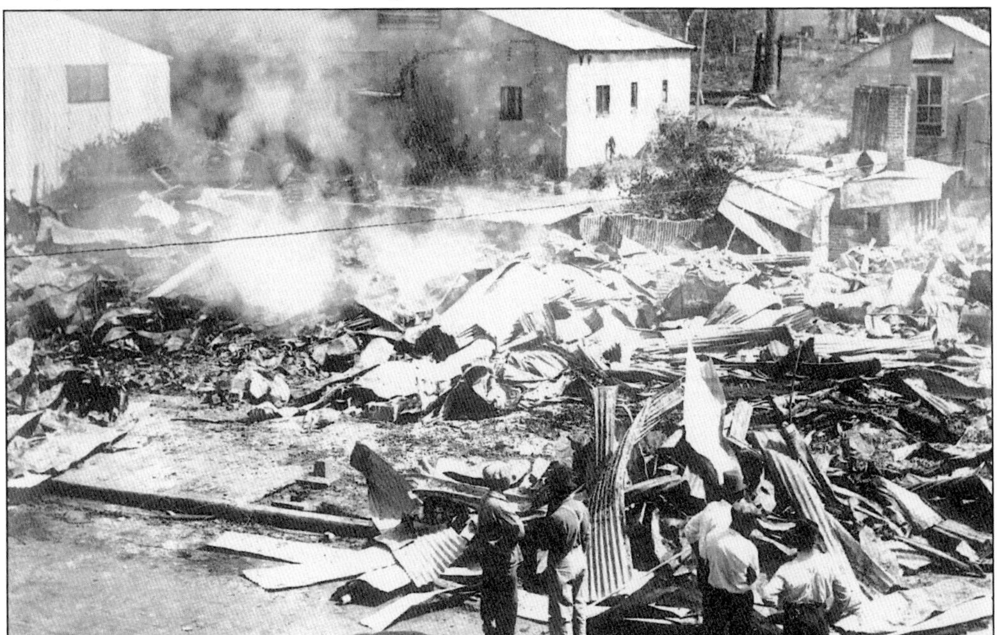

As seen in this photograph, a fire in Mount Dora in 1922 destroyed part of the east side of the block between Fourth and Fifth Avenues on Donnelly Street. The citizens of Mount Dora considered themselves fortunate that it had not been worse. Many early Florida communities had suffered from catastrophic fires that destroyed hundreds of buildings and resulted in millions of dollars of damage.

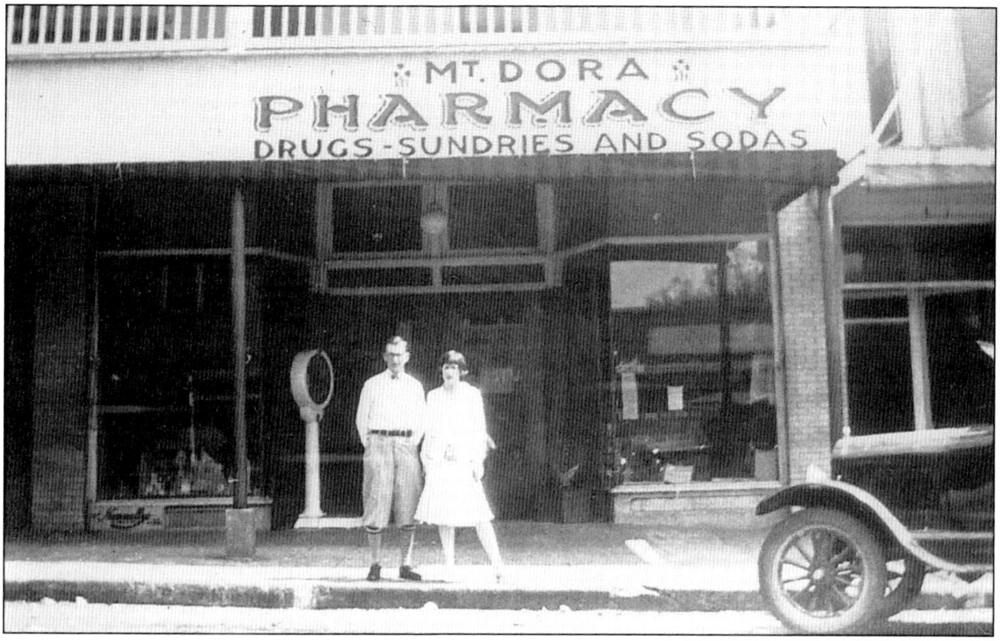

The Mount Dora Pharmacy was a spot where tourists and residents alike were able to sit back and relax with a beverage from an old-fashioned soda fountain. The pharmacy was originally established in 1901 by Dr. T. Newton Lewis, a transplant from Michigan. Upon the death of Dr. Lewis in 1910, the store was sold to Dr. Harry T. Fenn. By 1932, the pharmacy was operated by Cort Helms, pictured here with his wife.

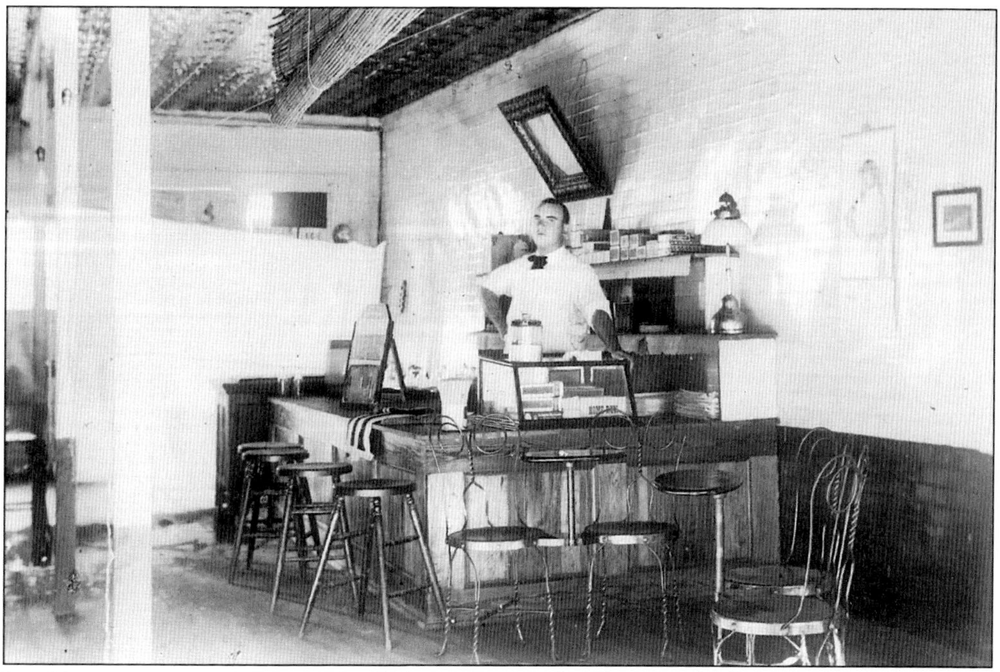

In addition to acting as proprietor of Silas's Meat Market, Raymond Silas, in 1915, also operated the city's ice-cream parlor. A thick and cold ice-cream soda made a perfect treat on a hot Florida day.

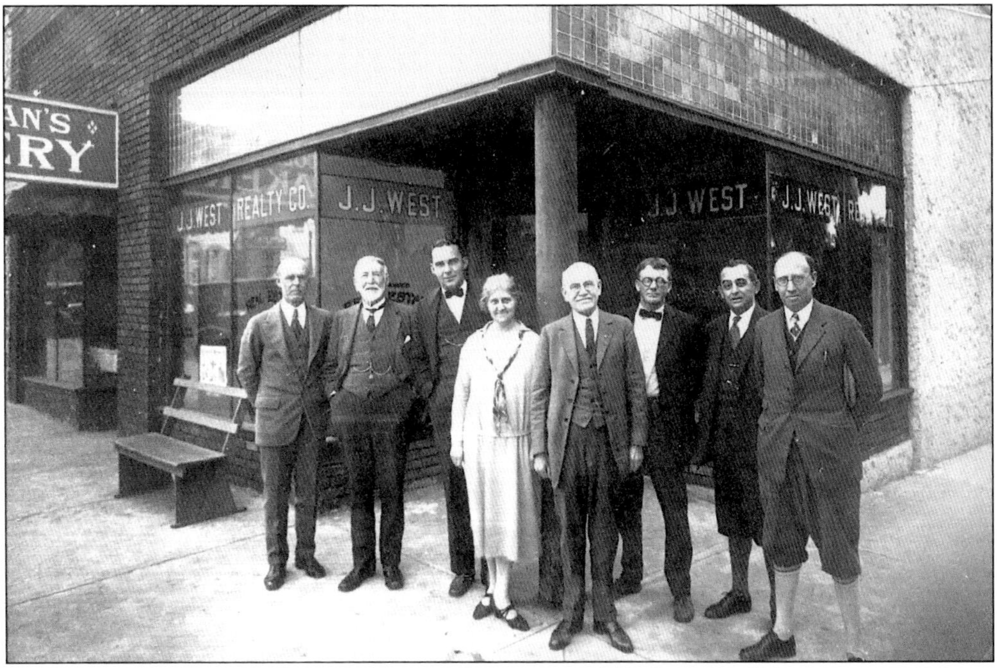

During Florida's 1920s real estate boom, John J. West, fifth from the left, was one of Mount Dora's most prodigious builders. West, owner of the J.J. West Realty Co., told a newspaper reporter after a 1926 visit to the north, "Things are dull up there. There is not the activity up there that we are experiencing in Florida. I am glad to be back in Mount Dora to take hold and help in building the prettiest town in America."

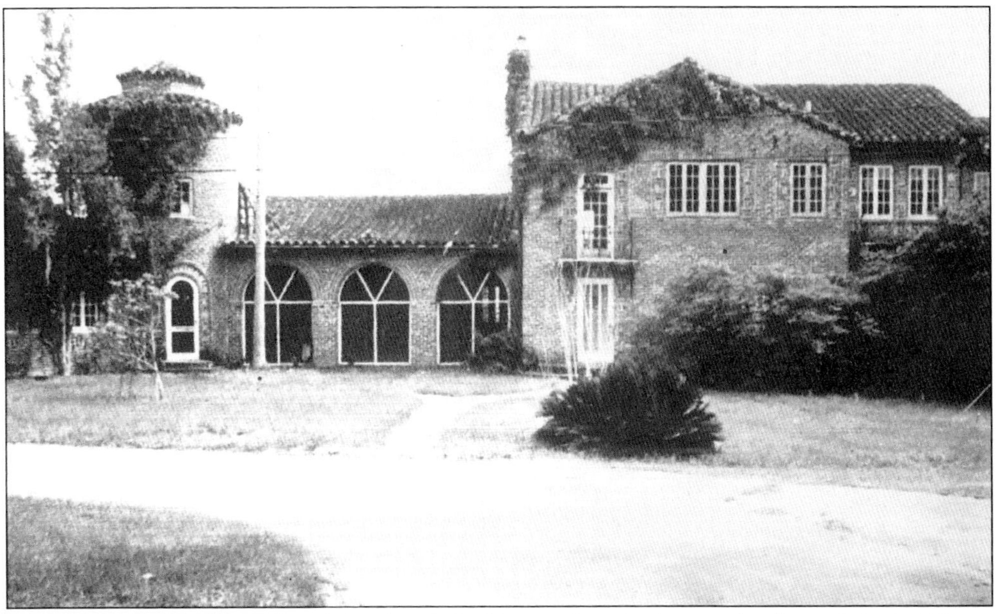

As have many of Mount Dora's landmark buildings, the Castle met the fate of the bulldozer. Designed in the Mediterranean Revival style of architecture, the Castle was reportedly built by Arthur Frothingham, a New York builder and relative of Washington Irving, author of *The Legend of Sleepy Hollow*.

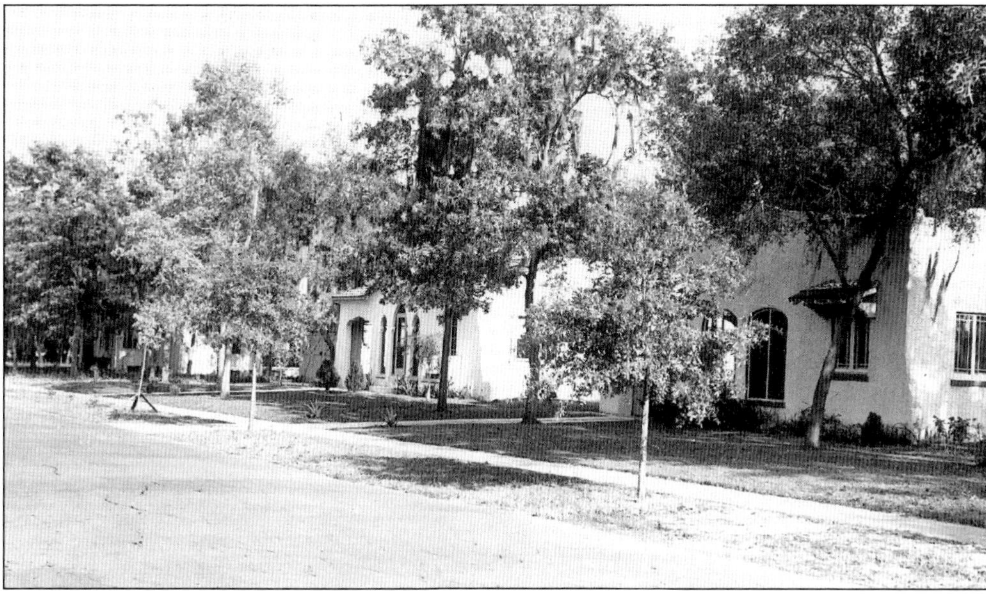

L.R. Heim and his family came to Mount Dora, from Danbury, Connecticut, in the early 1920s at the height of the land boom in Florida. As did others, he expected to make money on land speculation and the construction of housing developments. He bought the property that had once been the site of Chautauqua Park and began the development of Sylvan Shores. Almost weekly, full-page advertisements for Sylvan Shores appeared in local newspapers. Heim, like many other Florida developers, had not reckoned on the Great Depression, however. Financial difficulties forced him to sell off his land at rock-bottom prices.

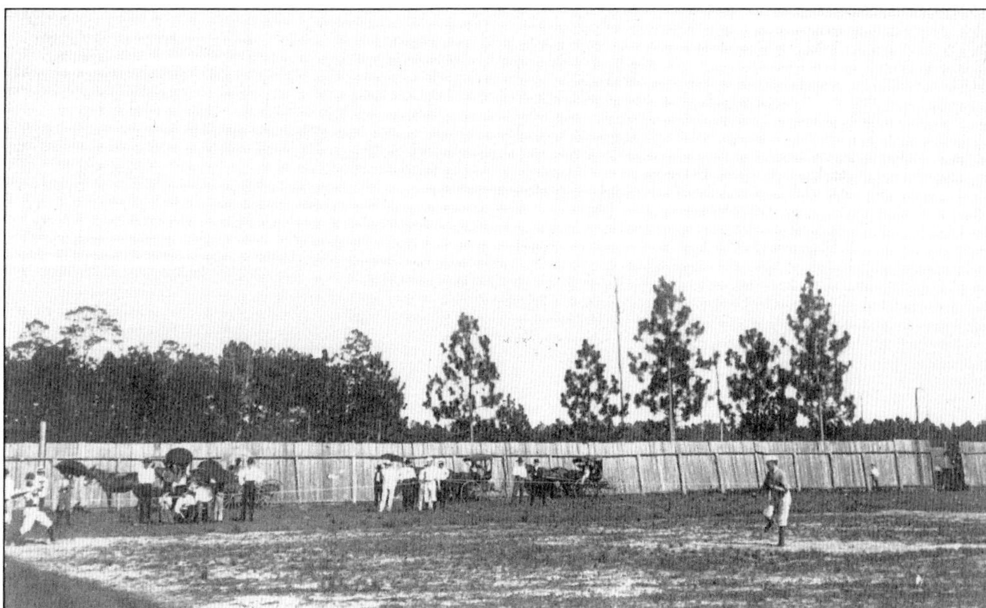

While Heim had money, he put it back into the community. In 1926, the developer of Sylvan Shores bought several acres of ground and had a baseball field constructed, complete with general seating, grandstands, and dugouts. When completed, according to the *Mount Dora Topic*, Heim presented it to the city's baseball organization "all ready to move into."

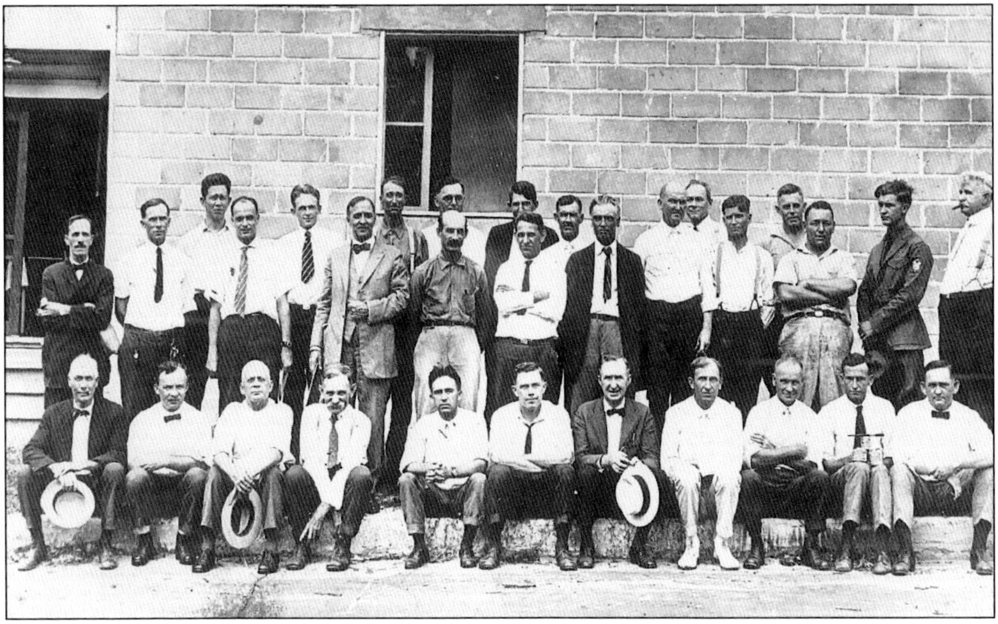

This august body of men, all members of the Noonday Club, represented many of the best-known families of Mount Dora. The membership roster included Tremains, Simpsons, Rehbaums, Waltzs, LaDues, and Donnellys. Originally chartered in 1925, the Noonday Club became a chapter of the Kiwanis Club on February 4, 1926.

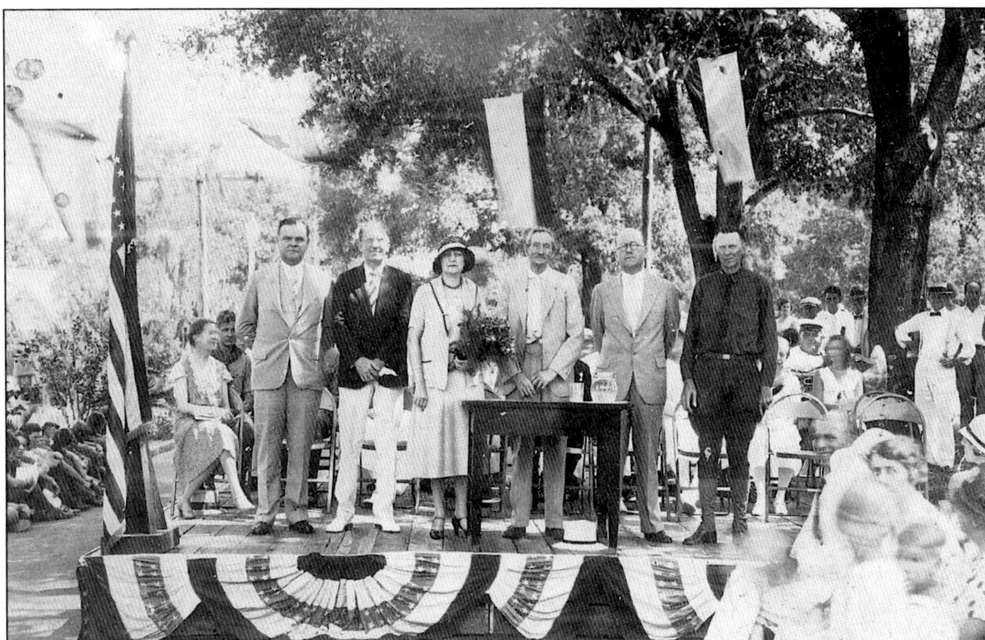

Citizens of Mount Dora, like most other small town American cities, reveled in their annual Fourth of July celebration. On July 4, 1931, Mayor W.E. Lackey, fourth from the left, officiated at the day's events that no doubt included patriotic parades, good food, and speeches by past and future politicians.

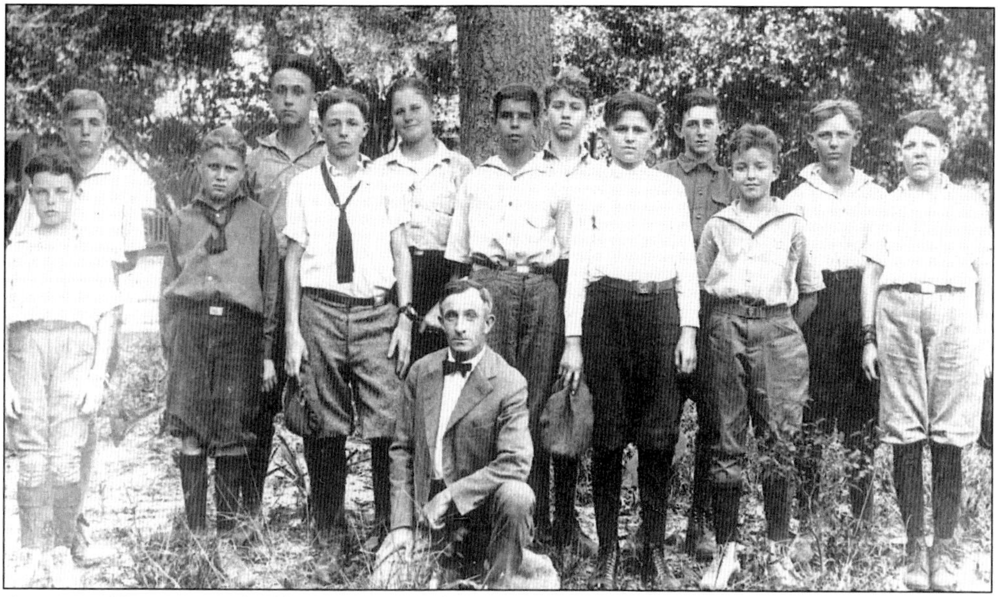

A troop of Boy Scouts had been a part of the youthful social scene in Mount Dora almost since the incorporation of the Boy Scouts of America on February 8, 1910. From the Tenderfoot to the First Class ranks, Mount Dora offered an ideal location for young men to pursue merit badges in archery, backpacking, bird study, camping, canoeing, and fishing, as well as many other areas.

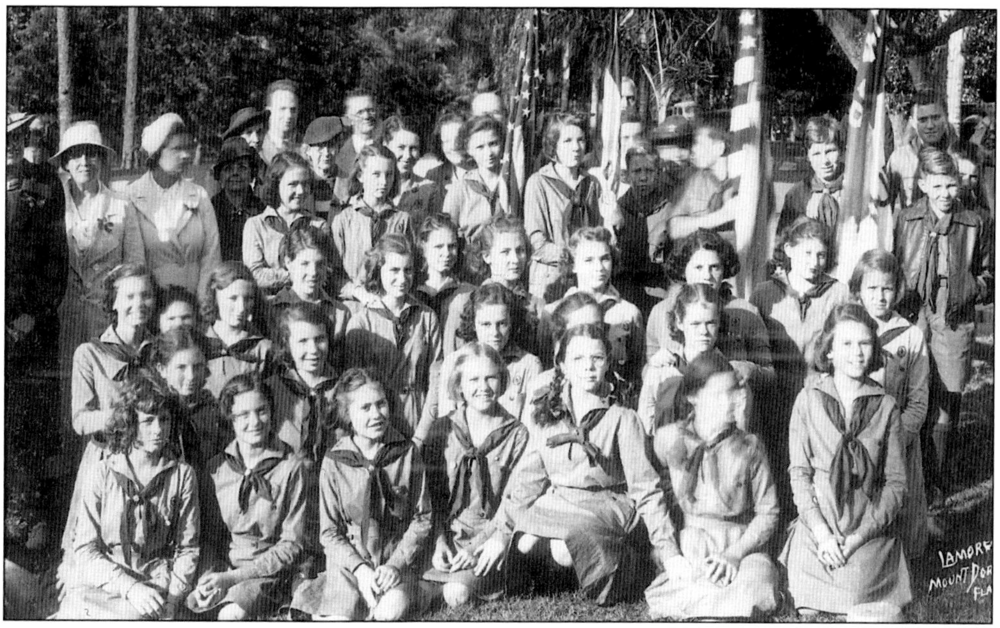

Lilah Spooner organized Mount Dora's Girl Scout troop in 1923, only 11 years after Juliette Gordon Low established the first troop in Savannah, GA. The purpose of Girl Scouting was to "inspire girls with the highest ideals of character, conduct, patriotism, and service." Mount Dora's Girl Scout leaders undoubtedly believed in these tenets and strove to insure that the young girls in the green uniforms were inspired toward becoming "happy and resourceful citizens."

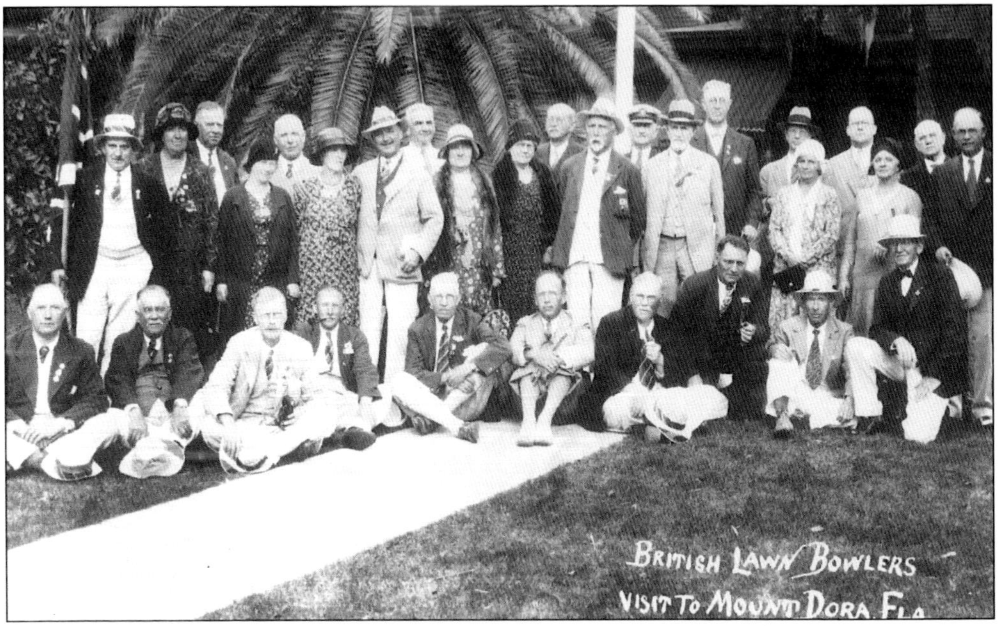

By the time these British lawn bowlers visited Mount Dora in 1931, the Mount Dora Lawn Bowling Club had been a thriving organization for three years. A lawn bowling court was first proposed to the city council in 1925 by a pair of winter residents, Willard M. Bryant and Fred S. Thompson, from Hartford, CT. Councilmen were receptive to the proposal, but nothing was done for several years.

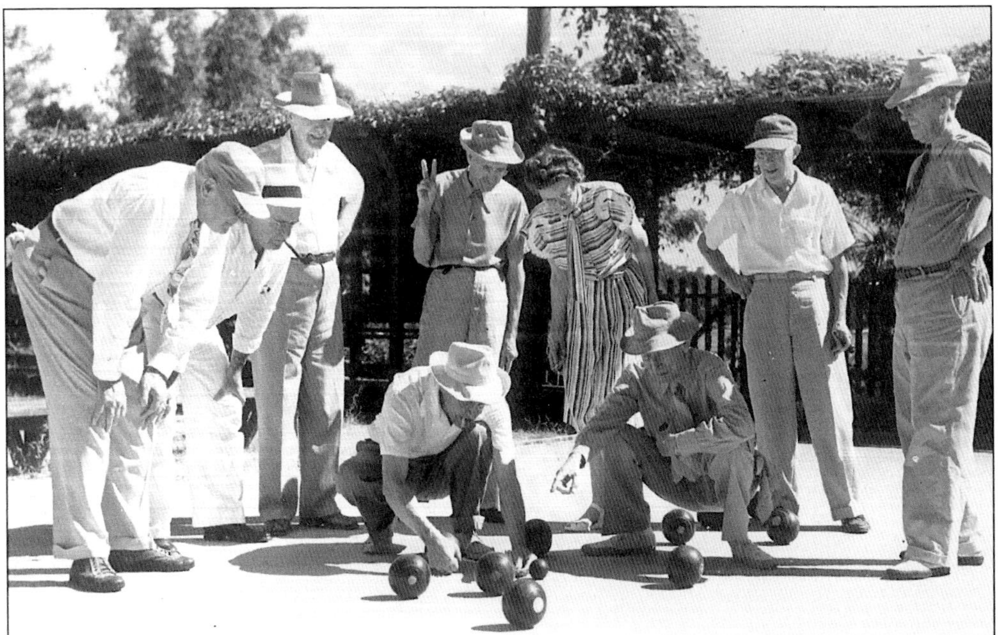

Fortunately for these lawn bowlers, the city council obtained land at the foot of Donnelly Street for a lawn bowling club. By April 1928, the Mount Dora Lawn Bowling Club boasted 20 charter members.

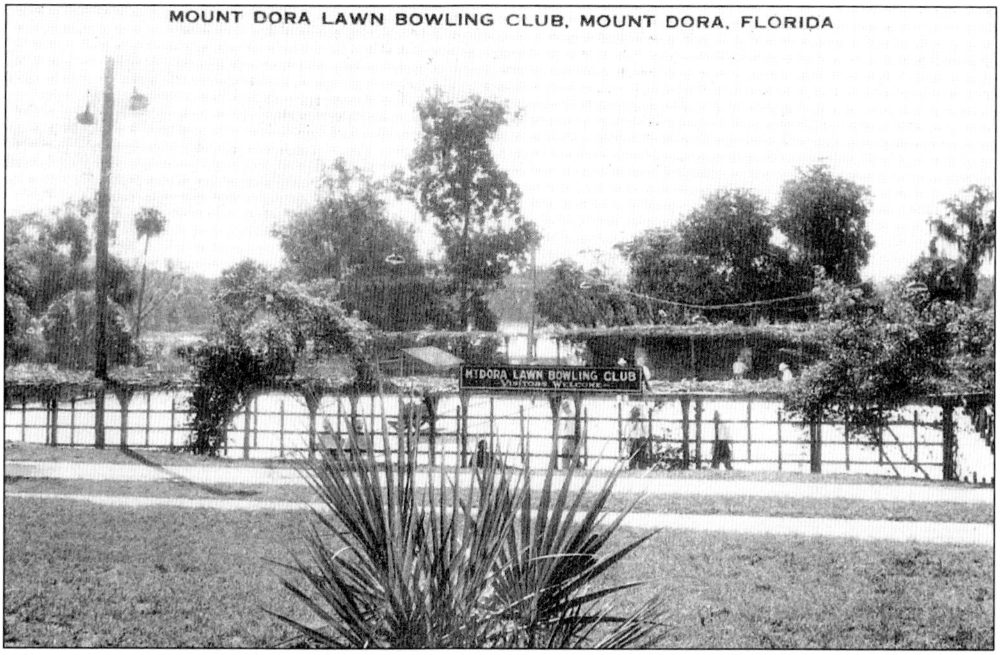

Three lawn bowling rinks were constructed shortly, and the club's membership grew. In 1930, the park commission constructed a clubhouse, along with grandstands and lighting.

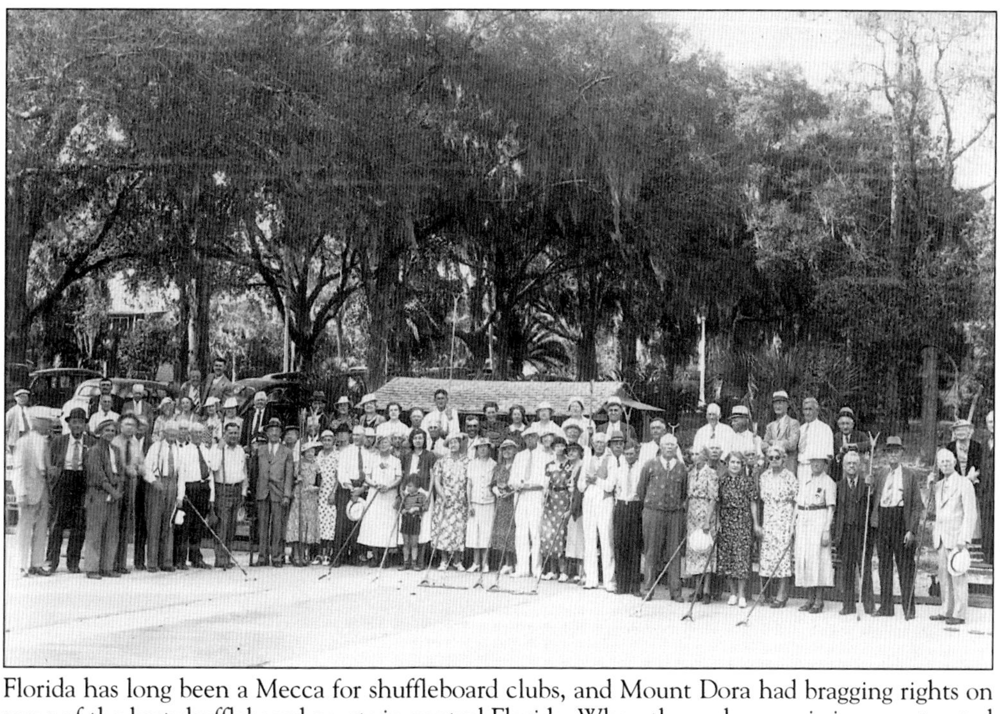

Florida has long been a Mecca for shuffleboard clubs, and Mount Dora had bragging rights on some of the best shuffleboard courts in central Florida. When the park commission constructed a pair of shuffleboard courts in Donnelly Park in 1926, the city's first shuffleboard club was organized. In its first year, membership totaled 20 people. Each year, the membership grew, as did the number of courts.

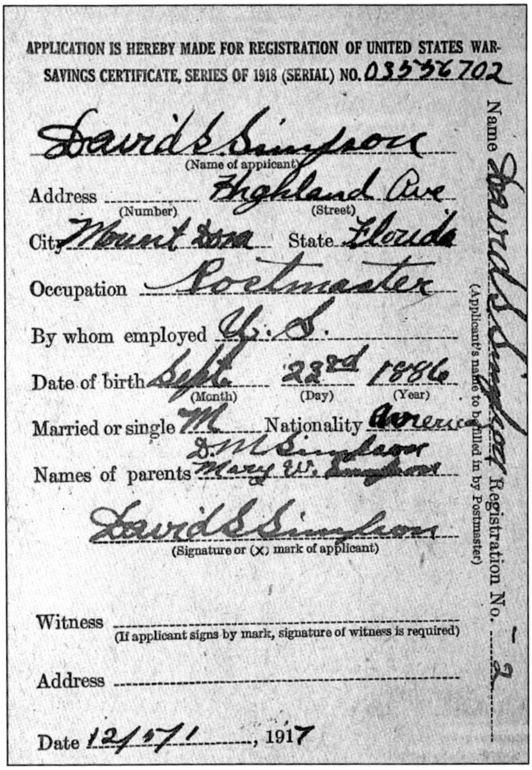

APPLICATION IS HEREBY MADE FOR REGISTRATION OF UNITED STATES WAR-SAVINGS CERTIFICATE, SERIES OF 1918 (SERIAL) NO. 03556702

David S. Simpson
(Name of applicant)

Address ______ Highland Ave
(Number) (Street)

City Mount Dora State Florida

Occupation Postmaster

By whom employed U. S.

Date of birth Sept. 22nd 1886
(Month) (Day) (Year)

Married or single M Nationality American

Names of parents D. M. Simpson, Mary W. Simpson

David S. Simpson
(Signature or (X) mark of applicant)

Witness ______
(If applicant signs by mark, signature of witness is required)

Address ______

Date 12/17/, 1917

Name David S. Simpson (Applicant's name to be filled in by Postmaster) Registration No. 12

During World War I, patriotic citizens of Mount Dora did their part on the home front for the Allies. One way of contributing toward the push for victory in Europe was the purchase of United States War Savings Certificates that would allow America to build more tanks, ships, and airplanes. As did many other men, women, and children from Mount Dora, David S. Simpson, the town's postmaster, made his contribution with the purchase of war savings certificates.

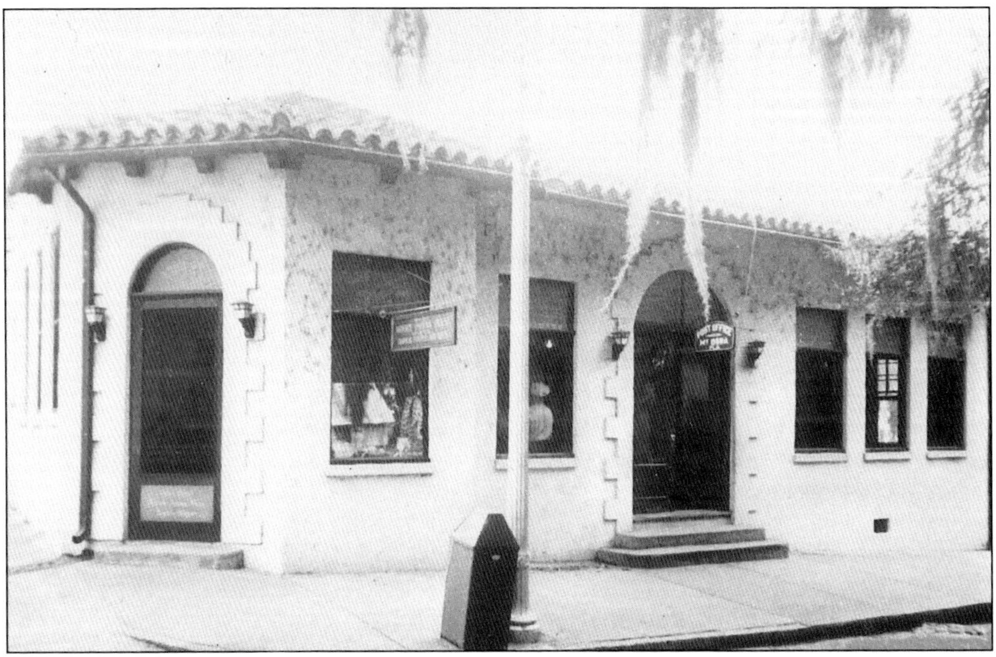

This building served as Mount Dora's post office from 1925 to 1962. For many years, David S. Simpson had served as the town's postmaster, taking the position in 1911 when the town's population was less than 400 people. He retired in July 1930, after 19 years of service with the postal service. One year later, he died in an accident.

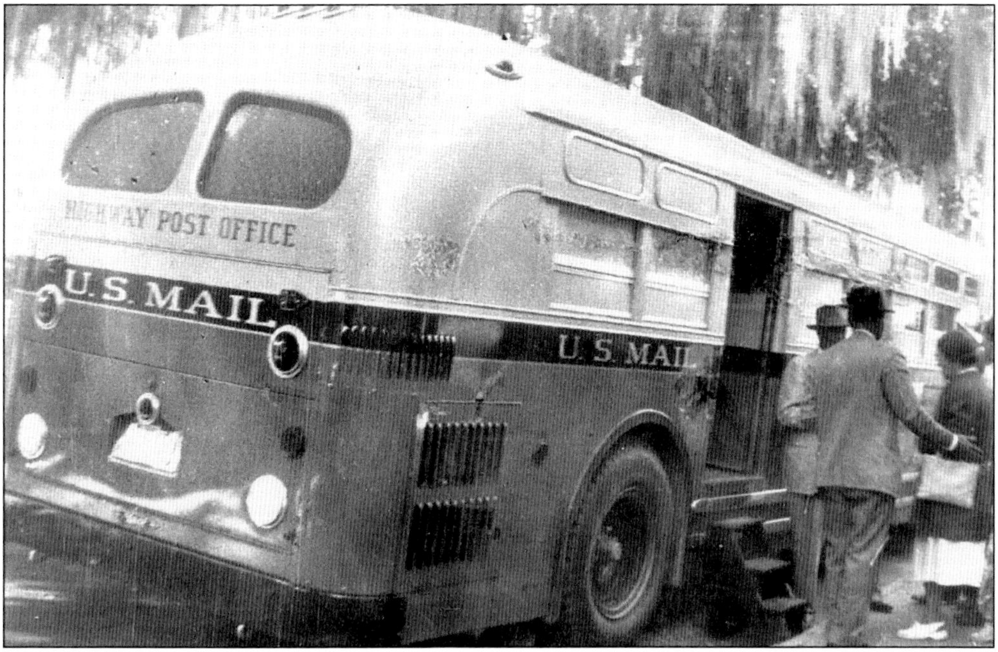

In November of 1949, the United States Postal Service inaugurated its latest example of postal efficiency. Housed in a converted bus, the Highway Post Office provided mail delivery and other postal services to customers along the route between Orlando and Leesburg. As residents lined up to take advantage of the new facility, envelopes were stamped with a special first-day cover denoting the new service.

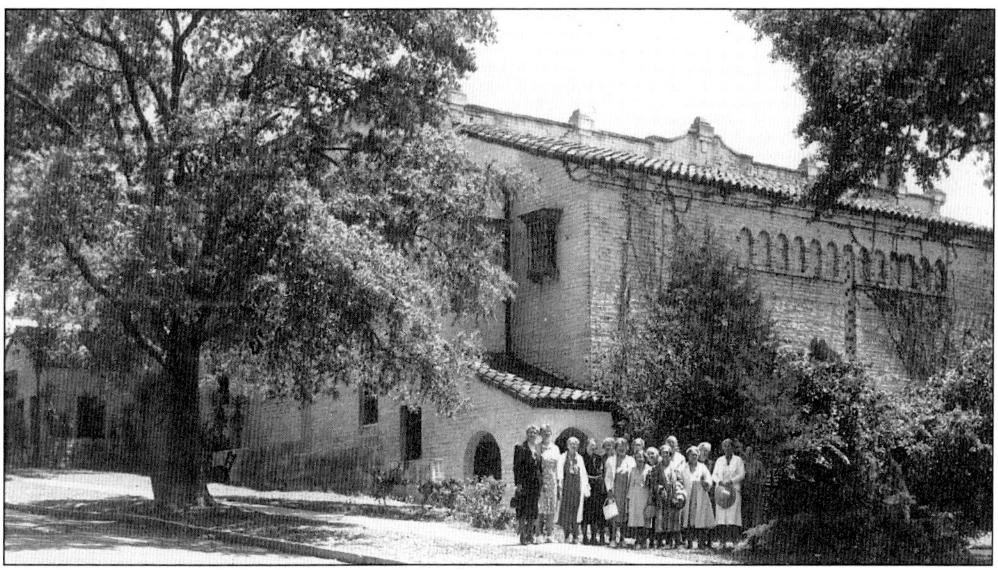

During the height of the Great Depression, Mount Dora's councilmen and voting citizens went out on a tremendous limb in recommending a community hall. Banks were facing closings, and many people could barely pay their taxes, but a bond issue in favor of the construction of Community Hall passed by a vote of 80 to 59. Constructed in 1929 at a cost of $35,000, the Mediterranean Revival Community Hall was a source of pride and hope for the town of Mount Dora.

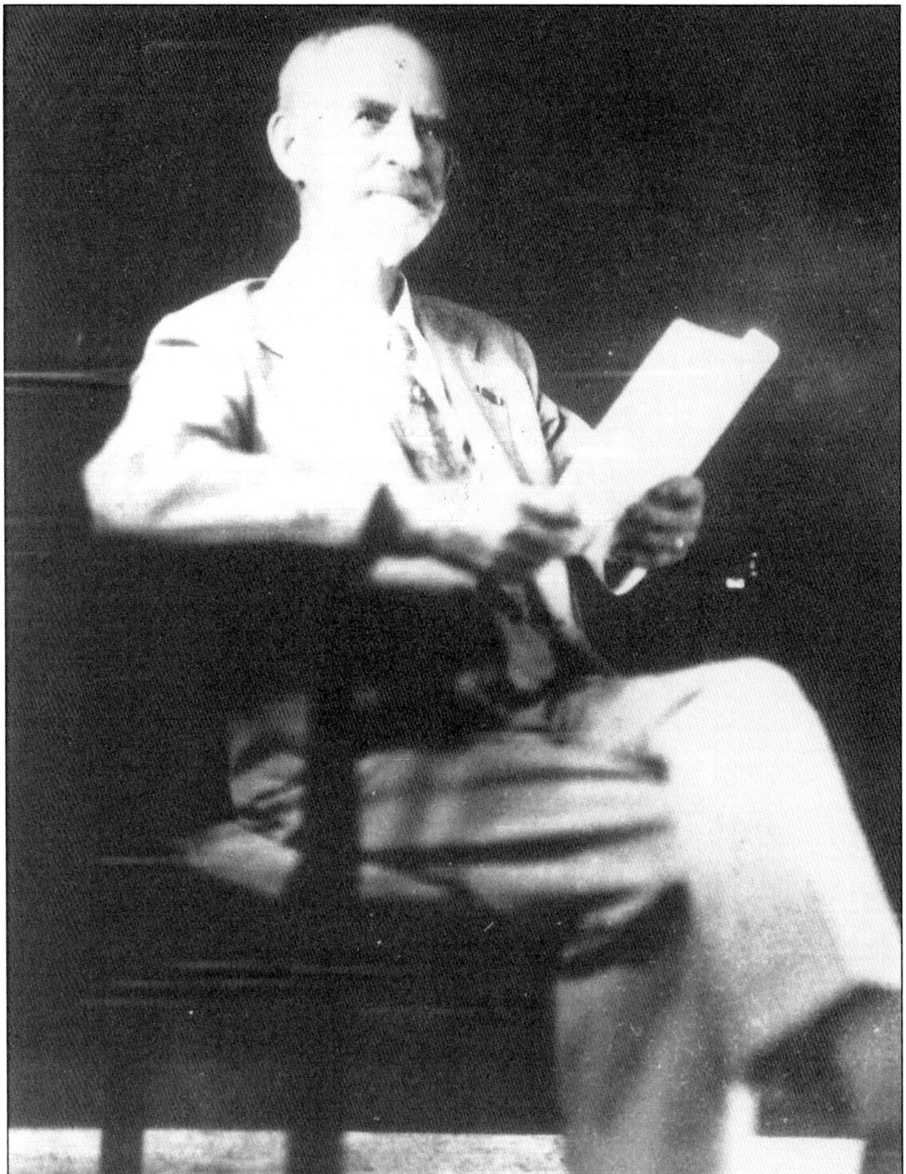

People settled in Mount Dora for their own reasons. Few stories were more interesting than this man identified only as Mr. Sanborne. In 1938, he wrote, "I am today 85 years old. Going strong. Began early, Keokuk, Iowa. In 1864, Civil War, was with 27th Iowa Infantry; Mississippi, Tennessee, Louisiana. Enlisted as a boy, twice commended for services rendered. There met Bill Cody, 7th Kansas. Early in '70s went west, Missouri River to the coast, Winnipeg to the Gulf. Knew Great Plains in the days of the Indian and the buffalo, the sod house, the dugout, and the stagecoach. Those years I was a cowboy, sheepherder, gun toter, trail rider, bank clerk, stockman. Buffalo Bill, Major Burke, 'Wild Bill' Hickcock, were among my friends. Captain Jack Crawford, chief of scouts to General Custer, was my old partner. Pioneered in Dakota before the Indians left. Deaf from terrible freezing in worst of blizzards while getting settlers to cover. Two of reserve party died of freezing. I nearly did. Came here from Cleveland, Ohio, in '24; like it, may decide to stay and 'grow up with the country.'"

Five

Always the Lake

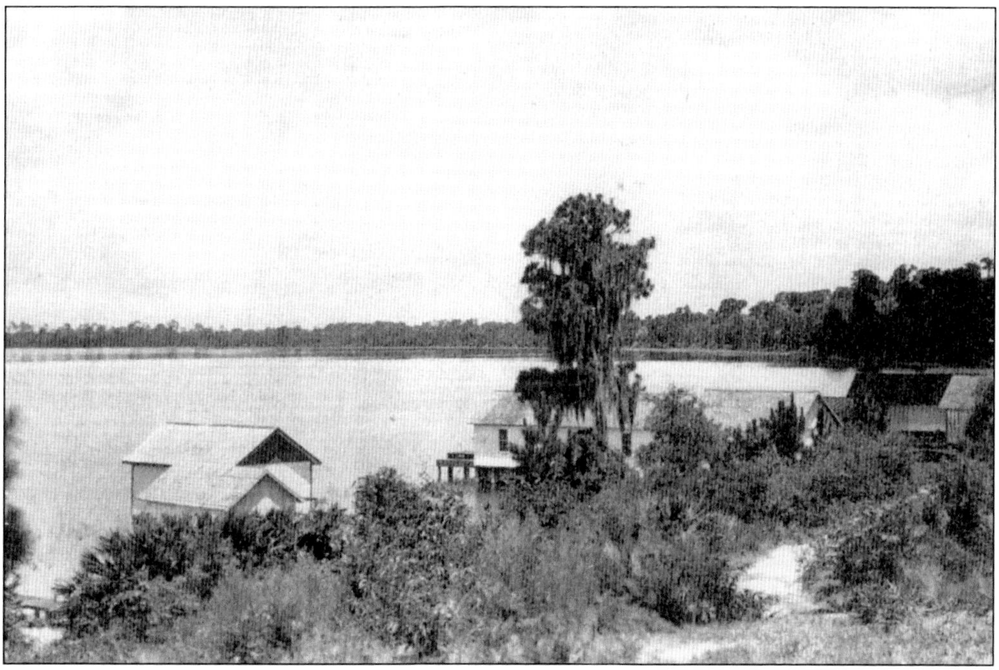

From the beginning, much of life in Mount Dora centered upon the lake. Narrow winding roads that were less than wonderful in the best of weather deteriorated markedly during the rainy season. Quicker and more reliable than overland transportation, steamboats traveling the St. Johns and the Ocklawaha Rivers that interconnected many of the lakes in the area brought both visitors and goods from more urban Florida communities. Excellent fishing in the lake provided bountiful dining. Whether as a means of transportation to the cultural pursuits of the Chautauqua or as the site of the outdoor sports of boating and fishing, Lake Dora played an important role for visitors. With the exception of the boathouses, this scene looked much the same in the 1920s as it would have when the first settlers arrived in the region.

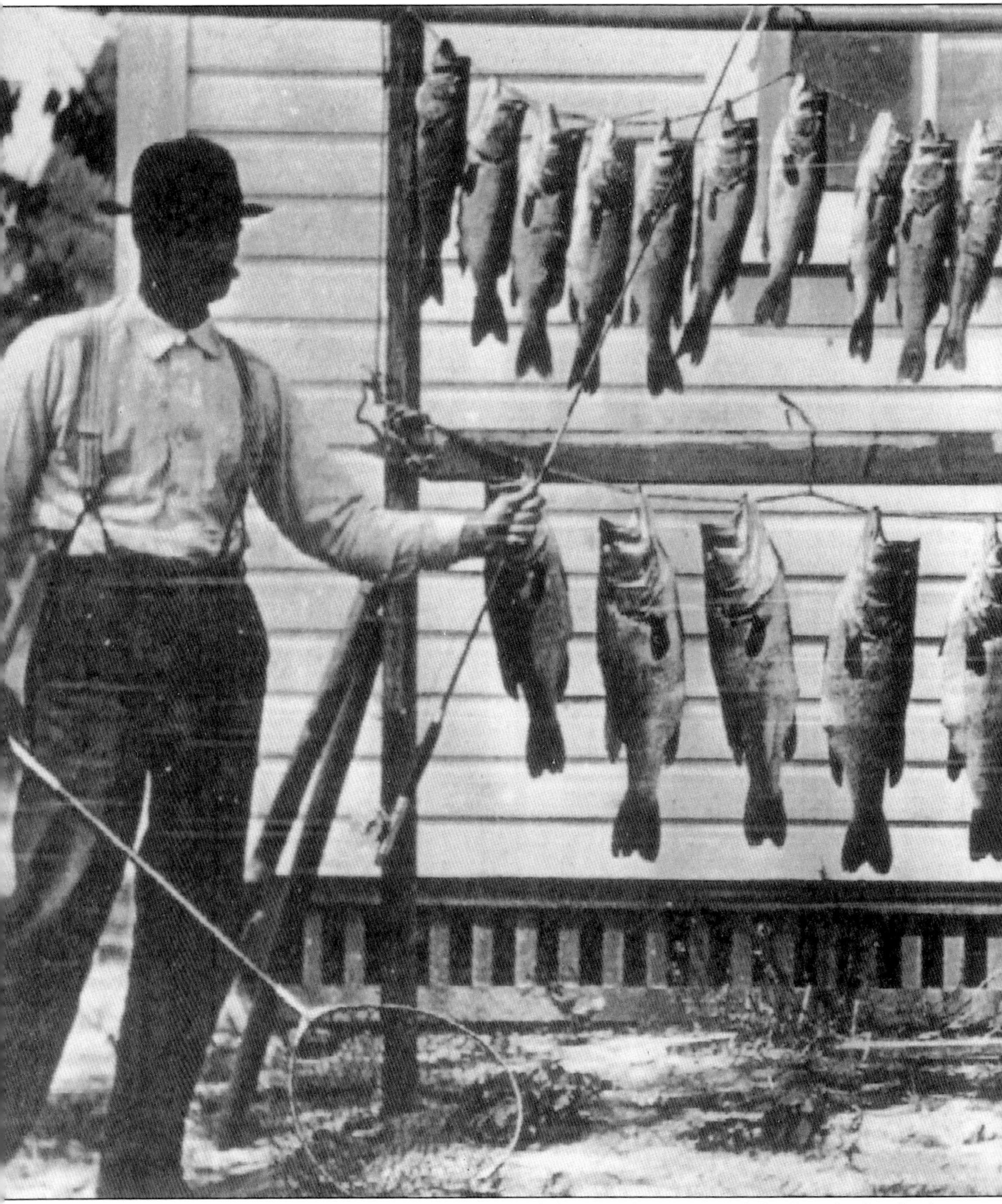

Famed throughout the country for its excellent fishing, Lake Dora and the hundreds of other bodies of water in Lake County drew avid fishermen from near and far. While this may have been a posed photograph of a record catch, such occasions were not at all uncommon. *Kim's Guide to Florida* in 1939 contained advertisements encouraging visitors to "Catch a RECORD BASS" and bragging "World's best bass fishing...giant size large-mouth...world's record small-mouth came from these waters." Unfortunately, the fertile marshland surrounding the lakes also

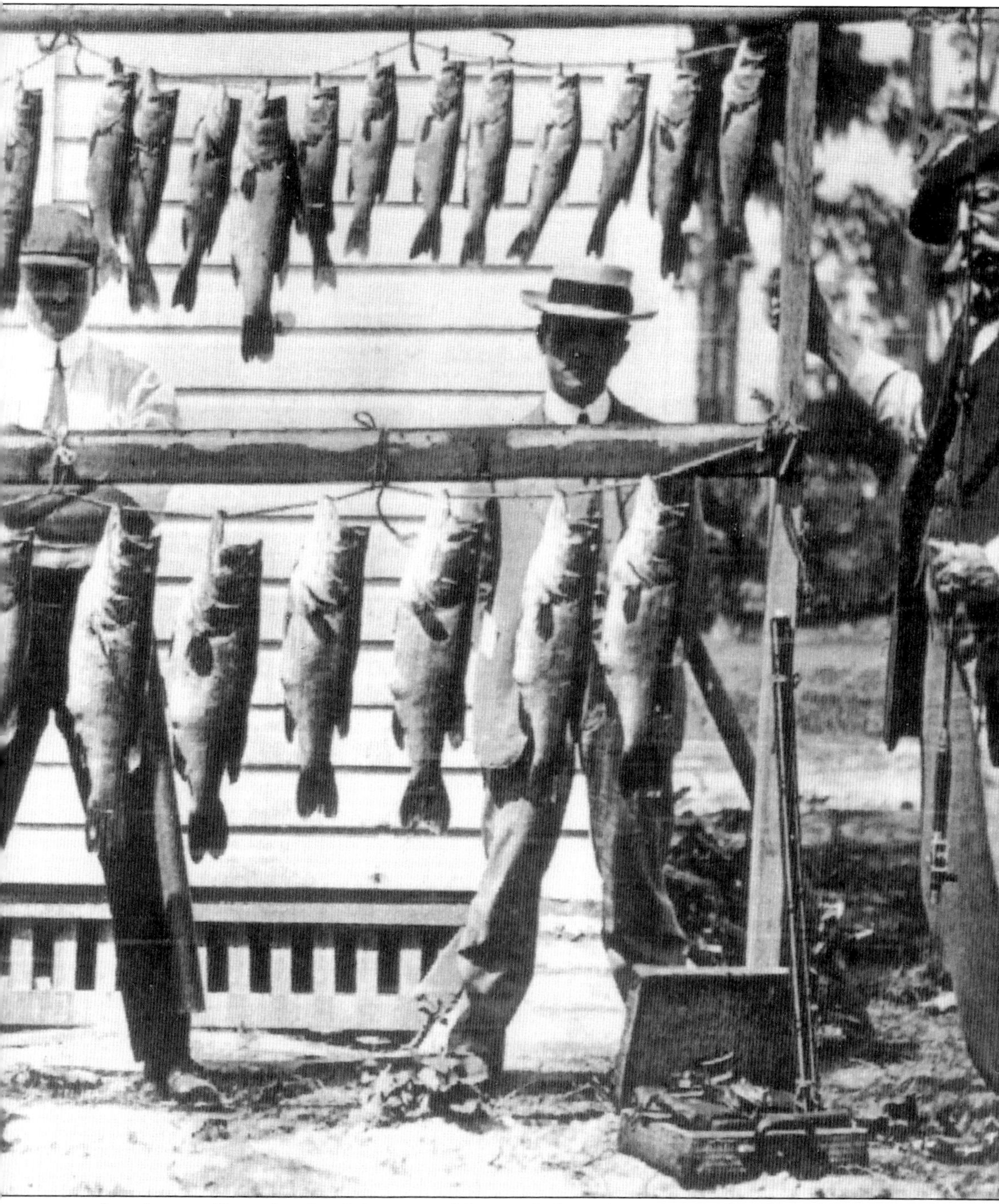

proved to be excellent farmland for vegetables, including the renowned Zellwood corn. As the farming increased, so did the runoff from the agricultural fertilizers and pesticides used to produce ever-increasing harvests. One by one, the interconnected lakes slowly died. Now part of a massive clean-up begun in the 1980s, the lakes are being returned to a healthy condition, increasing the probability of "record catches" again in Lake Dora.

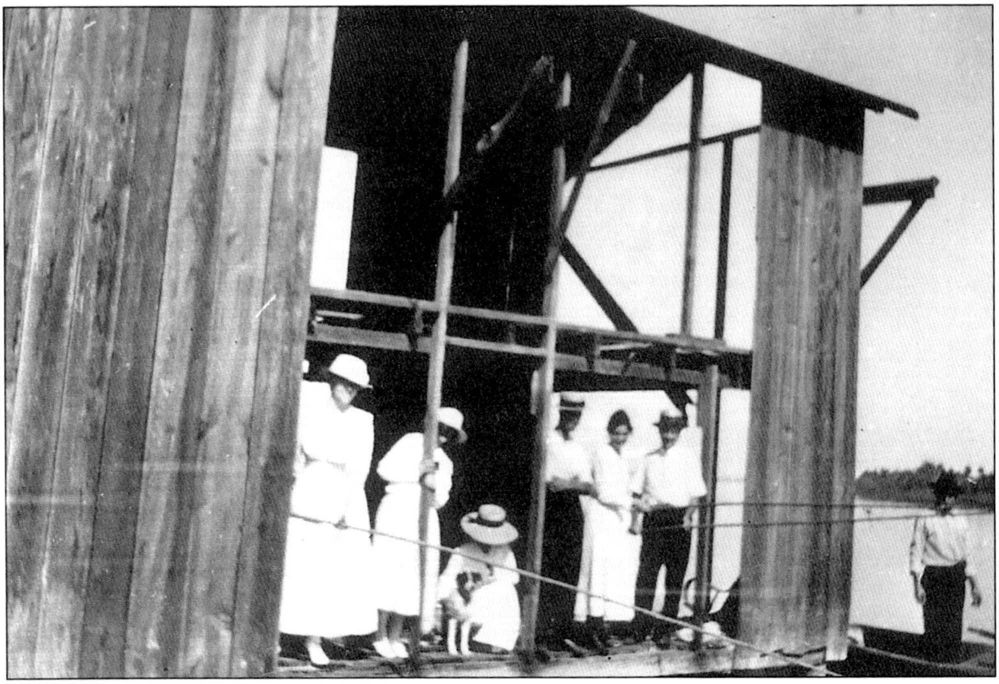

Judging from this photograph, an afternoon spent fishing from one of the Mount Dora boathouses was an activity that involved the entire family, including the dog. Using long bamboo fishing poles, anglers could land dinner, set a record, or win a prize. In 1928, a fishing contest sponsored by the Mount Dora Hardware Company reported more than 100 entries.

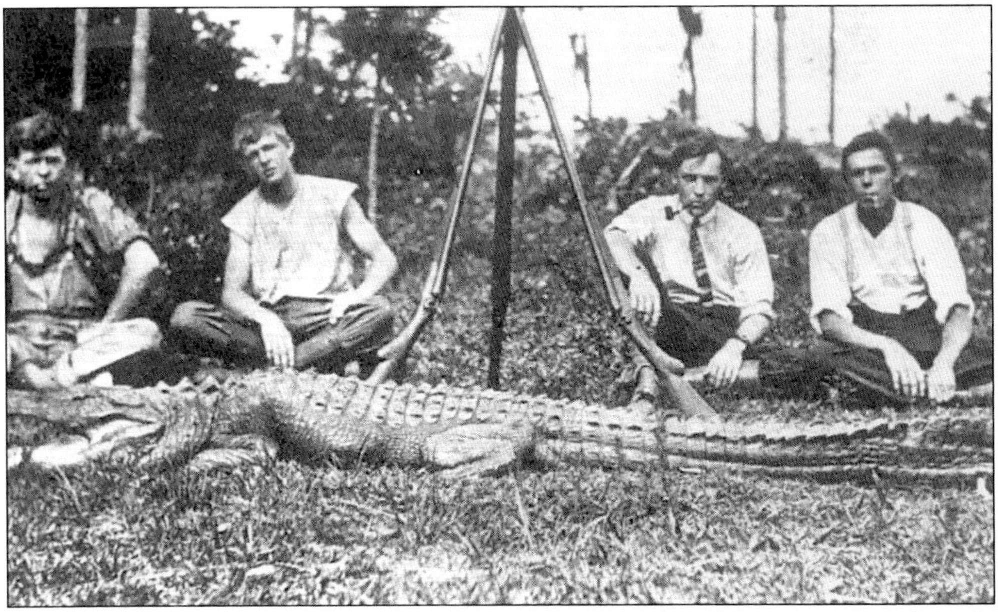

Fish were not the only creatures that lived in Lake Dora and the adjacent streams and canals. Raymond Orton, Burgess Thayer, Marcellus Javens, and Darragh Javens posed with this 14-foot alligator that they had just killed along the Apopka Canal in 1911.

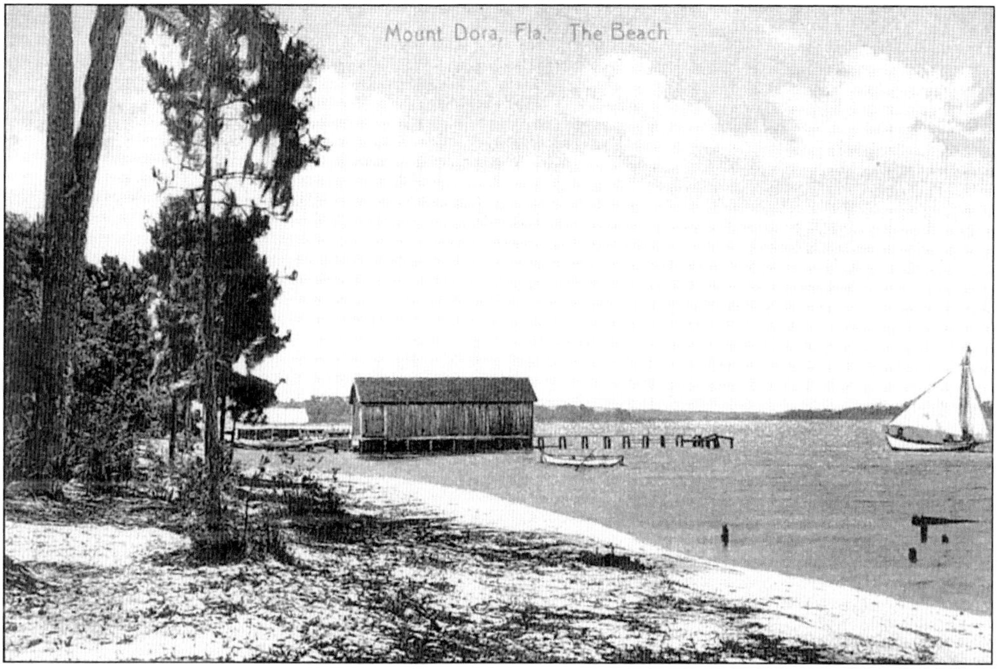

Postcards from the 1920s pictured the idyllic life along Lake Dora's beach. Whether fishing, boating, picnicking, or just relaxing on the warm sand, seasonal visitors found their days far more pleasurable than shoveling snow during the icy winter up north. While some visitors stayed only a short time, many came for the entire winter season, earning themselves the nickname of "snowbirds."

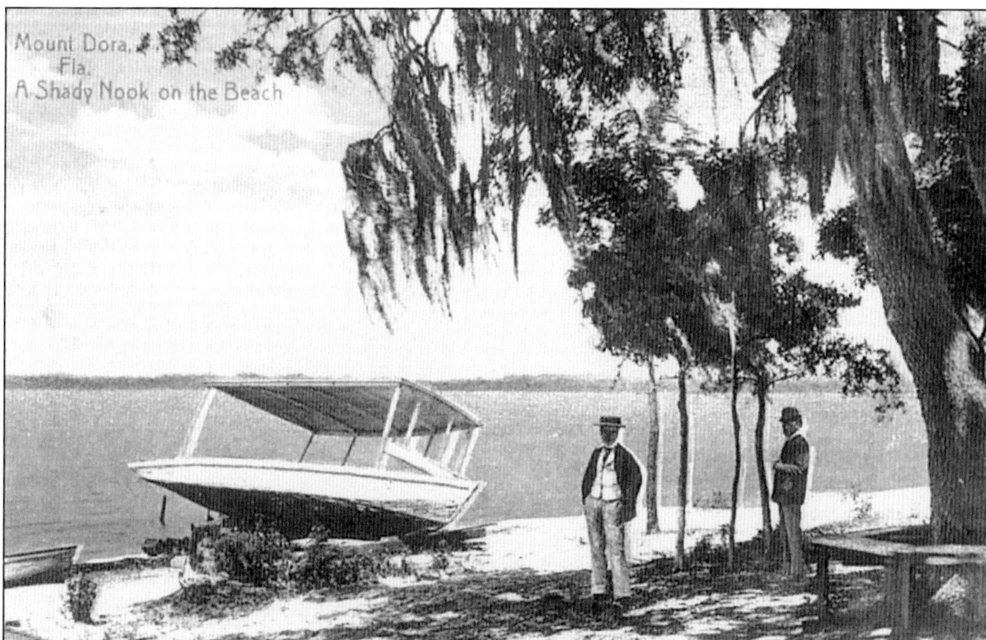

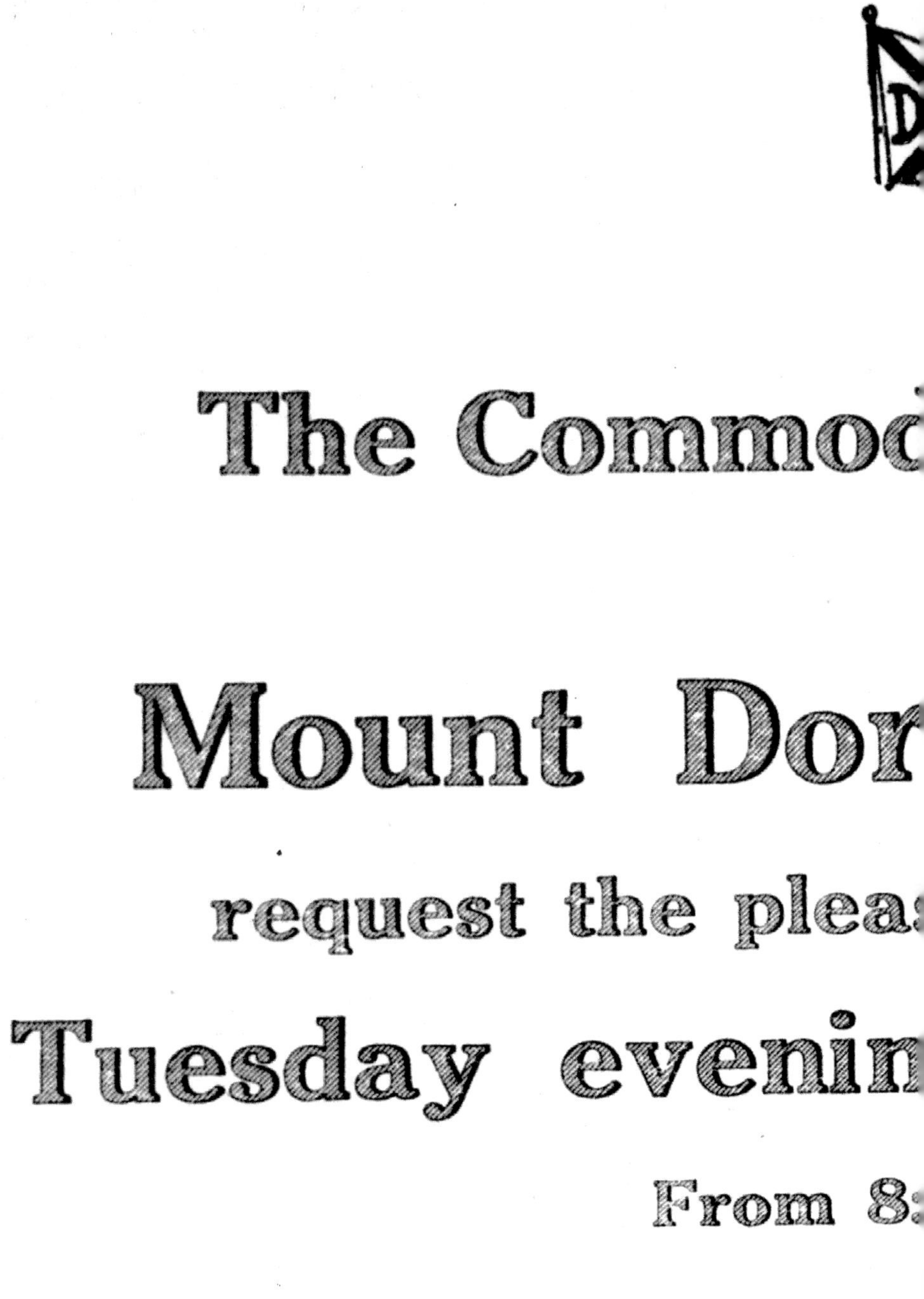
The Commod
Mount Dor
request the plea
Tuesday evenin
From 8:

From its founding in 1913, the Mount Dora Yacht Club played a pivotal role in the social life of many Mount Dora residents. The membership list of the yacht club was synonymous with a "who's who" in Mount Dora, while the club provided the setting for many social functions. In 1913, the local newspaper reported, "Perhaps Mount Dora was never the scene of a more brilliant social function than that given at the Yacht Club House on Friday evening last by the Flag officers of the Club, who received in full uniform. Attended by beautiful matrons and maids

re and Officers

the

Yacht Club

'e of your company

March the sixth

to 12 P. M.

in costly costumes and diamonds, handsome and gallant men in full dress, music, refreshments and elegant surrounds, two hundred invitations had been issued. The spacious rooms and piazzas of the Club House furnished ample room for that number, aside from floor space for dancing. A hard thundershower had only just cleared away for guests to gather and view the crescent moon sitting behind a cloud. An orchestra from Eustis played."

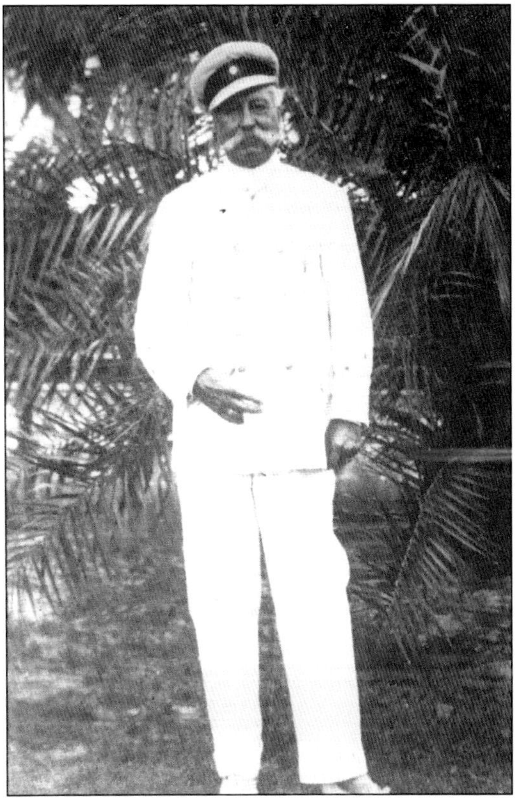

In 1913, along with J.P. Donnelly, Charles Geer, M.V. Simpson, H.R. Miller, and Raymond Silas, H.C. Fuller formed the Mount Dora Yacht Club. Pictured with his trademark walrus mustache, captain's hat, and sparkling white suit with brass buttons, H.C. Fuller served as the club's first commodore from the organization's founding until 1921.

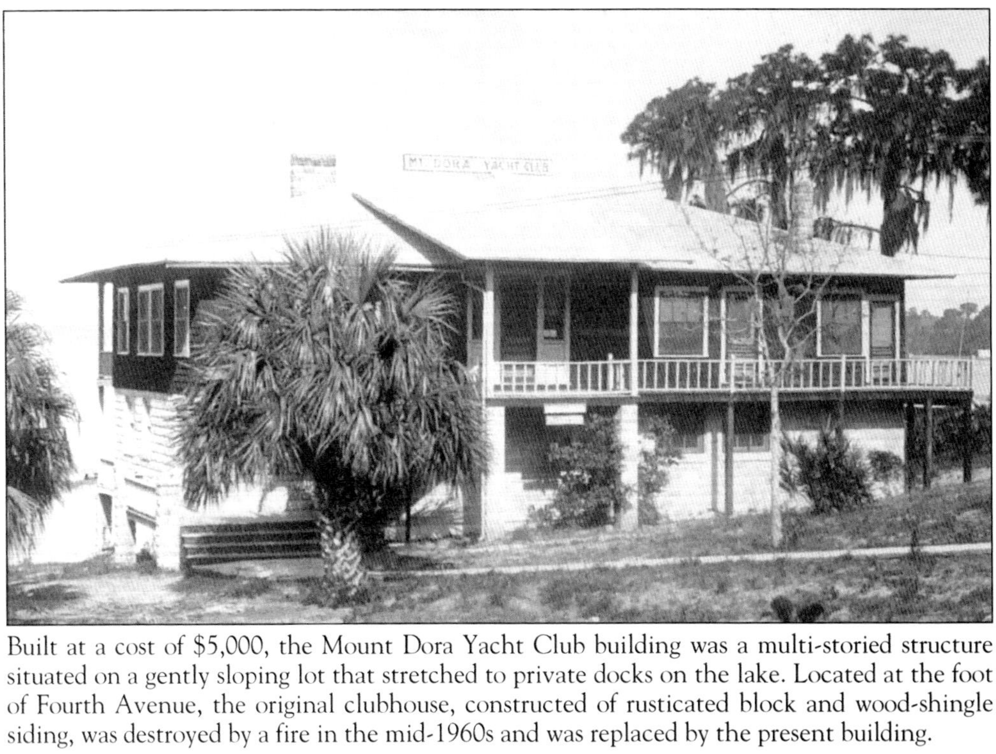

Built at a cost of $5,000, the Mount Dora Yacht Club building was a multi-storied structure situated on a gently sloping lot that stretched to private docks on the lake. Located at the foot of Fourth Avenue, the original clubhouse, constructed of rusticated block and wood-shingle siding, was destroyed by a fire in the mid-1960s and was replaced by the present building.

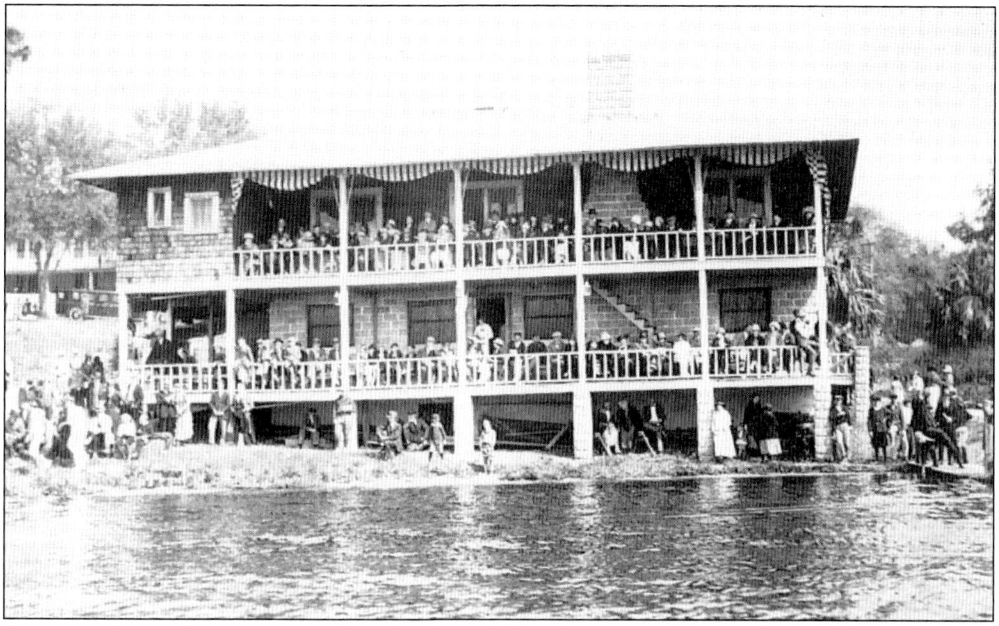

As the oldest inland waterway yacht club in Florida, the organization has a long-standing tradition of hosting successful regattas and other boating competitions. In fact, ownership of a boat was one of the initial requirements of membership. This photograph shows the porches of the Mount Dora Yacht Club packed with spectators at a regatta in 1922.

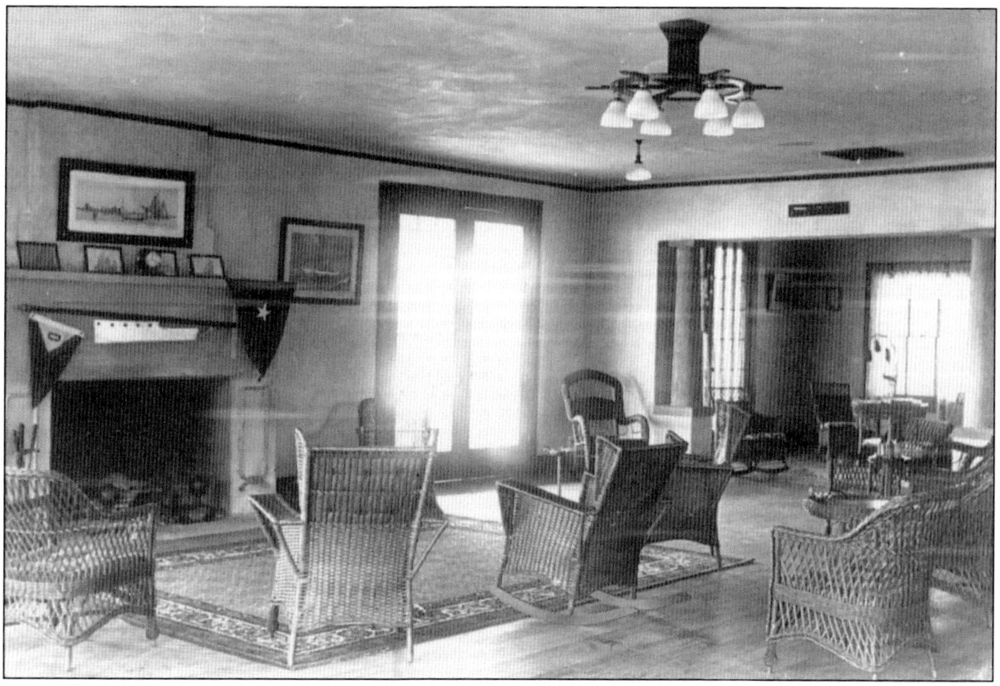

Not all of the activities at the Yacht Club centered upon the water. In addition to the various regatta balls and dances held there, the *Mount Dora Topic* reported, "There will be a card party next Wednesday night at the Mount Dora Yacht Club where card players may find pleasure in playing 500 and other card games besides bridge."

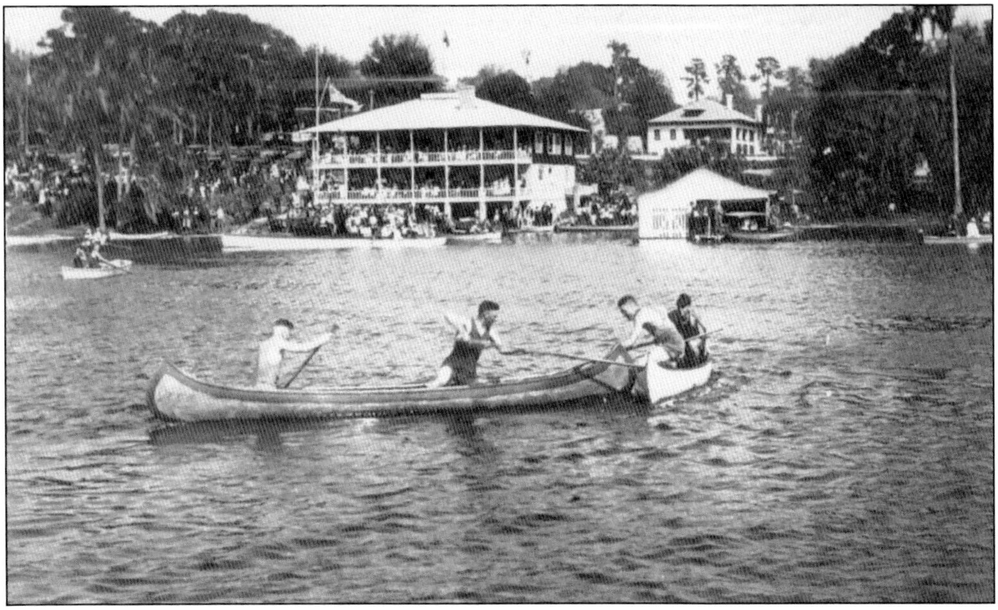

Canoe tournaments took place frequently at the Mount Dora Yacht Club. In this photograph dating from 1920, it is difficult to tell whether these teams of canoeists from Rollins College were assisting or opposing each other.

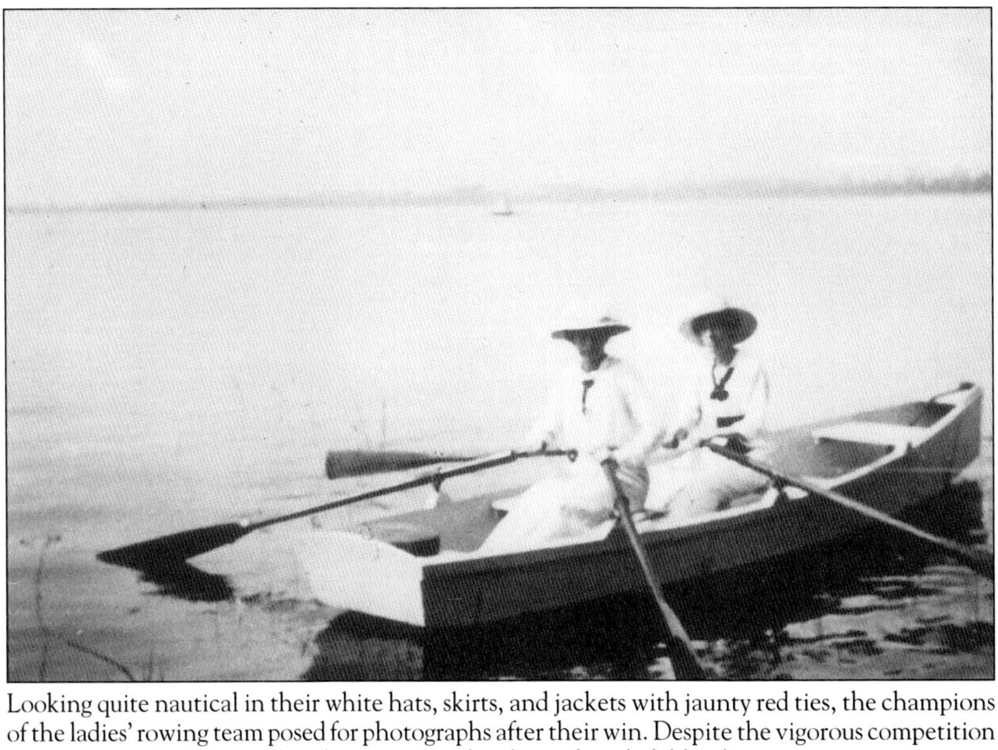

Looking quite nautical in their white hats, skirts, and jackets with jaunty red ties, the champions of the ladies' rowing team posed for photographs after their win. Despite the vigorous competition in the warm Florida sun, they have managed to keep their ladylike demeanor, appearing quite fresh and pristine.

Sailboats were, and still are, a frequent sight on Lake Dora. This particular sailboat was named the *Mary C.* A sailing regatta is held every April, while an antique boat show takes place each March in Mount Dora.

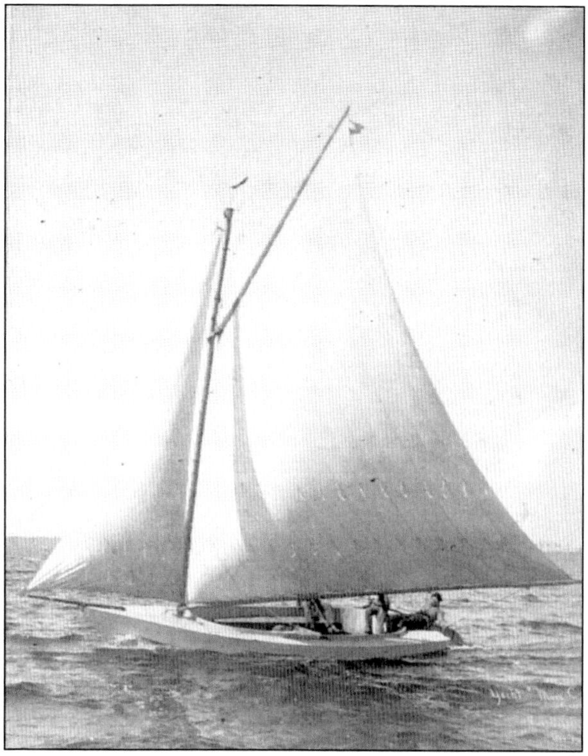

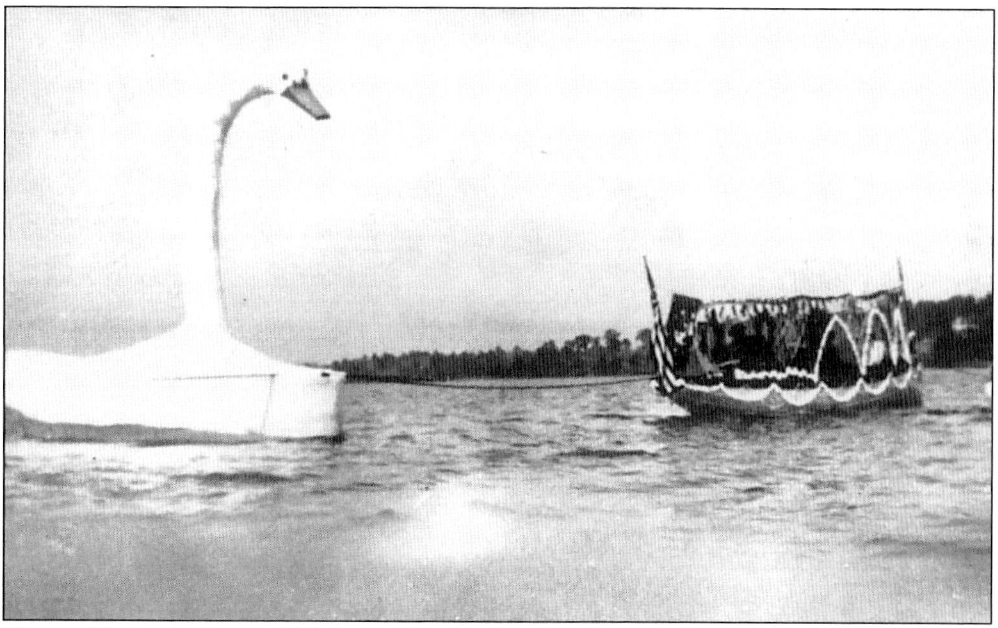

These elaborately decorated boats participated in a regatta in the neighboring community of Eustis. The large swan appears to be an especially imaginative adaptation of a motor cruiser. A lighted boat parade on the lake is part of the annual Christmas holiday festivities in Mount Dora.

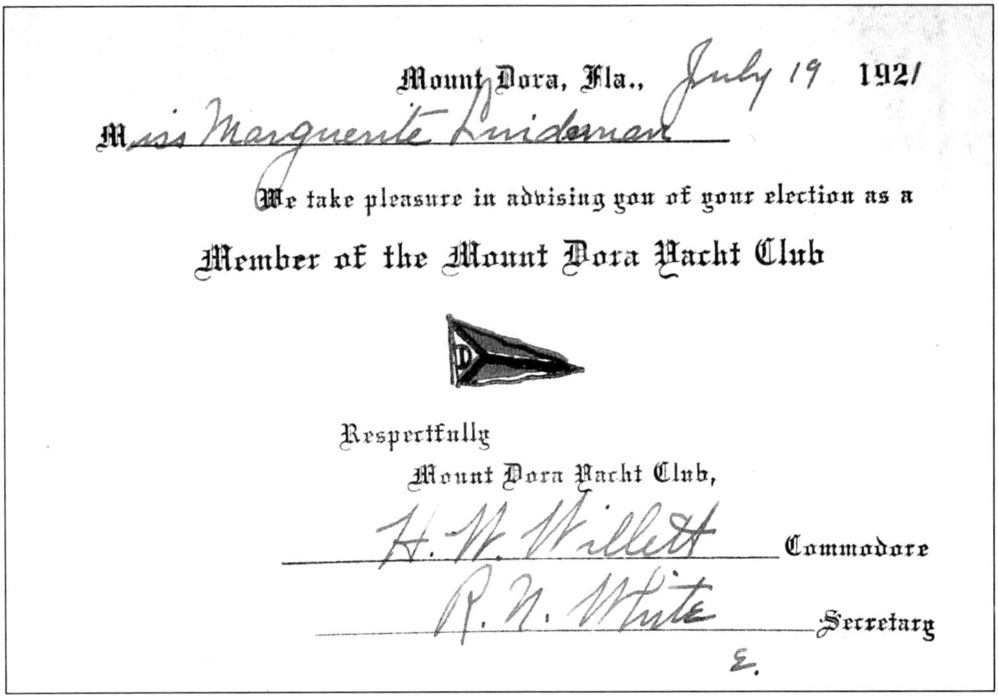

Mount Dora, Fla., *July 19* 192*1*

M*iss Marguerite Lindeman*

We take pleasure in advising you of your election as a

Member of the Mount Dora Yacht Club

Respectfully

Mount Dora Yacht Club,

H. W. Willett Commodore

R. N. White Secretary

E.

Unlike many organizations whose membership was restricted to only men, the Mount Dora Yacht Club permitted women to join. A special "Lady's Membership Card" was bestowed upon female members following their election. Certain areas of the clubhouse were, however, considered to be off-limits to women, regardless of their status as members or guests. Special events such as "smokers" were also open only to males.

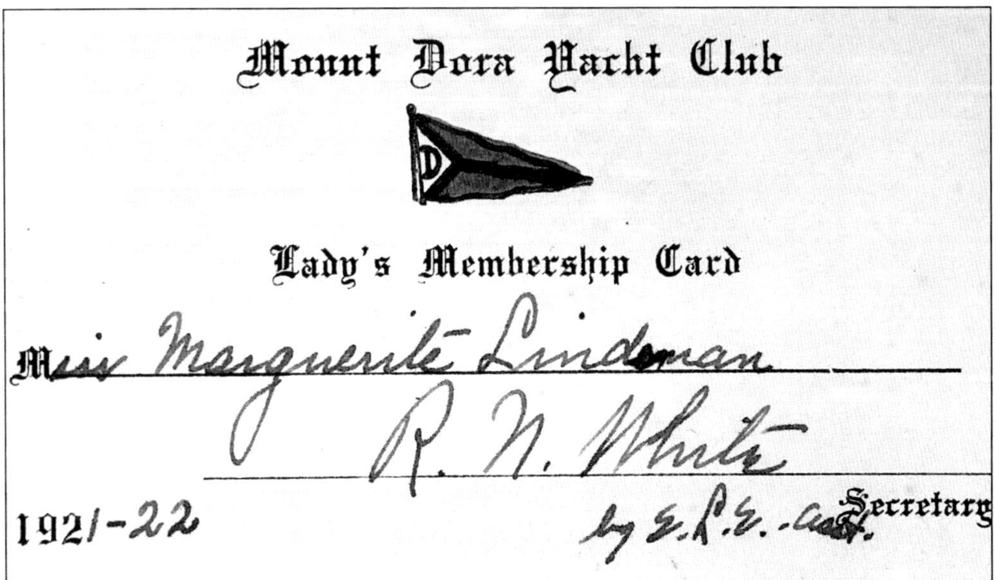

Mount Dora Yacht Club

Lady's Membership Card

M*iss Marguerite Lindeman*

R. N. White

192*1-22* *by E. P. E. - Asst.* Secretary

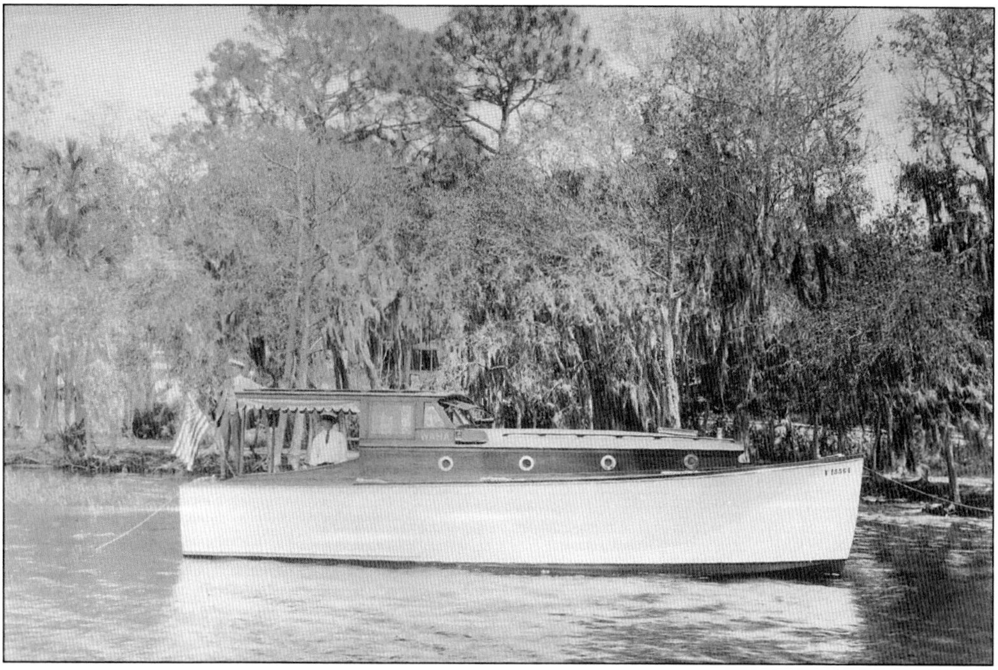

Affluent winter visitors frequently came to Mount Dora aboard their private yachts via the interconnecting lakes and rivers. Reciprocal memberships between yacht clubs across the nation allowed the yachtsmen to participate in the activities of the Mount Dora organization.

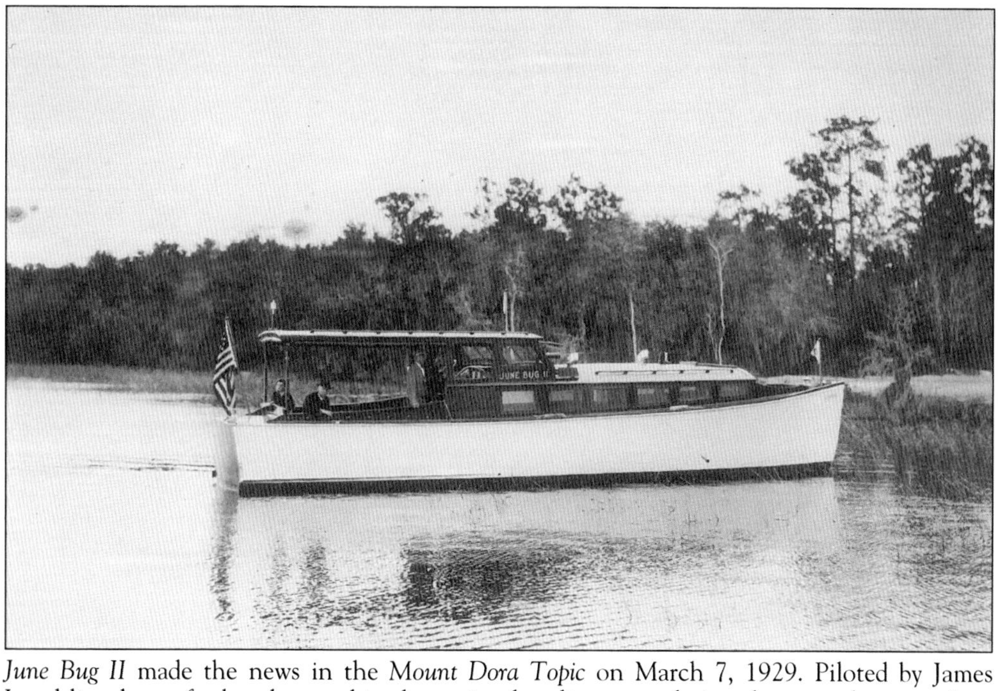

June Bug II made the news in the *Mount Dora Topic* on March 7, 1929. Piloted by James Laughlin, the craft placed second in the cruiser handicap race during the annual regatta. *June Bug II* also participated in the rescue of the pilot of *Hot Ziggetty* when his Class B outboard caught fire during a race.

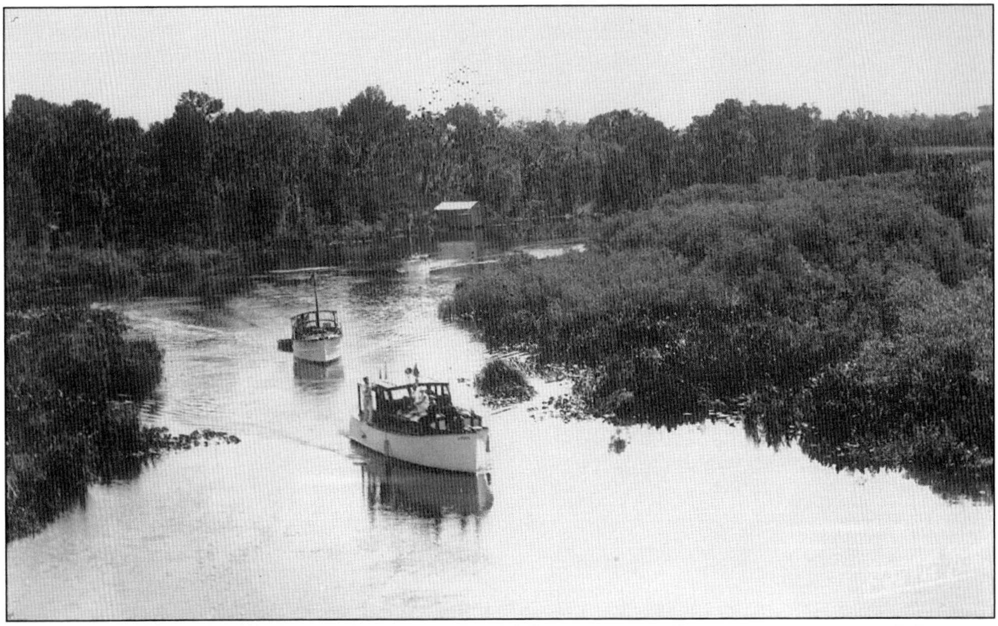

Each year, members of the Mount Dora Yacht Club were invited to participate in a club cruise or "boatacade" to various Florida or South Georgia cities via the interconnecting waterways. In fact, in 1915, one member was reported to have piloted his yacht from Lake Dora to Canada and back again. Harold Fowler of Eustis took these two photographs of a procession of motor cruisers making their way up one of the streams in the area in 1919. While the circumstances are unknown, Fowler may have been recording the beginning of another club cruise.

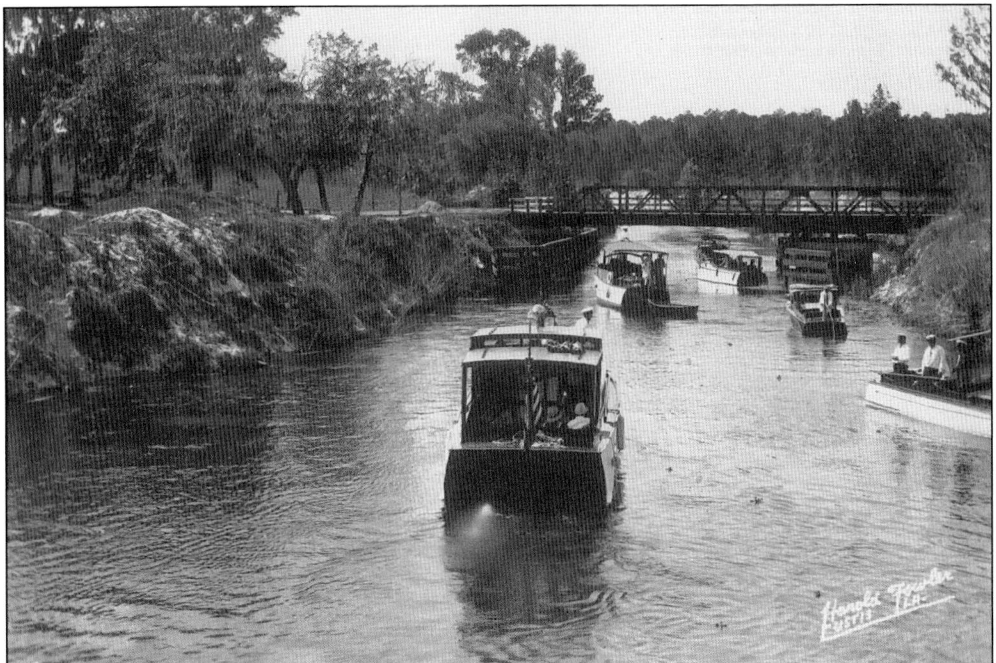

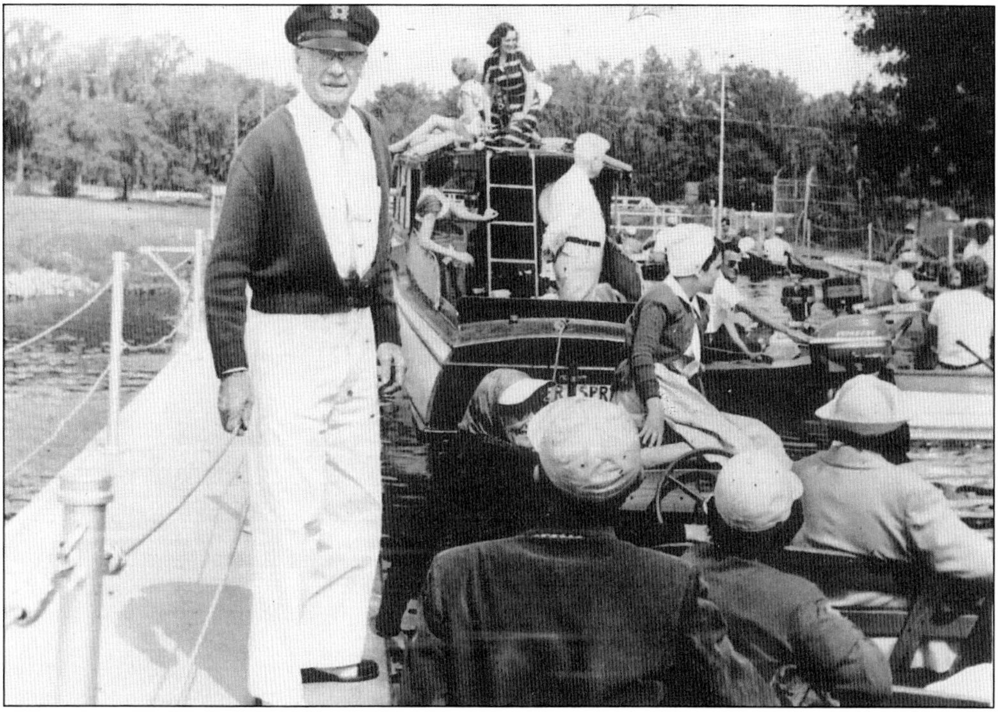

Captain Harry Wise came to Mount Dora from Wayzeta, MN, and started the southern branch of the Wise Boat Works. According to local lore, Wise received an honorary life membership in the yacht club in exchange for a sailboat that he built for the organization. Along with the various boats that he constructed for Mount Dora residents, Captain Wise also supervised the rebuilding of J.P. Donnelly's old boat. Rides on the *City of Dora* quickly became a popular excursion for both visitors and residents.

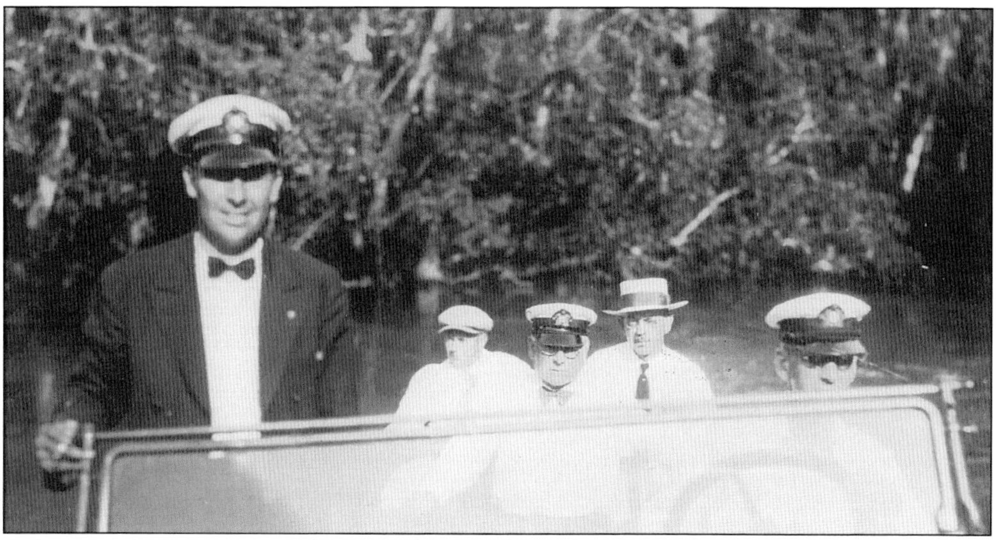

Sightseeing boat cruises on the area's lakes and canals were a pleasurable way for visitors to spend an afternoon. Complete with a guide to point out interesting flora and fauna, tourists could experience nature from a safe and comfortable setting. Several companies still operate such tours today.

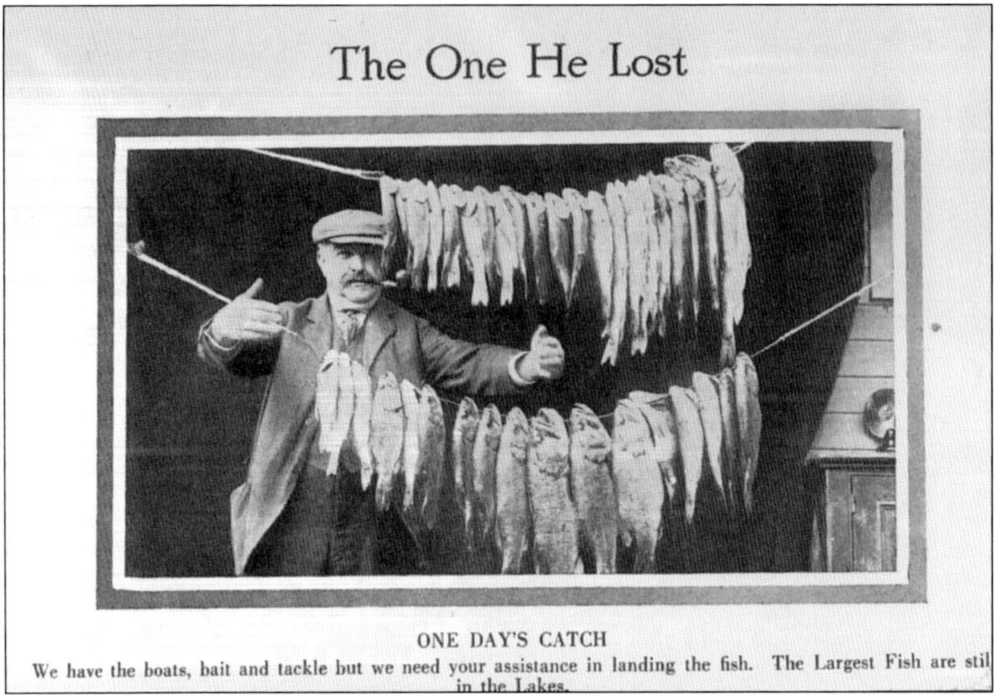

As these two old postcards prove, advertising campaigns are not a new invention. Throughout the 20th century, using hyperbole and tongue-in-cheek witticisms, promotions were designed to attract tourists to Mount Dora. Many proved successful. From the Midwest and the Northeast, the visitors came—some just for a few days or weeks, others for "the season."

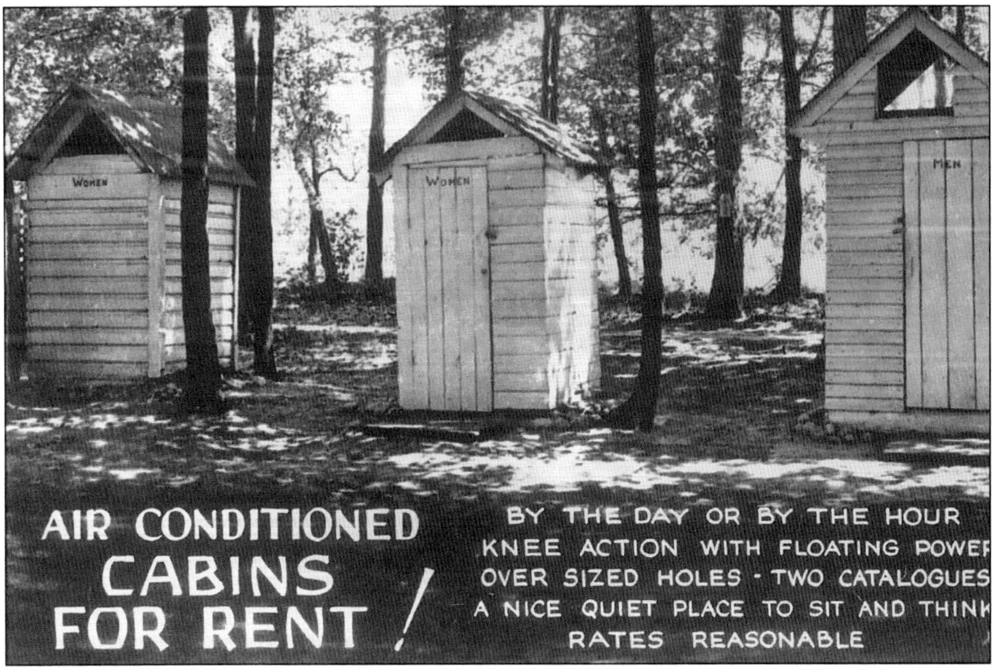

Six

HOUSING THE VISITORS

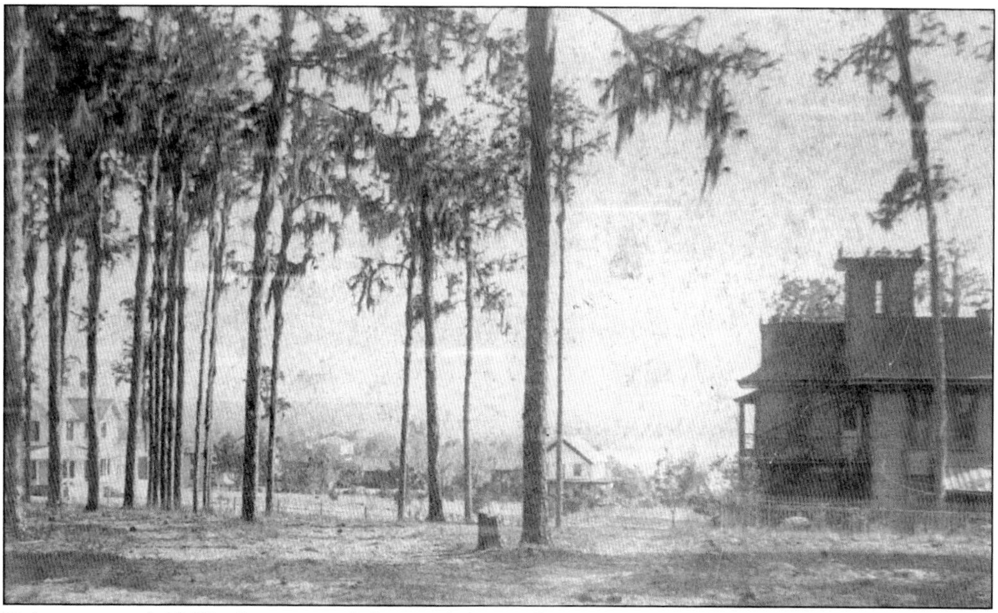

Taken around 1895, this view of three of the early Mount Dora hotels includes the Edward Smith home on the right that would one day become the Villa Dora Hotel. The Grandview Hotel is in the center, while the Lake House is barely visible in the distance. The large white house on the left that is partially obscured belonged to Mrs. A.J. Armstrong, a teacher in the Mount Dora school system from 1894 to 1896. The early hotels offered winter visitors some gentility in the midst of what was really little more than wilderness. Early settlers to Mount Dora lived much as early settlers in any other section of the country did. Self-sufficiency was certainly important; people tried as much as possible to live off the land. They raised cattle, hogs, and chickens. There were good yields of vegetables and citrus. Many of the early settlers had black servants. One woman wrote, "We like the people very much and the warm air is lovely. But the alligators in the backyard, snakes fighting in the orange grove, lizards racing back and forth across the tea towel line over the kitchen stove catching flies—yes, and something gnawing at the kitchen door after we retire at night..." Life in Florida did require some adjustments.

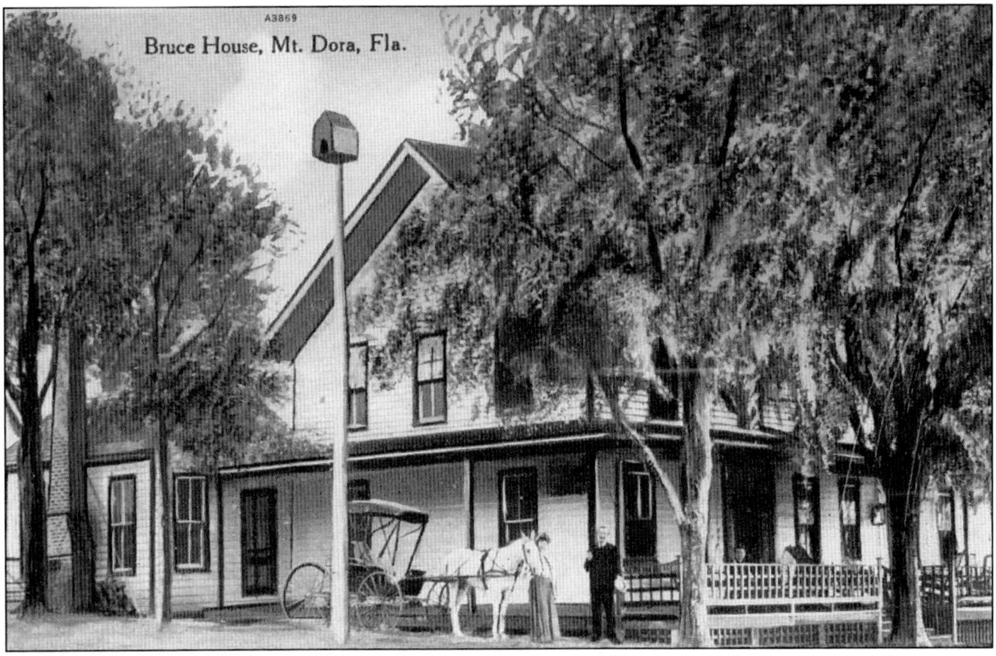

As were so many of Mount Dora's founders, Byron M. Bruce and his wife, Caroline, were newcomers to Florida and Mount Dora. Arriving from Ohio in 1882, the Bruces purchased several lots on Lake Dora and constructed the Bruce House hotel. While Mrs. Bruce operated the hotel, Byron Bruce became involved in the citrus business and, in 1911, served as a Mount Dora councilman. Subsequently sold and renamed, the Bruce House became the Grandview (or Grand View, depending upon which postcard, local history, or newspaper account is credited).

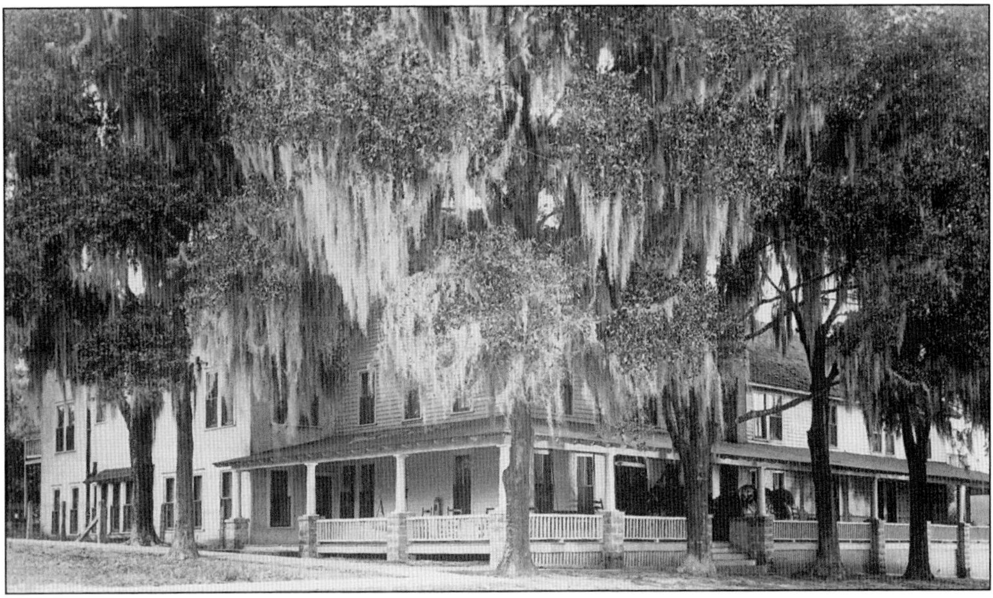

Ownership of the Grandview changed several times. In 1934, when Charles Edgerton acquired the Grandview Hotel, his sons operated it until it was again sold in 1938. Almost 50 years later, the owners of the Grandview Hotel received a certificate from the city of Mount Dora for the beautification of the property. Shortly afterward, the Grandview Hotel was demolished!

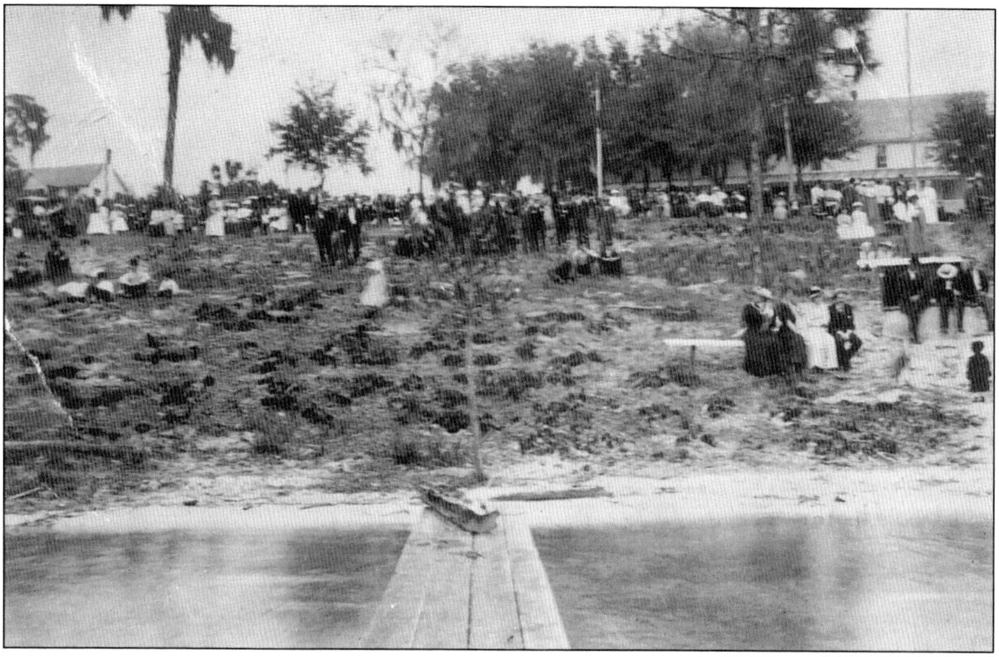

The Grandview Hotel sat on a prime piece of lakefront property on the southeast corner of Fifth Avenue and McDonald Street. Hundreds of people turned out on a Sunday afternoon to watch a regatta on Lake Dora from the hotel's lawn.

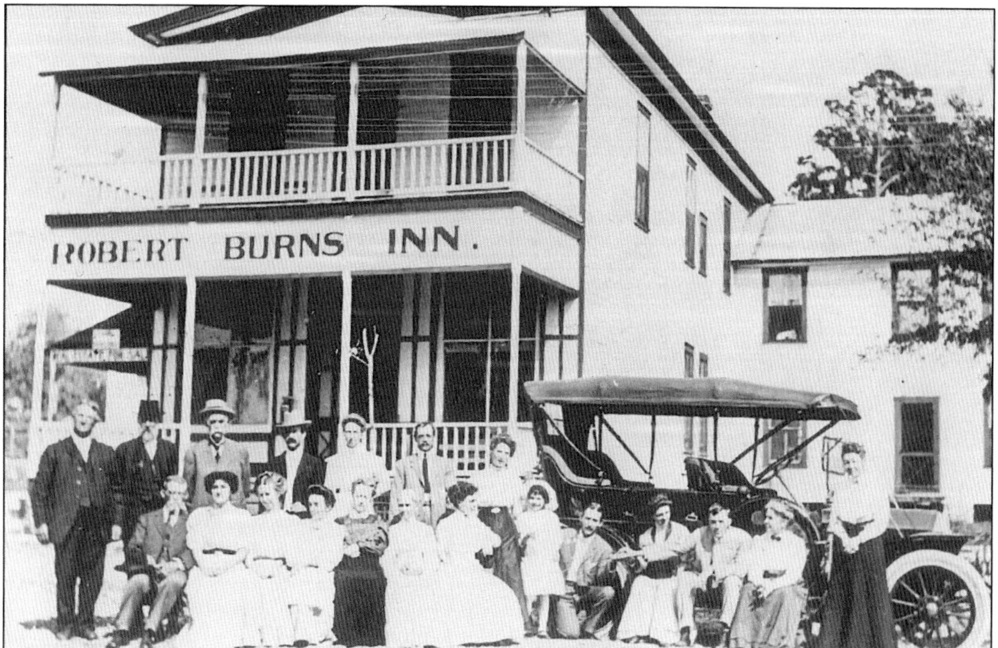

The Robert Burns Inn began business in 1908 when Charles Edson Little purchased a store on the southeast corner of Donnelly Street and Fourth Avenue. Following an extensive remodeling, the property reopened as the Robert Burns Inn. The hotel was named not after the famous Scottish poet, but in honor of Charles Little's son.

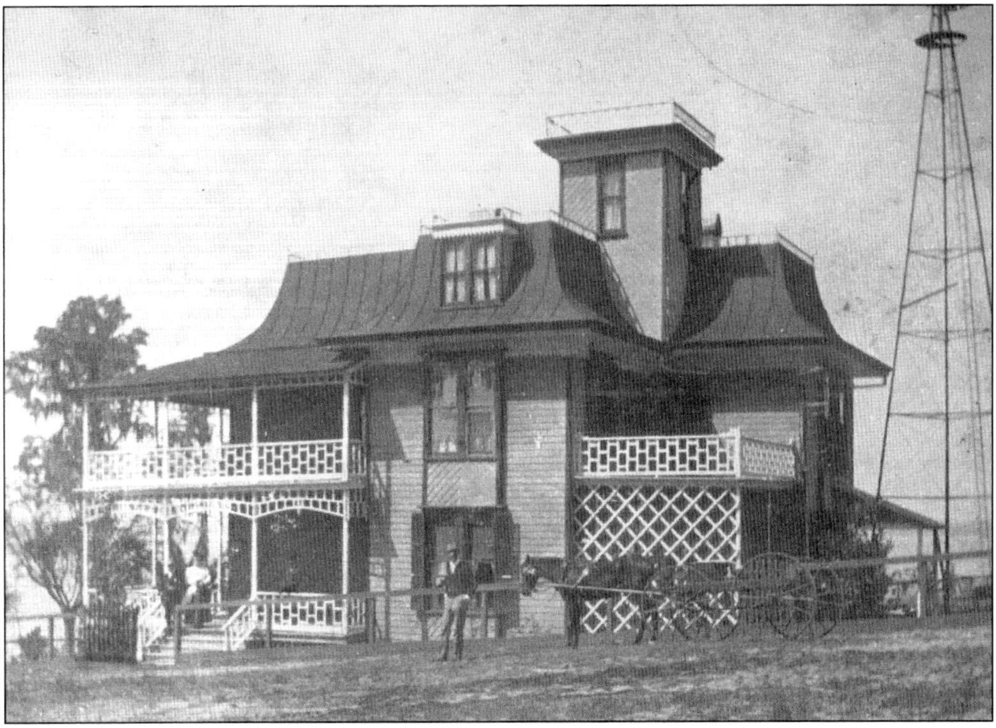

What would someday become the Villa Dora Hotel started out as the private home of Edward Smith and his family. Gertrude Thorne of Toronto, Canada, purchased the Smith residence in 1910 for $700. She owned and operated the property as the Villa Dora Hotel until 1925.

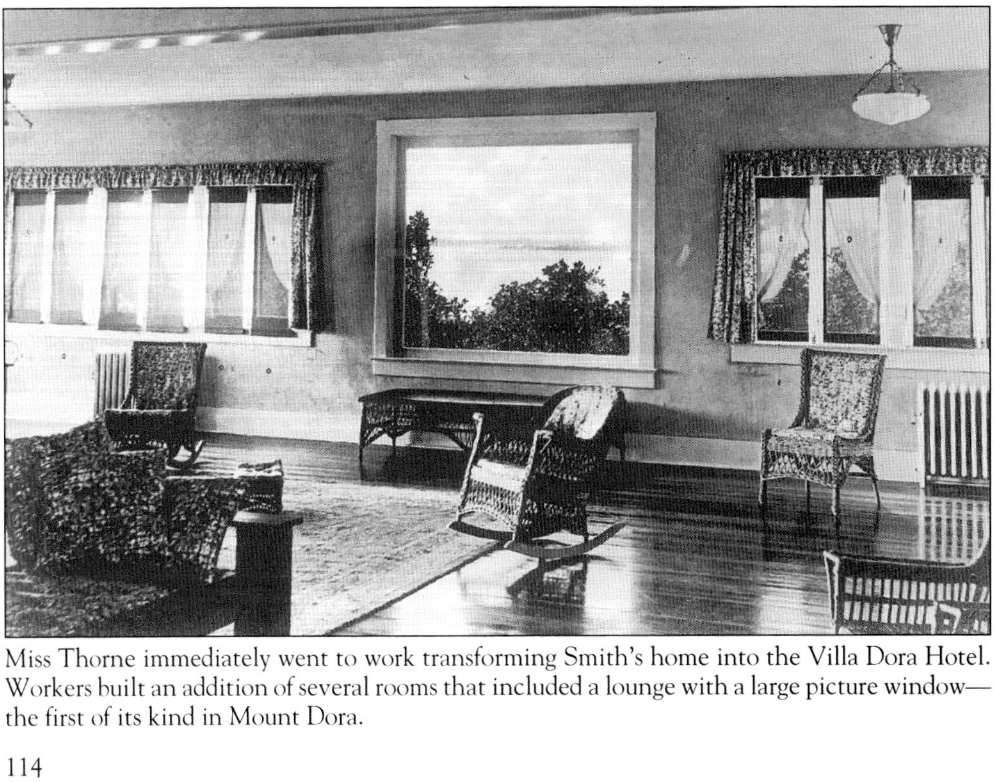

Miss Thorne immediately went to work transforming Smith's home into the Villa Dora Hotel. Workers built an addition of several rooms that included a lounge with a large picture window—the first of its kind in Mount Dora.

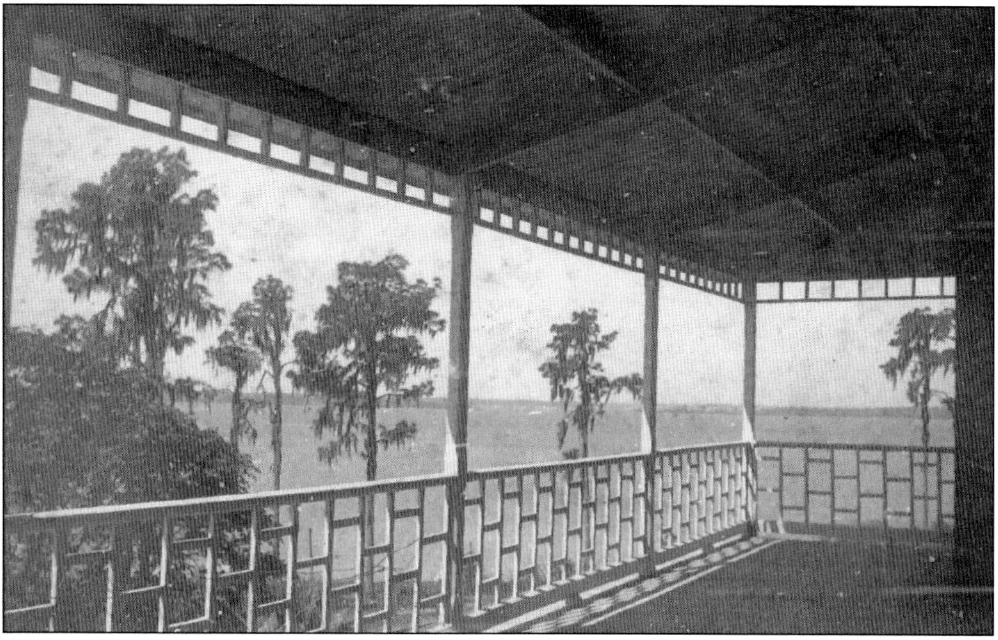

The porch of the Villa Dora had a commanding view of Lake Dora. An early brochure promoted the Villa Dora as the place "Where Hospitality Is A Pleasure." Guests of the hotel sometimes referred to examples of their landlady's eccentricity and frugality. No rocking was permitted on the hotel's rugs, lest the motion wear them out. While the hotel could accommodate 60 guests, there were but three bathrooms.

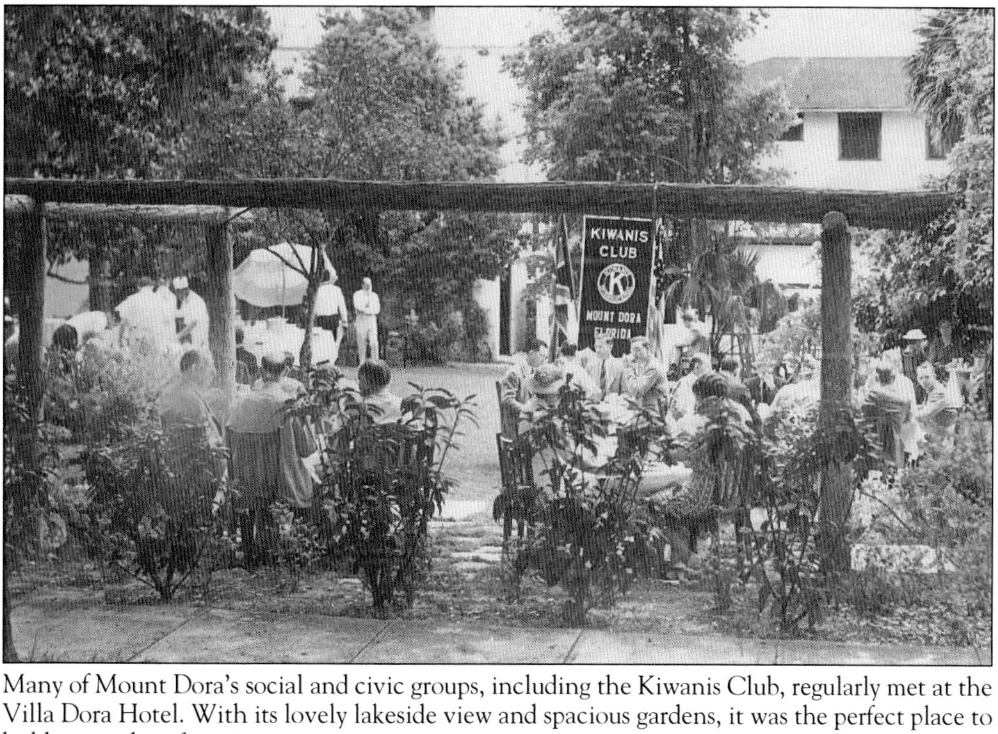

Many of Mount Dora's social and civic groups, including the Kiwanis Club, regularly met at the Villa Dora Hotel. With its lovely lakeside view and spacious gardens, it was the perfect place to hold an outdoor function.

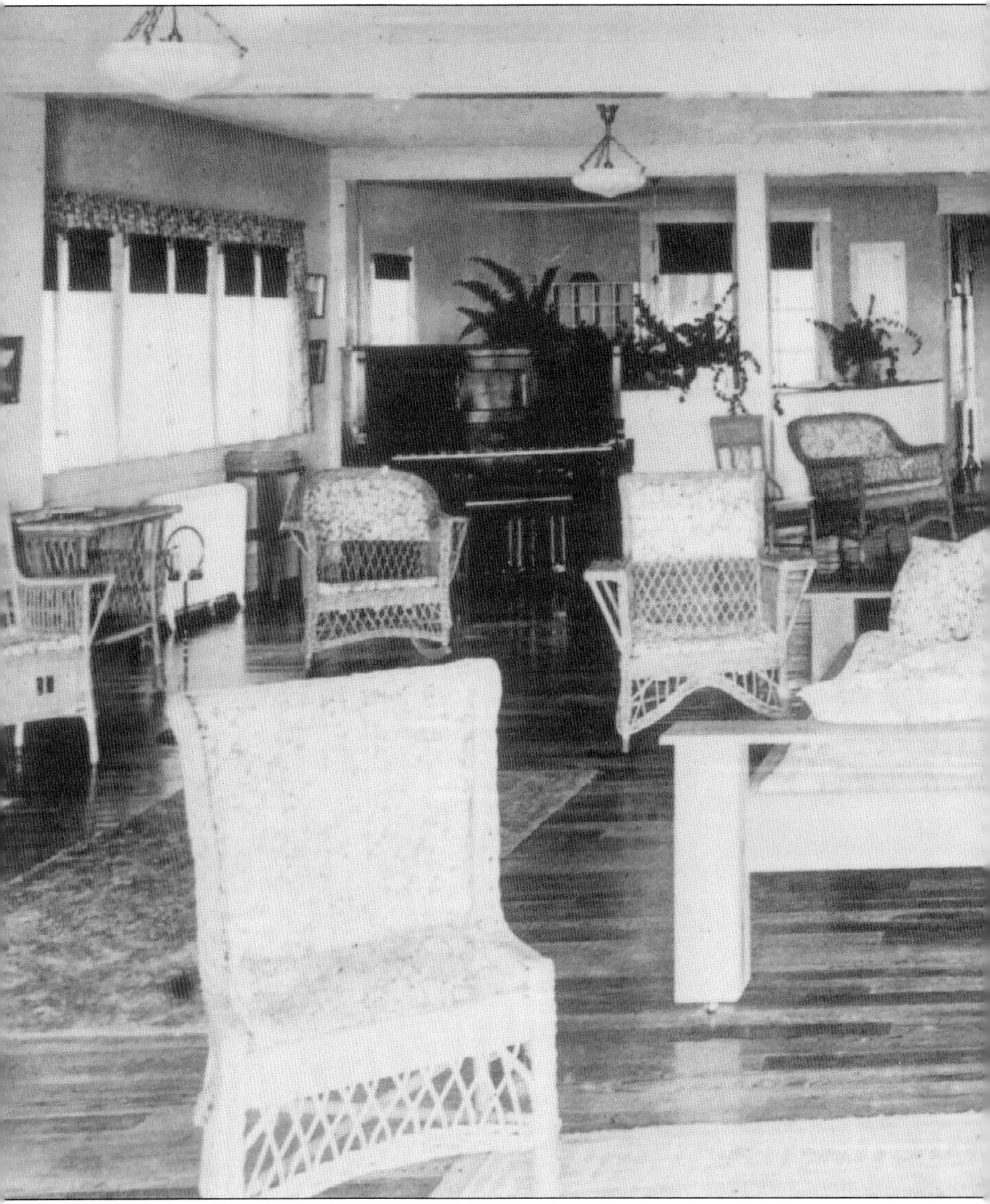

Offering a wonderful view of Lake Dora, the Villa Dora Hotel had a wide lobby adorned with white wicker furniture, ferns, oriental rugs, and a spinet piano. With a mix of hyperbole and folksiness, an early Villa Dora brochure claimed, "In the shadow of live oaks, with a background of fertile orange and grapefruit groves, overlooking one of Florida's most beautiful lakes, is the setting for the Villa Dora. A home-like hotel owned and personally supervised by the same

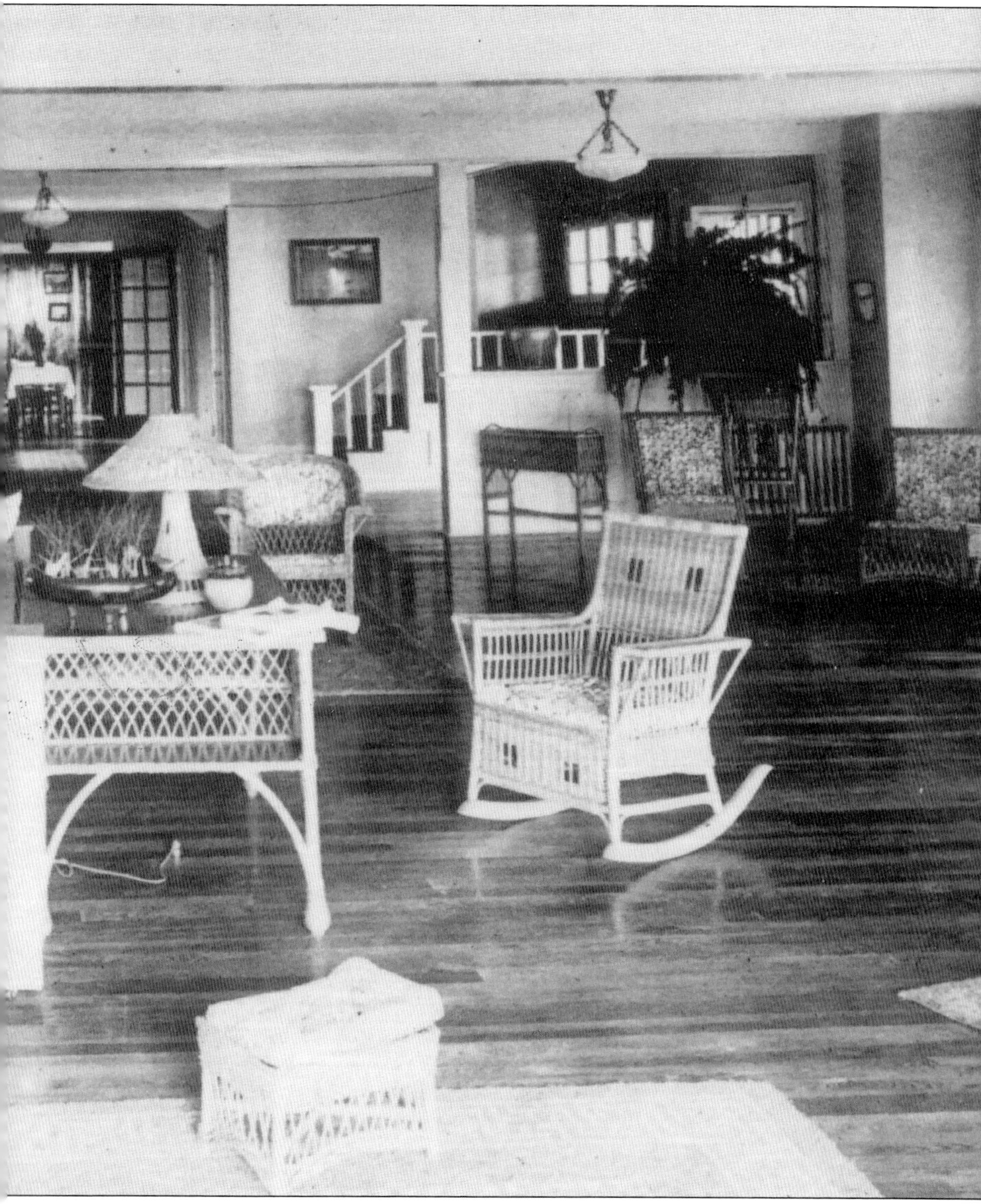

management since 1925. A hotel offering to its guests a home of comfort and convenience at rates within the reach of all. Rooms with and without bath. A menu simple but completely satisfying with an abundance of fresh fruits and vegetables, and the best quality of meats served always...pure drinking water, free from sulphur, is a boast of which we are proud."

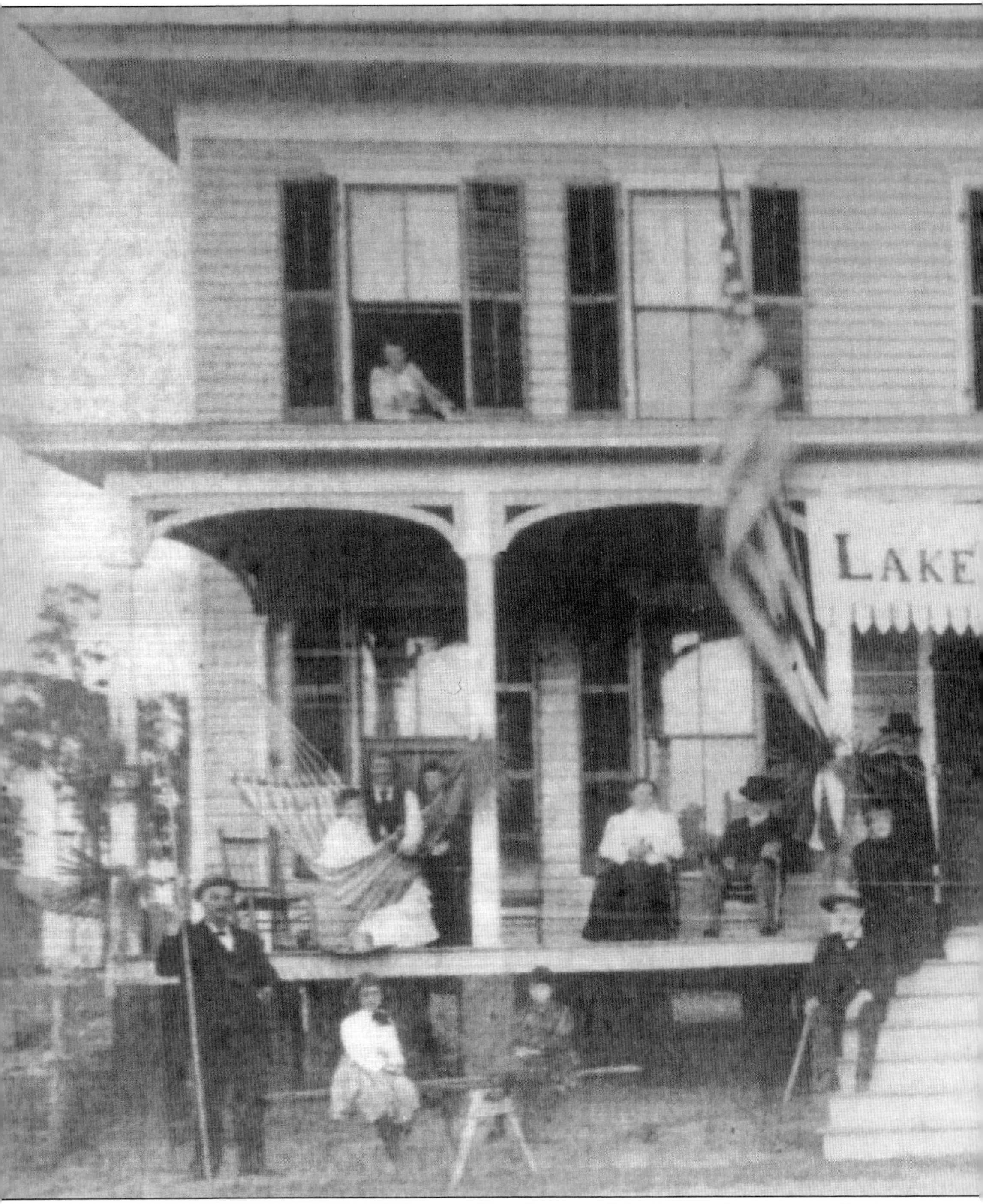

In 1883, a partnership was formed that would make one of the longest lasting contributions to Mount Dora's history. John M. Alexander, John A. McDonald, and Annie McDonald Stone became the impetus behind the construction of the town's newest hotel—the Alexander House. Involved with their many other interests, the partners hired Caroline Bruce to manage the ten-room inn. The name, Alexander House, was retained until 1895, when the hotel was

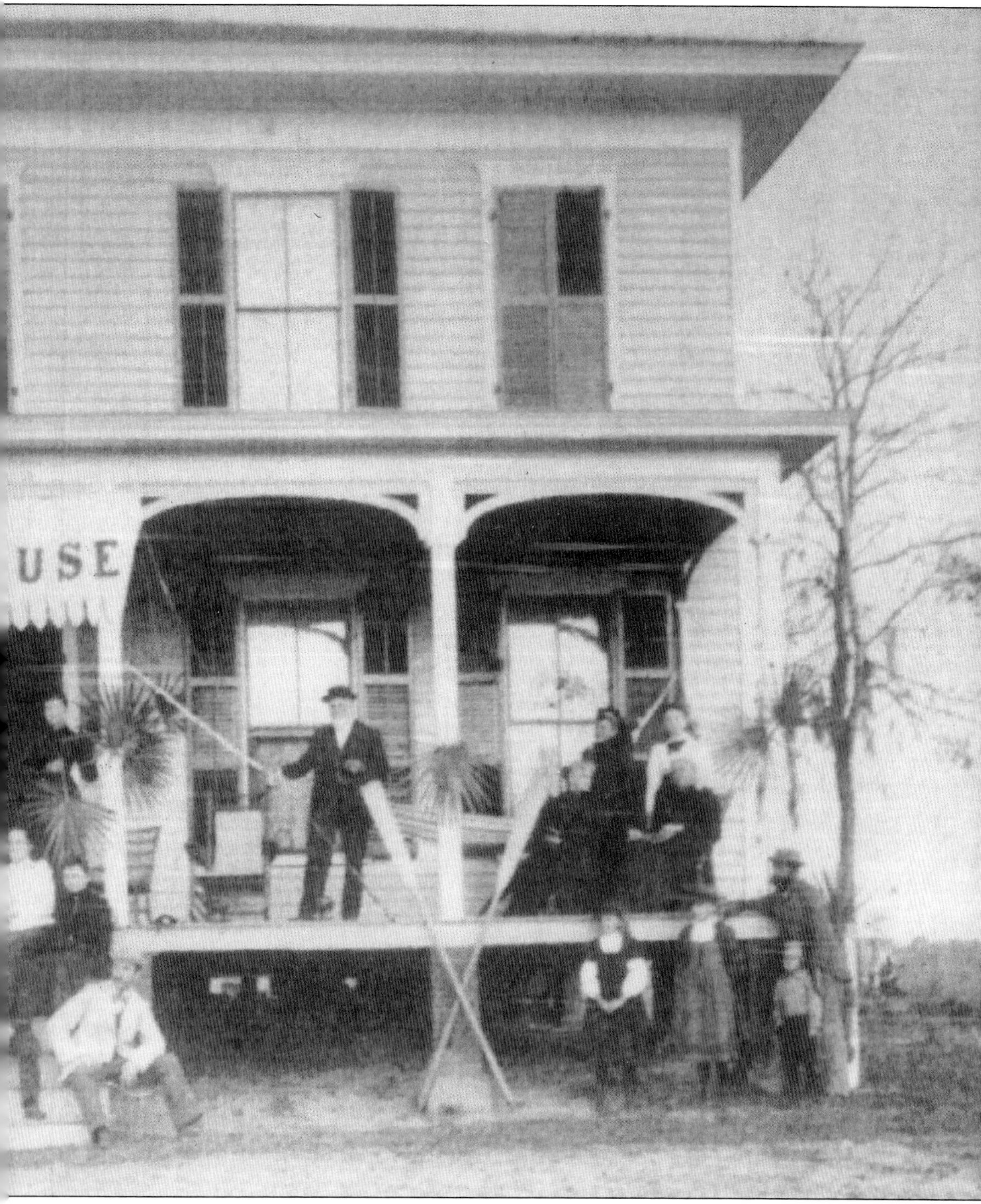

rechristened as the Lake House. While the occasion for this photograph is unknown, everyone in the vicinity seems to have been anxious to take part in the event. With a large American flag waving in the breeze, men, women, and children are posed in hammocks and rocking chairs, on the porch steps, seated on a seesaw, standing in front of the hotel, and leaning from an upstairs window.

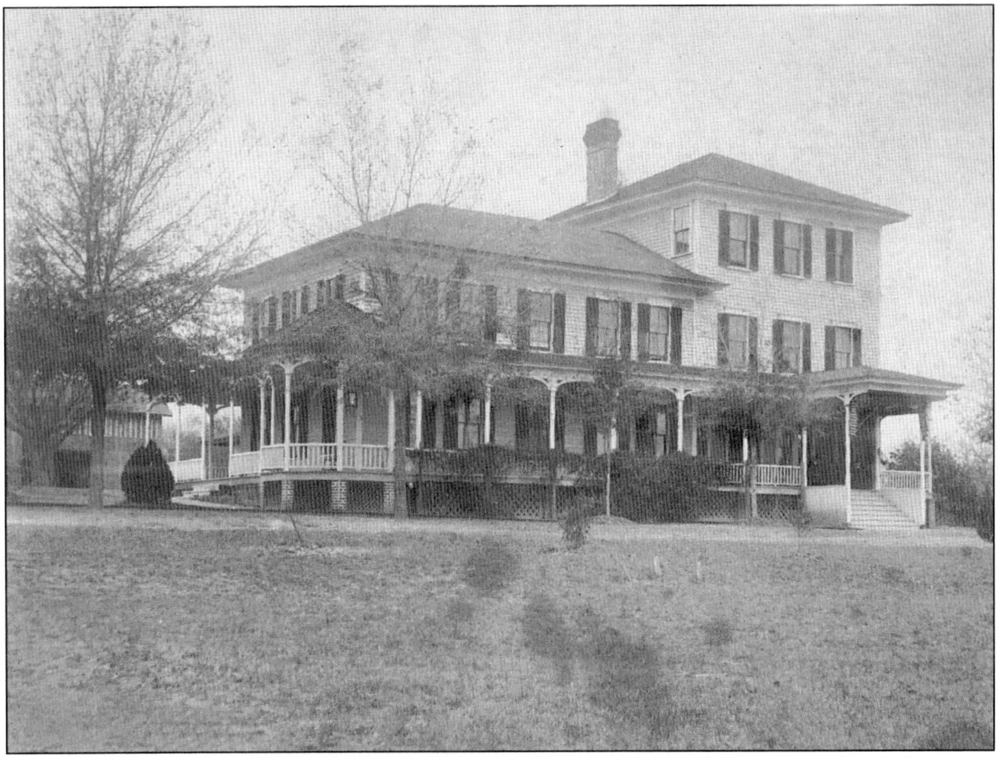

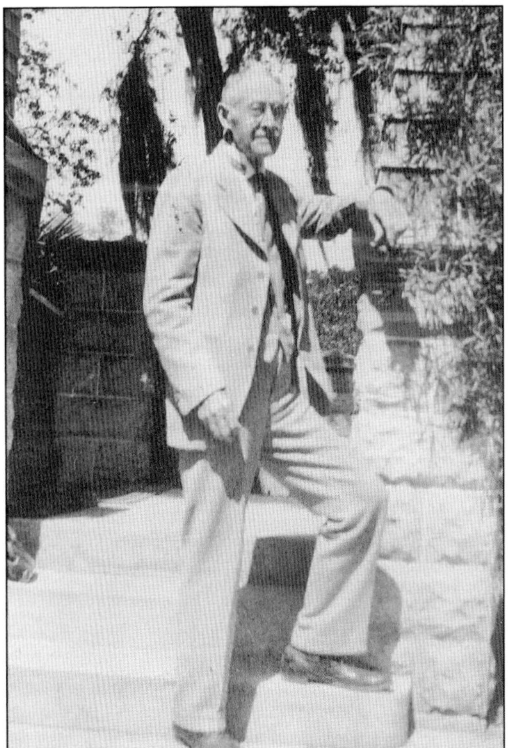

Caroline Bruce left as manager of the Alexander House in order to run her own establishment, the Bruce House. In 1895, Emma Boone of Boston, MA, became the hotel's new manager and quickly changed the name of the hotel to the Lake House.

George D. Thayer, a widower from Boston, moved to Mount Dora at the beginning of the 20th century for reasons of health. Following his marriage to Emma Boone in 1903, he formed a stock company to operate the Lake House. Although Emma Boone Thayer died in 1909, George Thayer continued to run the hotel until his retirement in 1924, making many changes and additions.

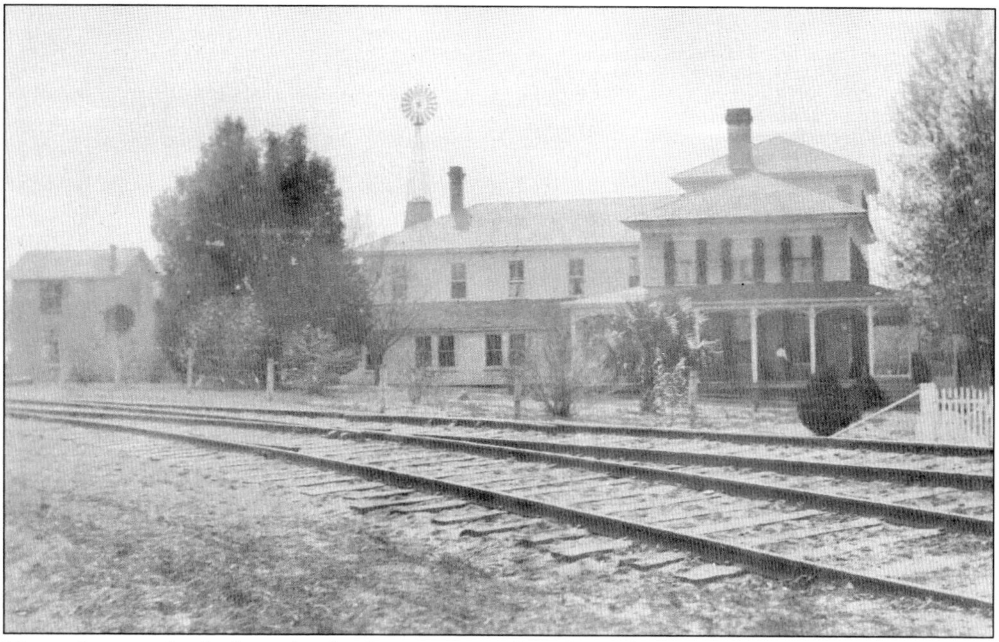

Horse-drawn vehicles brought the first guests to the Alexander House. When the railroad came to Mount Dora, its tracks ran along side of the renamed Lake House, putting the hotel in the perfect location to welcome guests as they disembarked.

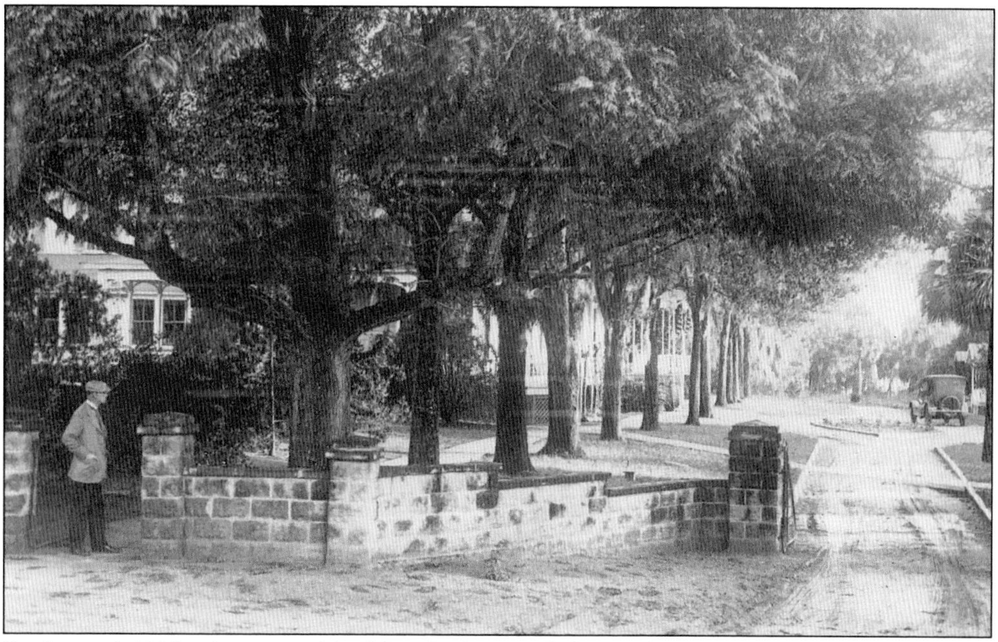

By the mid-1920s, the original building had expanded considerably, with a three-story center addition plus a new dining room and kitchen. The Gatehouse had been built in 1908; Sunset Cottage was added in 1914. A circular driveway facilitated the arrival of guests by automobile. In 1933, Lakeside Inn Properties, Inc., headed by Charles Edgerton and Fred Wentworth, took over ownership of the hotel. Richard Edgerton succeeded his father as owner-manager until 1980.

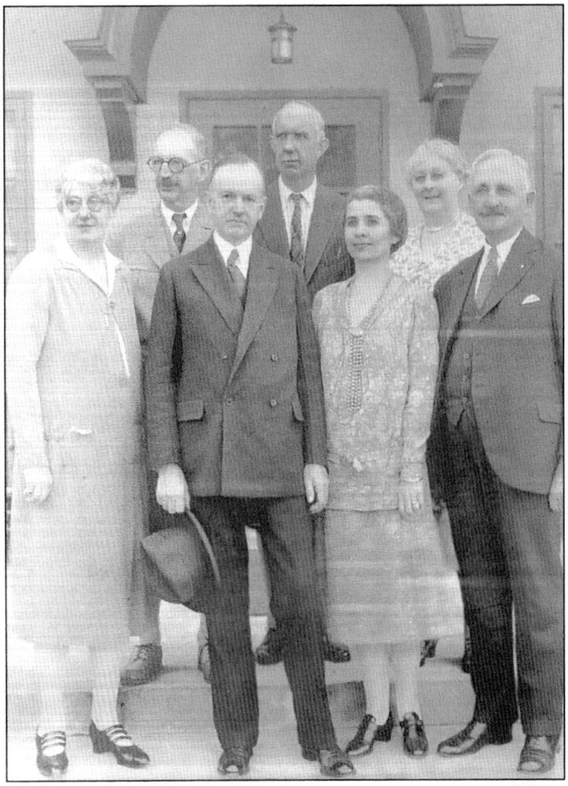

Undoubtedly one of the highlights in Mount Dora's social history was a visit by former President Calvin Coolidge and his wife, Grace. President and Mrs. Coolidge arrived by train on January 10, 1930, for what was expected to be a restful visit lasting four or five weeks. They were obviously the stars of the social season and were much in demand for tree plantings, building dedications, afternoon teas, and social activities of all kinds.

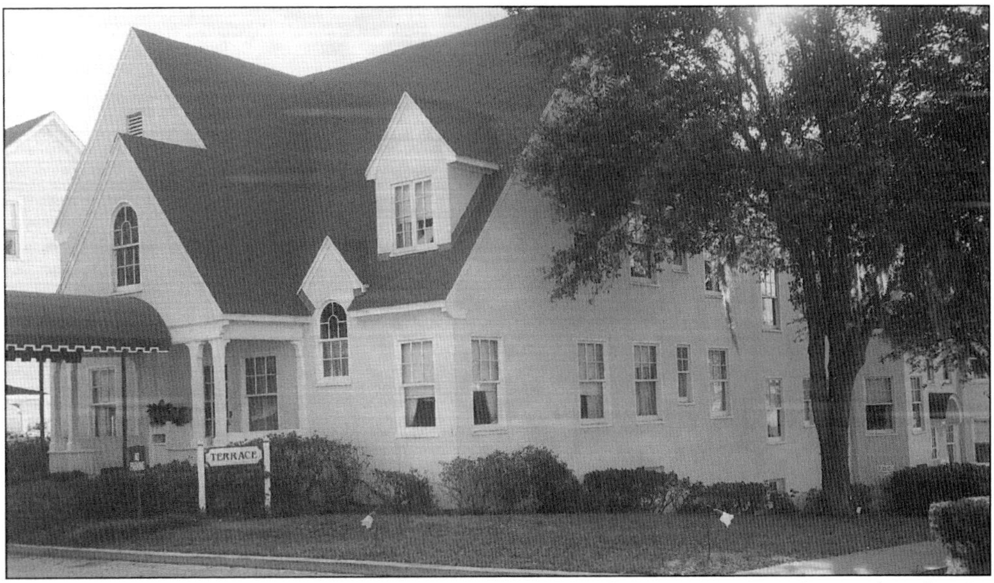

While in Mount Dora, the Coolidges were guests in the town's most elegant hotel—the Lakeside Inn. To the Coolidges also fell the honor of inaugurating the Lakeside's newest unit of 39 rooms, the Terrace. On January 15, 1930, at what the *Mount Dora Topic* described as "the most brilliant event in the history of Mount Dora and perhaps in Central Florida," President and Mrs. Coolidge hobnobbed with politicians and dignitaries from near and far. (Authors' collection.)

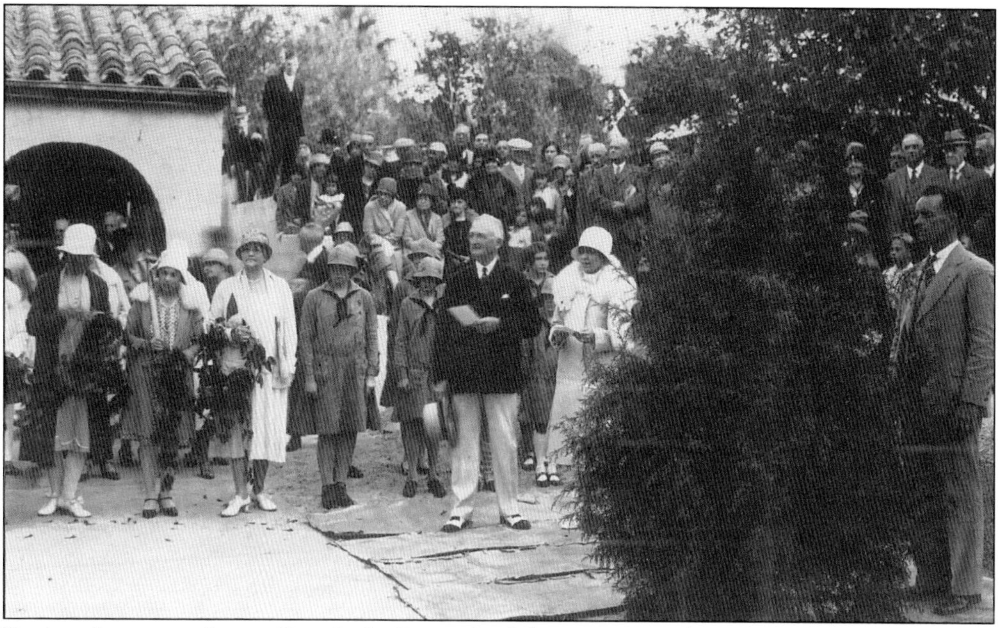

During their visit, former First Lady Grace Coolidge was as much in demand as her husband, the laconic ex-president. On January 24, 1930, dressed in a fashionable white suit and hat, Mrs. Coolidge listened to a speech by Mount Dora Parks Commissioner Charles Edgerton at the dedication of the town's new Community Hall.

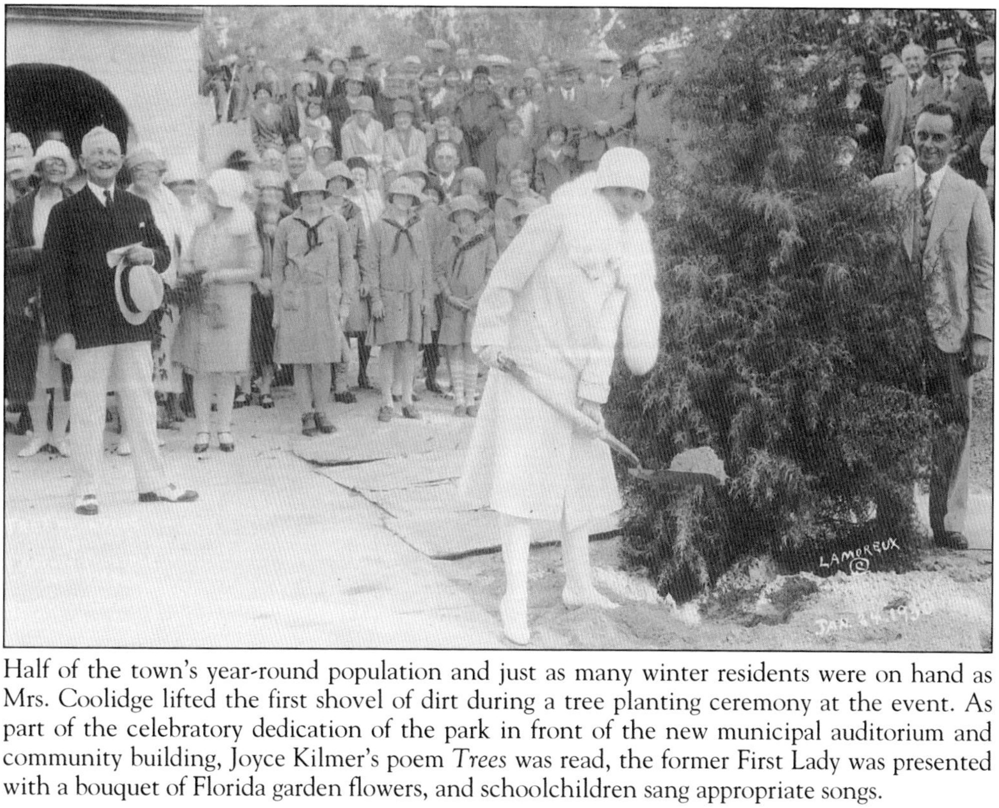

Half of the town's year-round population and just as many winter residents were on hand as Mrs. Coolidge lifted the first shovel of dirt during a tree planting ceremony at the event. As part of the celebratory dedication of the park in front of the new municipal auditorium and community building, Joyce Kilmer's poem *Trees* was read, the former First Lady was presented with a bouquet of Florida garden flowers, and schoolchildren sang appropriate songs.

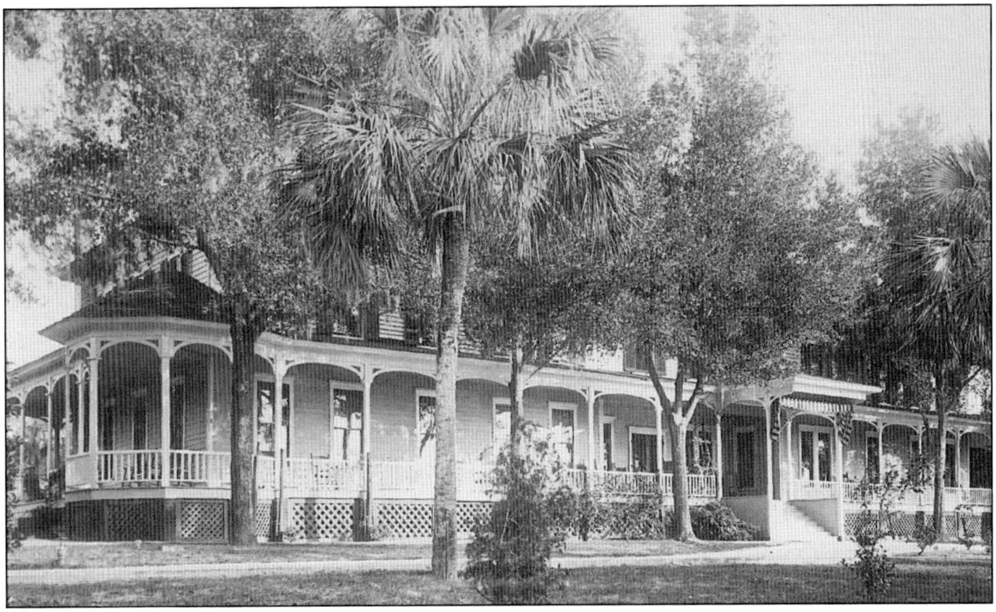

Shortly after this photograph was taken, the Lakeside Inn underwent major renovations. The Gables was built in 1928 next to the Gatehouse. With the completion of the Terrace in 1930, the *Mount Dora Topic* reported, "Over a quarter of a million dollars has been expended in additions and remodeling at the Lakeside properties and today the hotel and units take rank as one of the finest in the south."

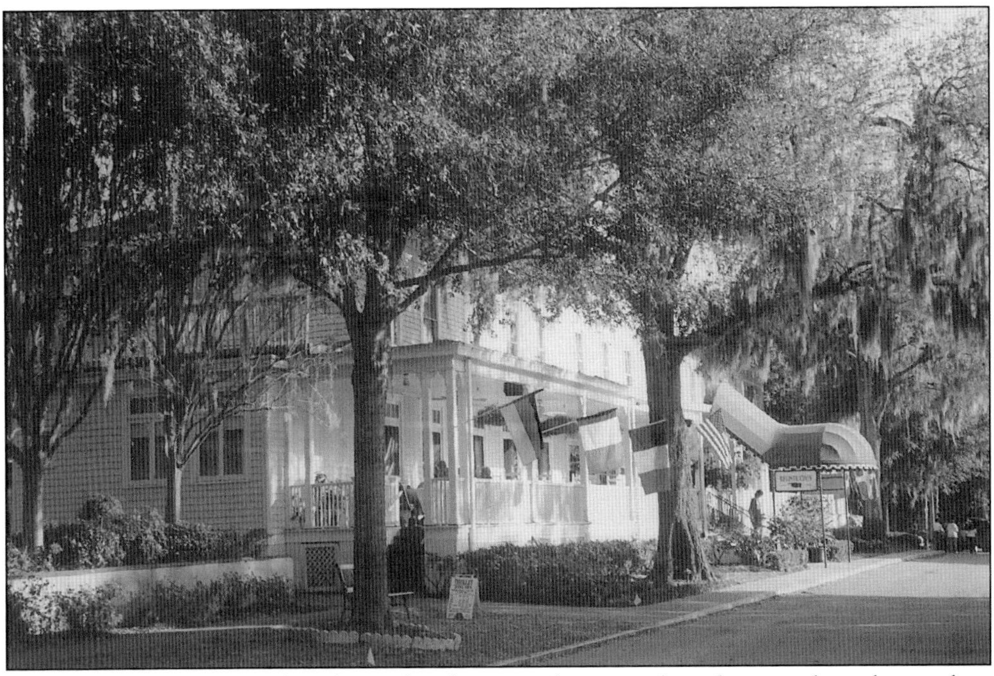

Although the landscaping has changed and certain alterations have been made to the porches, this recent photograph of the main building of the Lakeside Inn bears a marked resemblance to the 1920s-era version pictured above. The flags hanging from the porch represent several of the many nations that are home to the Lakeside Inn's international guests. (Authors' collection.)

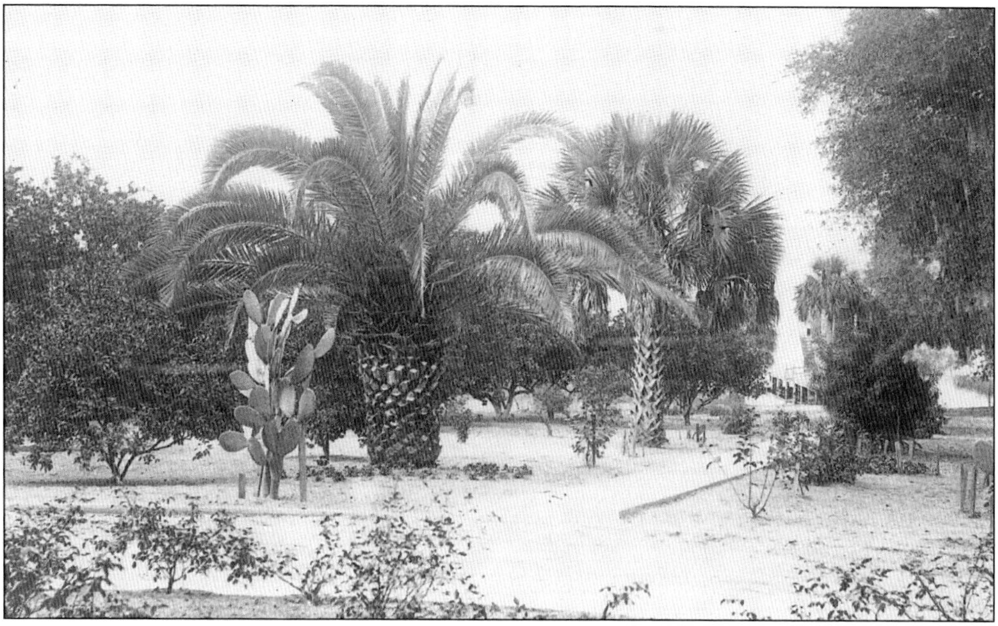

On the hotel grounds, different types of citrus, palms, cactus, and other exotic plantings gave visitors from cold climates the feeling that they had wandered into a tropical paradise. From the main building of the Lakeside Inn, a walkway led to the hotel's dock on Lake Dora, where guests could participate in a variety of activities, including swimming, boating, and fishing.

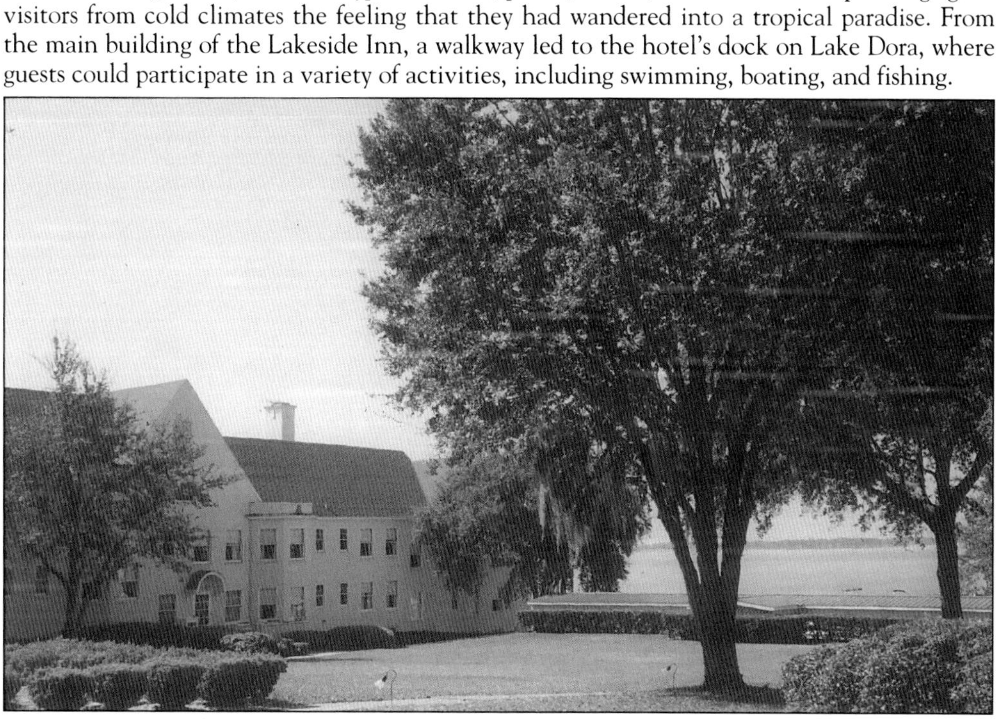

The hotel grounds today present a less tropical, more manicured appearance. Likewise, the lake is no longer the only site for swimming. As part of the renovations in 1930, an Olympic-sized swimming pool was constructed near the shore of Lake Dora between the Gables and the Terrace. When swimming and diving competitions highlighted the inaugural ceremonies, the local newspaper reported that "St. Petersburg swimmers carried away most of the honors at the opening event." (Authors' collection.)

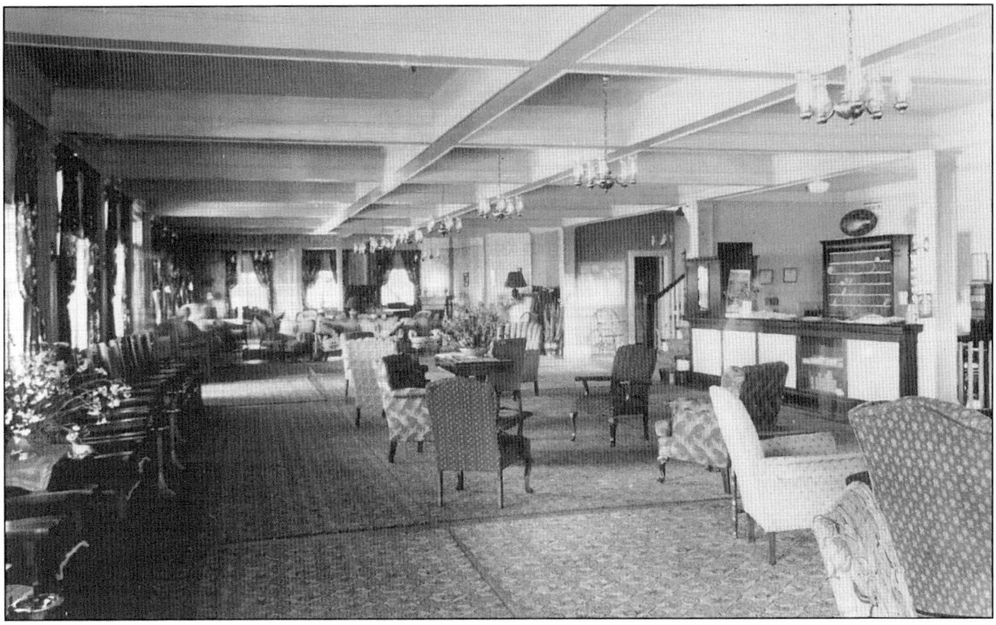

The dinner dances held at the Lakeside Inn were one of the highlights of the social season in Mount Dora. According to the local newspaper, following an elaborate dinner, "dancing was in order until a late hour, music being provided by a peppy Mount Dora orchestra." Located just outside of the ballroom, the hotel's lobby provided a quiet spot for conversation between dances.

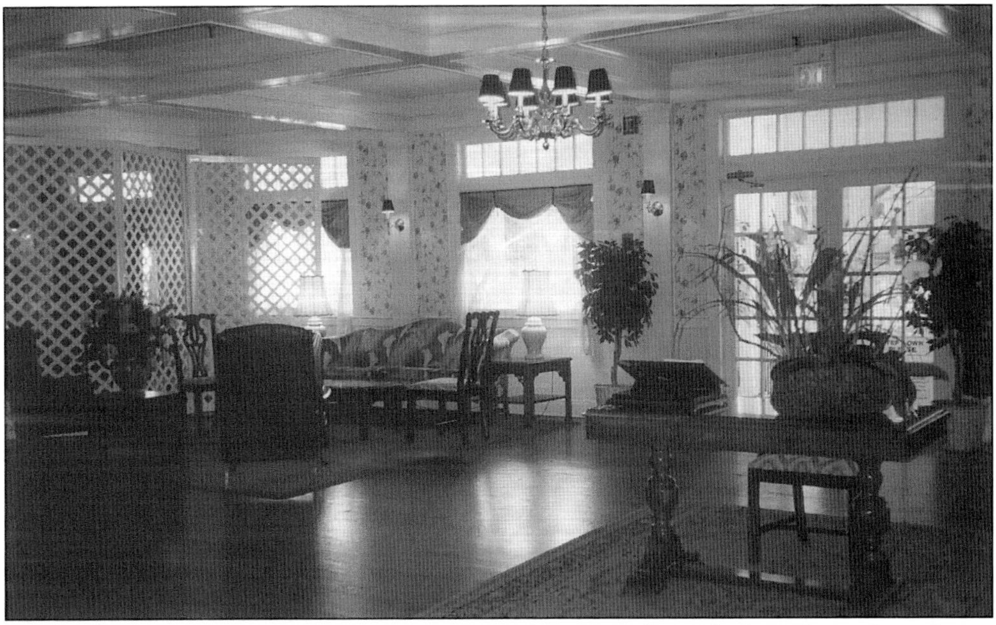

The lobby also presented a welcoming appearance for guests who wished to relax indoors during the daytime. Comfortable chairs arranged in conversational groupings facilitated discussions between visitors, many of whom returned each year to spend most of the winter at the hotel. As this recent photograph shows, the lobby retains many of the distinctive architectural and decorative elements pictured in the preceding image. (Authors' collection.)

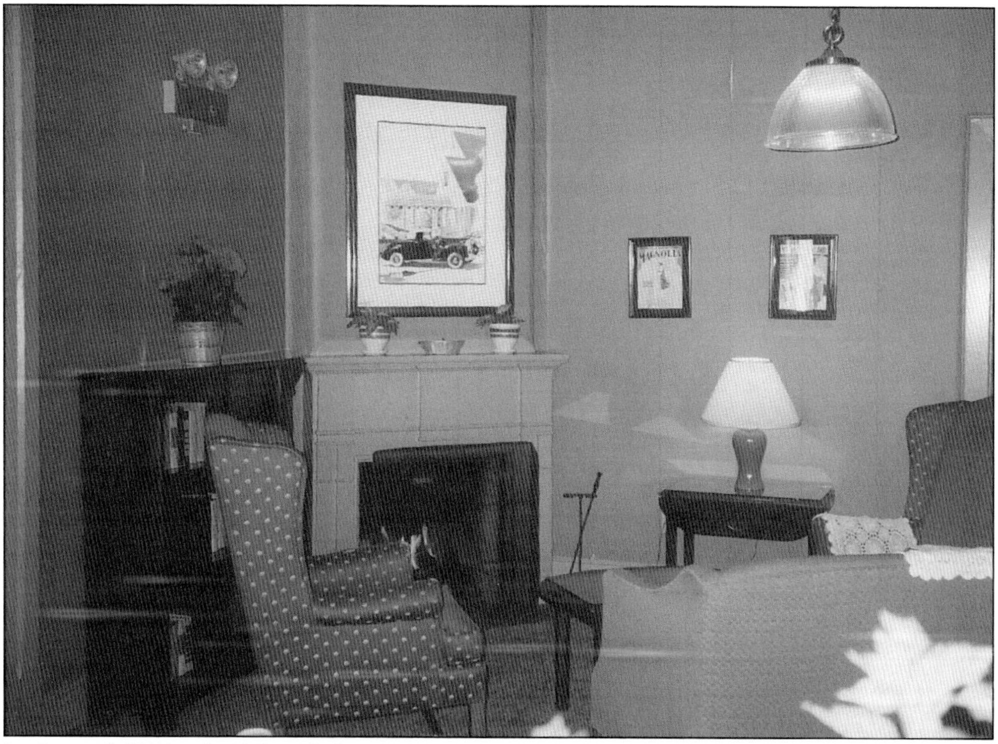

In the mid-1980s, the Lakeside Inn closed its doors during the winter season for the first time in its history. Following a $4-million renovation, it reopened as one of Florida's premier historic resort hotels. Special care has been taken to preserve important architectural details such as fireplaces and lighting fixtures that contribute to the traditional feel of the hotel. (Authors' collection.)

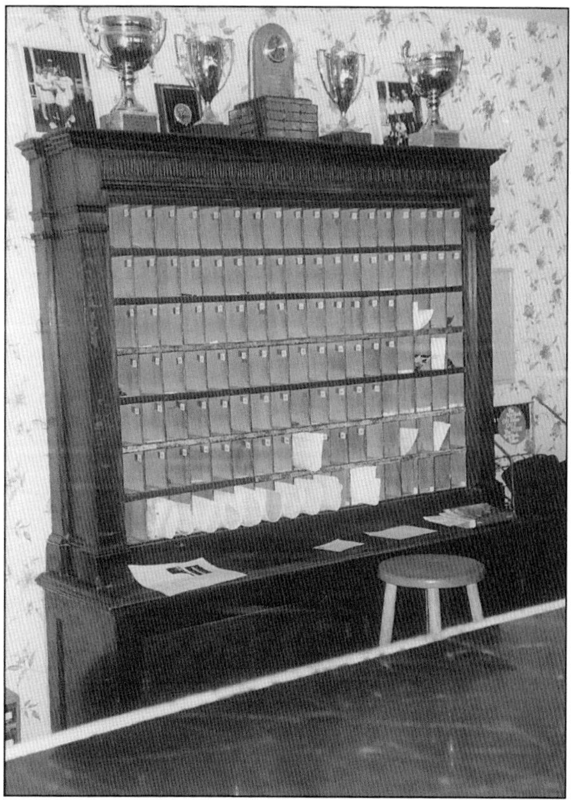

One of the special pieces of antique furniture that decorate the Lakeside Inn sits behind the registration desk in the lobby. In past years, many guests came for visits lasting weeks and even months; prompt mail delivery during their visit was important. Complete with pigeonholed compartments to hold both incoming mail and room keys for hotel guests, the elaborate wooden cabinet dates from the early years of the hotel's history. (Authors' collection.)

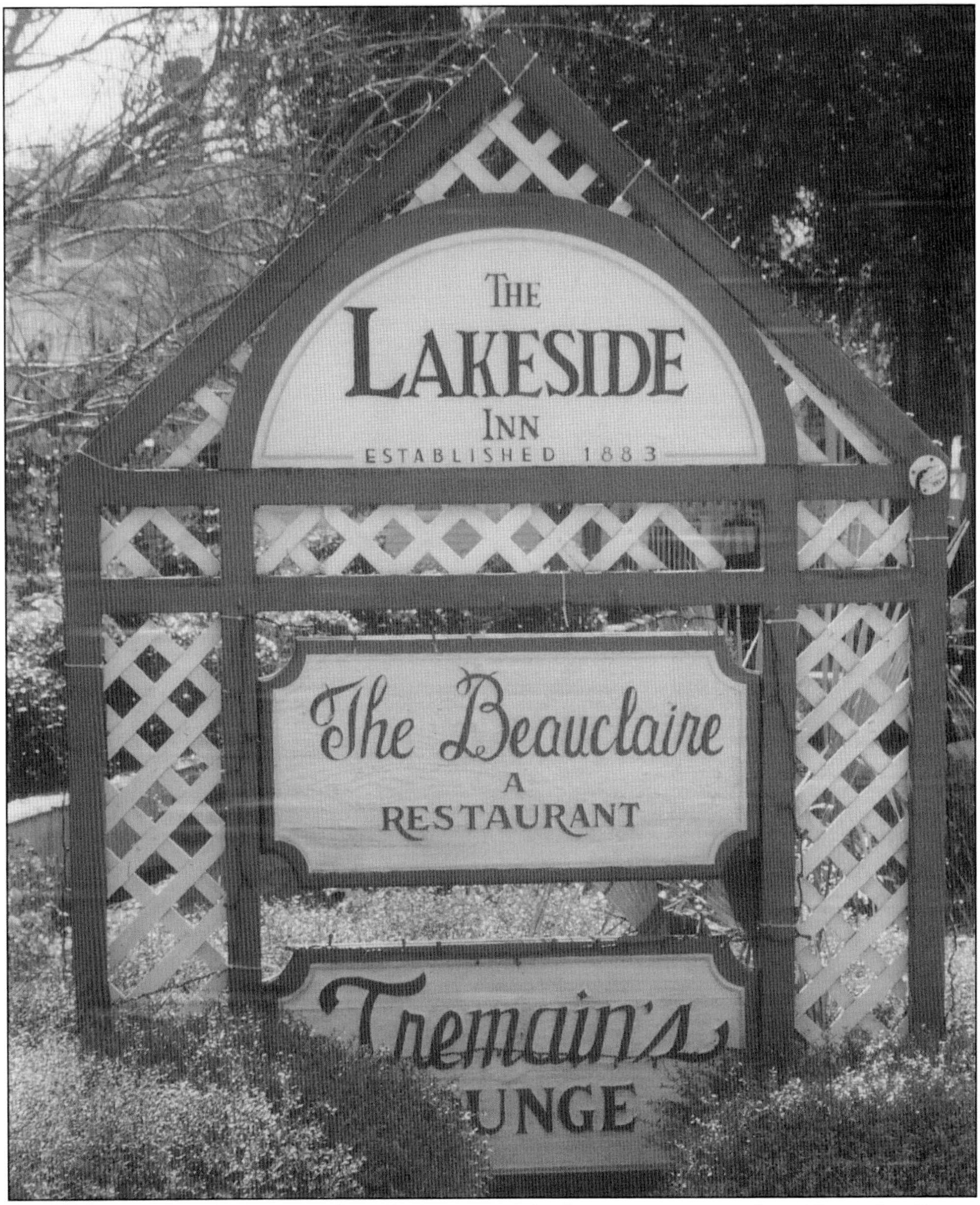

Reminiscent of a summer gazebo, this green and white sign sits at the Alexander Street entrance to the Lakeside Inn. In addition to the hotel itself, the sign advertises the Beauclaire Dining Room, recalling one of the nearby lakes, and Tremain's Lounge, named in honor of one of Mount Dora's founding fathers, Ross Tremain. Upon entering the Lakeside Inn, guests step back into time. Historical touches—traditionally styled lighting fixtures and furnishings, working fireplaces, ceiling fans, period artwork, and vintage music—abound. Special promotions tout "Romantic Rendezvous" and "Great Gatsby" getaways. Listed on the National Register of Historic Places and a member of Historic Hotels of America, the restored hotel advertises "Historic Hospitality Since 1883." Visitors are encouraged to "Experience the Lakeside Inn. Where what once was, still is." The same slogan could also be applied to Mount Dora today. (Authors' collection.)